how to garden

John Cushnie has run his own landscape design and contracting company in County Down for the last 25 years. He is gardening editor of *Ireland's Homes Interior and Living* magazine and writes for the *Daily Telegraph* and the Northern Ireland *Newsletter*. He also contributes to *Gardeners' World* magazine, hosted the BBC/RTE television series *Greenfingers* and is a regular panellist on BBC Radio 4's *Gardeners' Question Time*. His solo radio series, *John Cushnie Gets Down To Earth*, was broadcast on Radio 4 in 1999. His first book, *Ground Cover*, was published by Kyle Cathie in 1999 and *Trees for the Garden* will appear in autumn 2002. He lectures all over the British Isles.

Most importantly, John Cushnie i gardener first and a writer and broadcaster second. He has a d rooted understanding of the q that novice gardeners are likely to

D1534318

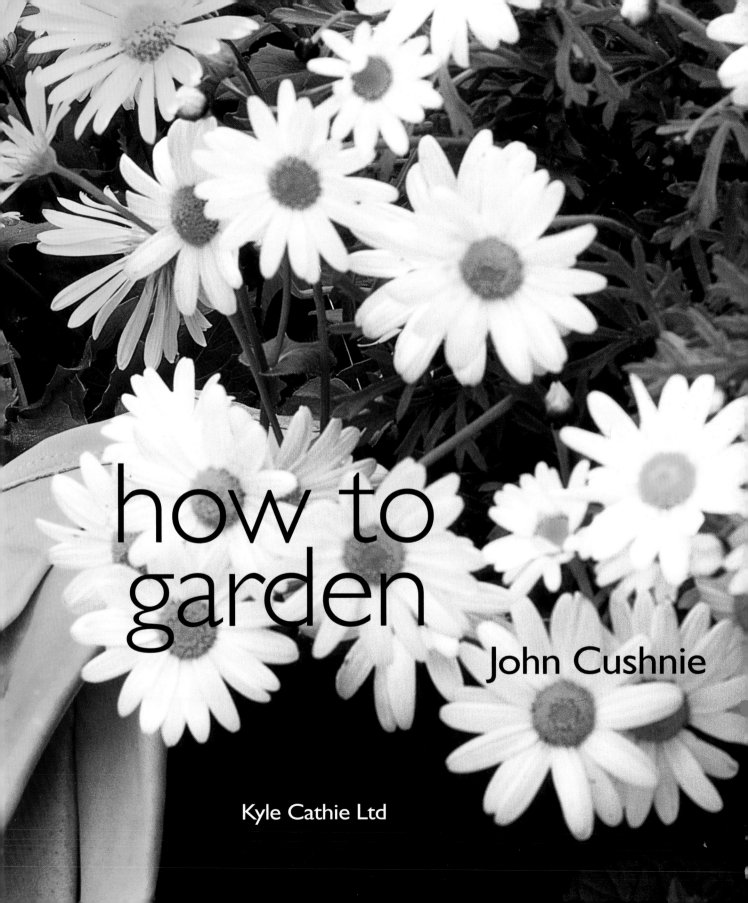

how to
garden

John Cushnie

Kyle Cathie Ltd

To Richard & Aisling
a couple of potential gardeners

First published in Great Britain in 2001 by Kyle Cathie Limited
122 Arlington Road, London NW1 7HP
general.enquiries@kyle-cathie.com
www.kylecathie.com

This paperback edition first published in 2002

ISBN 1 85626 438 6

Special photography by Steven Wooster
Project editor: Caroline Taggart
Text editors: Charlie Ryrie and Sharon Amos
Designed by Robert Updegraff • Illustrations by Elizabeth Kay
Production by Lorraine Baird and Sha Huxtable

John Cushnie is hereby identified as the author of this work in accordance with Section 77 of the
Copyright, Designs and Patents Act 1988.

A Cataloguing in Publication record for this title is available from the British Library.

Printed in Singapore by Tien Wah Press

contents

A garden doesn't happen overnight, but it is worth waiting for. After all your hard work, you will have a very personal place to sit and relax.

introduction

There is a difference between new gardeners and people who have new gardens. This book is written primarily for the former, whose gardens may or may not be new. You may have some experience, gleaned from helping in your parents' garden when younger, but more likely the concept of gardening will be a bit of a mystery, perhaps laced with a dash of apprehension or even a full measure of apathy. But if, for whatever reason, you find yourself the owner of a garden, you need to learn how to look after it and turn it into a source of delight rather than a burden.

There are many ways to become a gardener, some more painful than others. If you are serious about it, going to horticultural college or gardening evening classes is admirable. Reading gardening books and magazines, watching television programmes and getting tips from the radio are all helpful; joining a local horticultural society will introduce you to enthusiasts and enable you to pick their brains. One great way to get inspiration is to visit as many different gardens, large and small, as you can, making notes of ideas that might work in your garden and learning the names of plants that appeal to you.

But none of these is a substitute for getting out there in the garden, getting your hands dirty and setting about making plants grow. To do that successfully, you have to know the basics. The aim of this book is to teach you those basics – the rudiments of keeping your soil fertile and your plants healthy, of getting rid of weeds and minimizing pest attacks, of cutting a lawn and trimming a hedge – with just enough neat-and-tidiness to keep your neighbours happy, but without the whole thing becoming a millstone hanging over every weekend. It will also give you ideas for simple but successful plantings; for creating something you've always longed for like a cottage garden or your own patch of woodland; and for what to do with that dark boggy bit by the back fence.

Planting can be colour co-ordinated, as with the sea thrift, pansy 'Red Blotch' and pink forget-me-nots opposite; or an abundance of different hues complementing existing features, above.

You can start to garden at any age and the younger the better, because once you get the hang of it you will love it and wish you had taken it up earlier. It is also an advantage if you are fit enough for the donkey work, because there is bound to be some of that. Healthwise, gardening is one of the best hobbies, bringing lots of exercise, fresh air and the satisfaction of seeing plants maturing. People claim that it is therapeutic, but don't get too laid back about that – gardening can be pretty frustrating at times, most often because the weather is never what you wanted or expected.

In the meantime, while these encouraging words are being written and read, the weeds are growing like mad and the grass is growing like weeds, so I had better get on with some ways to garden.

Where do you start? There is no need for lots of paperwork but, in order to work towards your ideal garden, you should make a list of what is there already and whether you want to keep all of it. If you have a brand new plot, write down likes, dislikes and the features that you would love to have. With existing gardens, make notes of the things that you want to get rid of and all the jobs that you have to learn how to do, such as pruning and feeding plants.

What have you got? The perimeter may be a hedge, a fence or a wall, or a combination of all three. Some front gardens are what is termed open plan, with no demarcation screen at all, and only a kerb to mark the boundary. Whatever it is, measure it up and note the shape. Decide whether you are happy with it or if something different is needed for protection and privacy.

What size is your garden? Take measurements. Have the neighbours any interesting features or do you need to screen off an awful sight?

Is there a path? Do you want it, need it, like it? If there is no path does that matter? How will you cross the garden in periods of prolonged wet weather? Make a note of areas of shade in the garden and discover what is causing the shadow. Is the garden in full sun and at what time of day?

Think about the walls of the house, the boundary fence or the garden shed as areas that may be suitable for growing plants up – indeed, they may well benefit from a covering of climbing plants to disguise their appearance. There may well be lots of existing trees and shrubs or you could be the proud owner of a blank canvas with nothing but weeds.

Do you have a lawn? If so, is it big enough or even too big? Would you rather have more flowerbeds or a pond or a larger paved area for the barbecue and sun loungers?

Some plants are singularly unimpressive at certain times of the year and yet, when they decide to show off, the sight is unforgettable. Before making any decisions on the fate of existing plants, be patient and give them a year to show what they can do. Alternatively, call in an expert to label all the plants. Many excellent herbaceous plants and bulbs die down out of season and you risk throwing them out with the weeds before you get to see them in their full glory.

What do you want? The first question that demands an answer is: Do you want to be a gardener? It may well be that you are only interested to the point that you have an area of ground and have to do something with it. Don't worry, you are in the majority, and it is a fact that many fanatical gardeners grew out of reluctant plot owners who felt that they had to 'do' the garden.

If you want a garden that leaves you time to put your feet up and relax with friends and children, then you should aim for a low-maintenance plot. There is no such thing as a no-maintenance garden, unless it has been entirely paved over, but there are ways to reduce the hours spent on boring repetitive tasks.

A good starting point is to decide how much time you can spend working in the garden each week. There will be busy times such as in late spring when everything starts to grow – including the weeds and the grass – and there will also be slack times in the dead of winter when you can stay out of the garden for longer periods.

For lots of average gardens and indeed gardeners, a Saturday morning's work is sufficient to keep it in good condition. Grass areas can run away with your allocated hours, especially if a quality, weed-free lawn is your aim. Do you want to grow your own vegetables and fruit? What about flowers? Lots of gardeners enjoy cutting flowers for the house and a cutting border of suitable plants means that other ornamental beds in the garden won't be denuded of colour and interest.

How much can you afford to spend on the garden? I can't answer that for you, but even really small amounts of money can quickly make an enormous difference on the ground. Even gardeners can't get money to grow on trees, so it is a good idea to set a budget for each project or else your total allocation could disappear on one scheme.

Do you have children or are you planning for old age? Or perhaps you are one of those people who sees your whole life in front of you and are thinking of both!

Most people now use their garden for entertainment, whether it be for childrens' parties or adults' barbecues or a glass of wine on the terrace, and suitable areas should be allowed for in the overall plan.

Check list

• Try to identify all the existing plants, with expert help if necessary. Be patient and don't dig up something and throw it away until you are sure that it looks dull for a substantial part of the year.
• Learn the difference between annual weeds that seed and die in the same year and perennial weeds that are difficult to get rid of, such as gout weed (also known as ground elder) and nettles.
• Keep an eye on the sun as it travels around your garden. Note which areas are in full sunshine, as these will be sunny and warm, while shaded areas will be colder.

Mixed planting of roses, stachys, begonias and box leading to a vine-covered arbour. Notice how the curving beds create 'secret' areas of lawn.

Putting your garden on paper

Drawing a sketch of your garden is a simple task, but it doesn't achieve much unless it is accurate and enables you to determine whether or not there is sufficient space to accommodate extra features.

The answer is to make a scale drawing. All you need for the job are a pencil and some graph paper or squared paper. A long tape measure and someone to hold the other end, and you are ready to start. Measure the overall dimensions of the garden and transfer them to the graph paper using one square to represent 1 ft, 1 yd or 1 m, whichever you prefer. Alternatively, use a scaled ruler, on which 1 cm will represent 1 m of garden (it doesn't matter if you prefer to work in imperial, as long as your tape measure and your ruler correspond). Using a scale of 1:100 a sheet of A4 paper will easily accommodate a garden of 15 m x 25 m (50 ft x 80 ft).

Whatever means of measuring you choose, write the scale you are using on the plan (1 square = 1 m, for example), in case you forget. You should also measure and mark on the plan any immovable features such as a large tree or a shed that you want to keep.

Now you can start to redesign your garden. Decide on the overall shape of the beds, lawn and other main features and draw them on your plan. You may want a garden full of curves, or a more formal layout with lots of right angles and straight lines, or a mixture of the two. Once the shape of the feature you have drawn pleases you, measure its width and length and its position in relation to the rest of the garden and mark it out on the ground using sand, string, an aerosol marker or a length of hosepipe. Change the lines until you are happy with the size and shape, and mark the changes on the plan.

Lawns will be easier to cut if there are no sharp, tight corners that the mower cannot manoeuvre round, so design the paths and flower beds that border the lawn with gentle curves rather than sharp angles. Curving a bed also allows you to develop secret, hidden areas. Plant some of the taller evergreens, such as rhododendrons, in any area projecting out into the lawn and the area beyond, where the bed curves in, will be hidden from view. You might then plant it with smaller plants and bulbs that will be invisible from part of the garden but come as a pleasant surprise from a different angle.

A scale drawing will also help you to decide on suitable sites for larger plants, whether you want to move them from another part of the garden or introduce new species. Knowing how much space you have available will reduce the risk of overcrowding in later years. Small gardens can be made to look larger if your attention is drawn to a feature or plant at the farthest point from the house. If there is space, design in a tall, interesting plant such as the white-barked birch (*Betula utilis* var. *jacquemontii*) or a piece of statuary flanked by upright golden Irish yews (*Taxus baccata* 'Fastigiata Aurea'), making sure that, on paper, there is nothing to block the view.

The illustrations show four different approaches to the same 14 m x 20 m (46 ft x 65 ft) plot, drawn to a scale of 1:200. All of them can be worked out on paper before you put a spade in the ground, avoiding lots of hard work and potentially expensive mistakes.

Tips for a low-maintenance garden

• For ease of cutting, the lawn should be rounded at the corners rather than have tight angles where the mower won't fit.

• Deep mulches on the flower beds – of at least 5 cm (2 in) – will reduce the need to weed.

• Don't grass over steep banks: plant them with groundcover plants instead.

• Paths should be flush with the lawn to allow the mower to cut the edge of the grass.

• Use permanent shrubs for display rather than seasonal bedding plants as they don't need regular replacement.

• Don't plant hedges that require frequent clipping, such as privet or Leyland cypress.

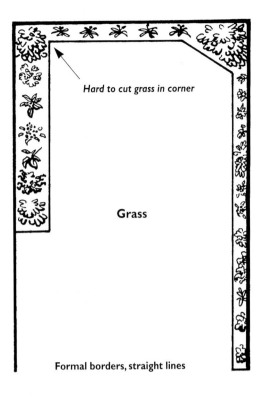

Hard to cut grass in corner

Grass

Formal borders, straight lines

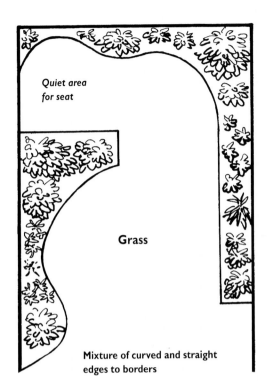

Quiet area
for seat

Grass

Mixture of curved and straight
edges to borders

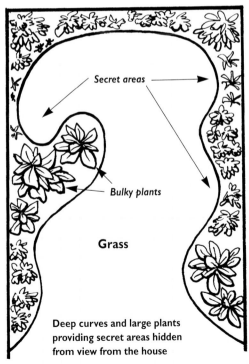

Secret areas

Bulky plants

Grass

Deep curves and large plants
providing secret areas hidden
from view from the house

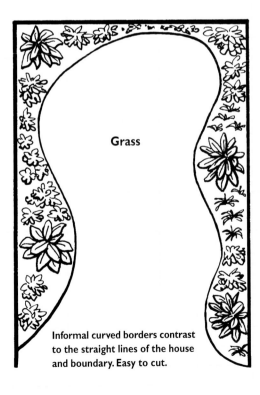

Grass

Informal curved borders contrast
to the straight lines of the house
and boundary. Easy to cut.

first things first

A first step towards succeeding at gardening is to get to know your plants: their likes and dislikes, the best food for them and the sites where they are happiest. So what exactly is a plant, and how does it function?

Well, plants can be thought of as a combination of roots, stems, leaves and reproductive parts – usually flowers.

What do roots do? One of the principal functions of a plant's root system is to take water from the soil and make it available to the plant. Without water, a plant will wither and eventually die. At the same time, the roots absorb minerals in solution that feed the plant; they also take up air. The root system also anchors the plant in the ground, keeping it from blowing over.

Some plants are adapted for drought conditions so that their roots can go deep in search of water; others, such as cacti, instead produce a shallow root system that spreads far and wide, ready to absorb any rain that falls before it can evaporate. The fine hairs at the ends of the roots are the collectors; the larger, thick roots transport the water and nutrients.

• Roots are easily damaged. Take great care when planting or moving plants and when using a hoe or spade around shallow-rooted plants such as rhododendrons, to avoid cutting roots.
• At planting time, soil should be loose and well broken up, to make life easy for the fine roots as they begin to move through the soil.
• Transplanting or shifting plants before they come into leaf allows the roots to become established before the plant starts to demand lots of water and food.

What do stems do? The thin, easily damaged stem of a young seedling is little different to the massive trunk of a mature tree, as both carry out the same functions. It supports the leaves of the plant in maximum light, as high as possible, and holds the flowers in a good position for insect and wind pollination. The stem passes water and nutrients from the roots to the leaves via xylem cells, which are not unlike our veins. It also sends a sugar-rich solution, manufactured in the leaves, down the phloem cells to provide energy for the whole plant.

The main difference between a plant stem and a tree trunk is that, in herbaceous plants – about which we shall hear more later – the stems die down each winter, with new ones forming the following spring.

• The outer protective layer of a tree trunk is called bark. It is easily damaged by animals such as rabbits, which like to eat it, and by overly tight tree ties which hold the tree to a stake and may strangle it. Bad garden planning, so that the lawn mower constantly hits the trunk of the tree, for example, is another cause of serious damage.

What do leaves do? The leaf can be as colourful and interesting as the flower and can be many shapes and sizes. It is also a very important part of the plant. It has two main functions: to manufacture organic substances using carbon dioxide from the air, plus water and minerals sent up the stem from the roots; and to dispose of unwanted substances such as surplus water in a process called transpiration – a bit like you and me sweating.

The energy produced in the leaf is dependent on its green colouring and on daylight; as a result, when green leaves become pale it usually means that the plant has a problem and the leaves can't do their job. In areas where there is less light – under trees, for example – coloured leaves can be an advantage. The white spots on variegated leaves magnify the available light and direct it on to the green parts. If the underside of the leaf is purple, the light is reflected back into the leaf rather than passing through.

What do flowers do? We tend to think of flowers as attractive, colourful and often scented and that is our main reason for growing lots of ornamental plants. The plant has a different agenda, however — it produces flowers in order to reproduce. In many plants a flower contains both male and female parts; others have separate male and female flowers, often on different plants. Insects such as bees carry the male pollen from one flower to another on their bodies. Some plants, such as hazels, are wind pollinated: the wind blows the pollen to the female flower. Fertilisation takes place when the male pollen lands on the female part of the flower and seed is formed after the flower dies. Peas in a pod are pea seeds in a case and an apple or pear is simply a seed container with the seed inside.

Different requirements for different plants No two gardens have exactly the same climatic conditions, and even within an individual garden there will be favoured areas. There may be a sunny sheltered wall and within the same garden, another site where the sun never shines and there is no protection from cold biting winds. The good news is that I have never come across an area where it was not possible to grow plants. There are plants to suit all situations and there is a section later in the book devoted to this subject (see page 115).

Plants with thick leaves that store moisture — such as the ice plant (*Sedum*) — are good for hot sunny sites, as are those with fine hairs that create a thin layer of still air next to the leaf surface, minimizing water loss. An example is lambs' ears, where the hairs on the leaves produce a silver upper surface. Other plants such as lavender, thyme and rosemary, give off essential oils, which saturate the air around the leaves and prevent water loss.

Areas in heavy shade will entertain butcher's broom, spotted laurel, ivy and periwinkle. The Labrador tea plant with the grand name of *Ledum groenlandicum* will tolerate the worst climatic conditions imaginable, including freezing winds, shade and prolonged rainfall, and still manage to flower in spring.

Rates of growth Some plants grow quickly and others are slow growing but still manage, in later life, to end up large. It is worth noting that there is a difference between the descriptive terms 'slow growing' and 'dwarf', in that the former will remain small only for a period of time, whereas the latter will never grow large. Other plants never grow very high but spread themselves over large areas of ground, which can be beneficial if you have bare earth to cover and need to suppress weeds. Quick-growing plants have their uses, too, especially for shelter and screening from the worst of the winds, or to provide privacy.

Most plant labels provide the important information, such as ultimate height and spread, preferred site and whether it is able to withstand harsh weather. If a plant can be grown outside without any protection it is referred to as being hardy.

Echium wildprettii **(with the red flowers) and** *Echium scilloniense* **require a frost-free climate and a well-drained soil. Given these conditions, they will throw out these spectacular columns of flowers.**

learning plant names

Do not be put off by long, hard-to-pronounce names. Usually someone long before you has had the same problem and has come up with a common name such as sweet pea, mock orange, birch or rose. Where the 'proper' botanical name has an advantage is that everyone uses it, so you can converse with anyone, anywhere, and know you are talking about the same plant. Common names change within counties, never mind countries, and two plants may have the same common name. *Pulmonaria saccharata* and *Phlomis fruticosa* are unrelated, but both are sometimes called Jerusalem sage.

Botanical names are made up of at least two words, conventionally written in italics. The first word is for the genus i. e. the group that the plant belongs to. Plants in the same genus share some characteristics but may differ widely in others – trees and shrubs can belong to the same genus, but different species within the same genus may be evergreen or deciduous. The second word refers to the species i. e. the kind of plant. Members of the same species are closely related – they will normally have the same height and spread, the same shape of leaf and flower, and can fertilize each other. Some plants then have a variety name, which is written without italics, enclosed in single quotation marks.

Quite often the species and variety names give you some description of the plant, so that *Rosa canina* is the dog rose and *Thymus vulgaris* is the common thyme, while the variety 'Aureus' is a common thyme with yellow leaves.

Most herbaceous plants have common as well as botanical names. *Verbascum* (the tall yellow spikes on the left) is also known as mullein; *Hemerocallis* (the orange flowers in the foreground) are daylilies.

Learning the language of plants

If all plants were just plants, a gardener's life would be rosy. But plants fall into categories, each with its own requirements. In time you will get to know the habits and needs of each type, but in the meantime you can grow the right plants by reading labels and finding out more information as you go along. There are dictionaries of plant terms containing lots of words you will never have need of – the following are the ones you are most likely to encounter.

Deciduous Plants that drop their leaves in winter, producing new foliage in the spring, such as oak or lilac.

Evergreen Plants that retain their leaves throughout the winter, including laurel and holly.

Hardy A plant that can survive outdoors all year round without protection. Obviously, plants that are hardy in a mild area may not be hardy in a colder area. North American gardeners are given guidance through a system of zones, of which zone 1 is the Arctic and zone 11 the southernmost part of the continent, where temperatures never reach freezing point. A plant may be hardy to, say, zones 7-9, which means you can leave it out of doors all winter if you live in Texas, but not if you live in New York.

Half-hardy Plants that need protection when the temperature drops to freezing.

Tender Plants that will suffer in cold weather, even before it reaches freezing point.

Acid loving Plants that grow best in soil that has a pH lower than 7 – i.e. soil that contains no lime. Such plants include rhododendrons and camellias, and are often also known as calcifuges (lime haters).

Alkaline (or lime) loving Plants that grow best in a soil that has a pH figure over 7 – i.e. soil that contains lime. Plants include lilac, the butterfly bush (buddleia) and fuchsia.

Rootstock The root and lower part of a plant on to which another variety is grafted.

Union The joint where the different variety is grafted on to the rootstock, usually causing a thickening of the stem.

Single, double and semi-double Single flowers have a single whorl of petals. Most wild plants have single flowers. Semi-double flowers have two or three rows of petals in layers. Double flowers have many rows of petals and usually no stamens.

Annual A plant that germinates from seed, grows, flowers and dies all in the same season; for example, snapdragons, marigolds and sunflowers.

Biennial A plant that is sown in summer, overwinters outdoors, flowers in the following spring or early summer and then dies; for example, wallflowers, sweet williams and Canterbury bells.

Herbaceous perennial Usually a plant that dies down in autumn or winter, reappearing in the spring and flowering in the second year. Perennials live for at least two years, some for much longer, and include the familiar Michaelmas daisy and hollyhock.

Shrub A plant such as hydrangea which produces many woody stems from the base rather than a single trunk, like a tree. A **sub-shrub** is a shrub that is woody only at the base of the plant, such as perovskia, or one that dies back to ground level in winter, such as fuchsia.

Tree Usually thought of as a large plant with a single stem breaking into a crown of branches, such as a chestnut. But there are trees of all sizes, including some that never become big, such as the dwarf Japanese acers that provide such wonderful autumn colour.

Conifer Usually an evergreen cone-bearing tree, such as a pine, but there are deciduous conifers, such as larch. Dwarf conifers are ideal for rockeries and small containers.

Bedding A general term for all those plants that provide seasonal colour in flowerbeds, especially in summer, and are then removed and disposed of in the autumn.

Climbers These plants clamber up and over walls, fences and other plants. There are three groups: those that are self clinging, using sucker pads, such as ivy; those that naturally twine around other plants (a good example is honeysuckle); and those that hold on using tendrils – sweet peas for example.

Bulbs, corms and tubers These are usually all called bulbs, but there is a difference. True bulbs, such as daffodils or onions, are made up of thickened leaves. Corms, by contrast, are thickened stems and are solid and hard. They include crocus and gladiolus. A tuber is a thickened root – a dahlia or a potato, for example – while a rhizome is a thickened underground stem, as seen in a bearded iris.

This deciduous azalea, variety 'Apple Blossom', requires an acid soil in light shade. If you provide the conditions your plants prefer – or choose plants to suit the conditions you are able to offer – they will reward you with health and beauty.

basic plant care

Get to know your soil — it's all that is keeping your plant alive. Is it light, dry, heavy, wet or even waterlogged? Some plants are fussy and they will be happy only if the soil is suitable for their needs.

Feeding the soil with the right nutrients can do a lot for a plant by encouraging growth, improving flower colour and increasing yields.

The right soil plus correct feeding equals happy plants.

your soil, for what it's worth

It may seem difficult to get excited about soil, but if you take a bit of interest before you start to garden I promise you that it will save you a heap of trouble later on.

Topsoil is the soil that gardeners are most interested in. It forms a layer overlying the subsoil which in itself covers the bedrock.

There are two types of topsoil, easy and hard. Easy includes soils that are loose and easily cultivated, such as sand, loam and peat types. Hard soils include stony, clay and wet – the types that are difficult to break up. Topsoil also comprises a mixture of minerals, water, oxygen and organic matter and if any of these is in short supply, plant growth is restricted. A good-quality soil contains earthworms, insects and bacteria which help to break down organic matter such as leaves and debris, enriching the soil and converting it into nutrients that the roots can collect and use as plant food. As earthworms move through the soil they form channels that aid drainage and introduce air. Grubs, centipedes and other insects also help to open up the soil.

Below every topsoil at varying depths is the **subsoil**, which is harder and poorer, with few earthworms and insects. Topsoil is simply improved subsoil.

A useful combination for a late spring border. Bluebells and lilac are both happy growing in an alkaline soil. The bluebells enjoy the partial shade and spread rapidly to cover the ground and help suppress weeds.

The soil is what gardening is all about and the more you respect it and care for it, the better your garden and plants will be. It is the soil that provides the nutrients plants need for growth and it stores the water and oxygen that the roots transport to the other parts of the plant.

Different soils have different characteristics and some are better suited than others to a plant's needs. The best soil to provide all that is needed should have a good structure where the individual crumbs of soil are loosely joined, leaving lots of small spaces that allow air and water to be retained, yet permit surplus water to drain freely. It should be rich in minerals that can be converted to plant food and contain organic matter. A slightly acid or neutral soil is suitable for the majority of plants.

Worms and soil

The more earthworms there are in your soil, the better. A rich organic soil may have as many as 25 worms per square metre, all tunnelling through the soil, helping drainage and turning debris into nutrients. As worms move through the soil they eat it and deposit it near or on the surface as casts. In this way, the nutrients that have been washed down through the soil are brought back to the surface.

Testing your soil It is worth doing a soil test to find out whether your soil is alkaline, neutral or acid, which is determined by the amount of calcium or lime it contains. Test kits are available from garden centres and are easy to use. When taking soil samples for testing, take them from different areas in the garden to obtain an overall picture of your soil. The test result will provide a pH reading on a scale where 7 is neutral, below that is acid and above that the soil is alkaline or limy. Alkaline soil rules out rhododendrons, camellias, pieris, azaleas, kalmias and a lot of the heathers. Incorporating large quantities of peat into the soil and top-dressing the surface with a mulch of peat twice a year will reduce the alkalinity, but it takes a lot to make much difference. It is probably simpler and cheaper to form a raised bed (see page 35) if you really want to grow these plants.

There is a great variety of soils from light, open, sandy mixtures to heavy, cold, waterlogged mud and in between there are clay, loam, gravel and peat. Some plants succeed in only one type of soil, so to choose suitable plants for your garden, you need to find out what type you have.

Loam soil has very few particles of clay and is free-draining yet moisture-retentive, with a high level of nutrients.

Clay-based soil has a large percentage of clay particles, which tend to stick together, leaving no air spaces. It is usually wet and solid, with poor drainage, slow to warm up in spring and eventually drying out to form a hard solid mass that is difficult to cultivate.

Peat soils are acid, wet and made up of partially decomposed organic matter. If they can be drained and a loam soil added they become a great growing medium for plants that like acid conditions.

Easy plants for acid soil

Calluna vulgaris (heather)
Erica cinerea (heather)
Camellia x *williamsii* 'Donation'

Easy plants for alkaline (limy) soil

Choisya ternata (Mexican orange blossom)
Syringa vulgaris (lilac)
Viola cornuta (horned violet)

Easy plants for sandy soil

Cistus x *purpureus* (sun rose)
Lavandula 'Hidcote' (lavender)
Thymus vulgaris (thyme)

Easy plants for clay soil

Chaenomeles x *superba* (Japanese quince)
Aucuba japonica 'Crotonifolia' (spotted laurel)
Potentilla fruticosa (potentilla)

Sandy soils contain practically no clay and are low in organic matter, so are free-draining and unable to hold moisture. Their nutrient content is low, with any minerals being washed down to below the root zone. Sandy soils warm up quickly in the spring, but require lots of irrigation and added nutrients.

The finger test A simple test for soil type is to rub some moist soil between your fingers. Loam will hold together and can be shaped. Sandy soils feel gritty and won't hold together; clay soil is sticky, heavy and has a sheen when it is smoothed over. Peat soil has a rich brown look and retains moisture – water appears when a handful is squeezed. Loam is the best choice for a whole range of plants and the addition of loam will improve all the other soils.

Most soils will benefit from regular applications of compost, bark or rotted cow or horse manure, either dug into the soil using one full wheelbarrow per 4 sq ms (40 sq ft) or spread on the surface of the ground 5–10cm (2–4in) deep as a mulch. As the material decomposes, earthworms transport it through the soil, helping to drain clay soils and make sandy soil more moisture retentive. Adding coarse sand or grit to a clay soil will open it up, separating the particles and allowing air pockets to form and surplus water to drain away.

The ideal time to incorporate materials into the soil is during cultivation or at planting time. Surface mulches can be applied at any time but the earthworms will move them more quickly in spring. Even the worst types of soil can be improved and, until the additives take effect, there are plenty of plants for all sorts of soils.

feeding plants

The mineral salts collected by a plant's roots in liquid form and transported through the plant via the stems are nutrients or food for the plant to use. Included are the main elements of nitrogen, phosphate and potash as well as trace elements – those that are needed only in small doses, such as magnesium, iron and zinc. Each nutrient serves a different purpose and knowing what part they play in growth allows you to feed the plant what it wants, rather than what it can manage to find.

Nitrogen (often referred to by its scientific abbreviation N) will help a plant make growth and so it is good for lawns, where lots of leaves have to be produced, and for leafy crops such as cabbage and lettuce.

Phosphate (P) encourages sturdy growth and good flower colour.

Potash (K) is needed for root growth and it also helps plants to resistance disease.

Magnesium (Mg) and **iron** (Fe) are the two trace elements most often in short supply. Not all soils contain all the trace elements that plants needs and a deficiency often causes mottling or discolouring of the leaves. Magnesium and iron can easily be applied to the soil or as a foliar feed (see box below) directly on to the leaves.

If the soil in which the plant is growing is in good heart and not exhausted of nutrients by decades of cropping with nothing being put back, then few, if any, nutrients need to be applied. A healthy plant in a rich topsoil with adequate water will grow away quite happily, but a lot of plants benefit from an application of fertilizer, either as a granular feed or as a quick pick-me-up in the form of a liquid feed.

When granular or powdered fertilizers are being applied to the soil, choose a calm day when the foliage is dry. This will prevent the fertilizer sticking to the leaves, absorbing moisture, converting to a liquid acid and scorching the foliage. Deciduous plants need feeding only from late spring until late autumn.

A feed at planting time will give a plant a head start. Mix 30 g (1 oz) of a fertilizer such as bonemeal, which releases its nutrients over a long period, into the soil from the planting hole. Return the soil around the roots and the extra nutrients will help the plant settle in its new site and grow away quickly.

Types of fertilizer

Powdered Fine powders such as bonemeal are apt to stick to damp foliage. They are best applied direct to soil and worked in before planting.

Granular These small clusters of fertilizer bounce off the leaves and break up in contact with moisture. Use them among growing plants or on lawns.

Concentrate Liquid feeds are usually sold as concentrates, to be diluted before use. They are frequently used for houseplants.

Soluble These are sold as granules or powders that you dissolve in water. Once in a solution, nutrients are quickly available to plants in need.

Slow-release One of the best types for long-lived plants such as shrubs. The nutrients are released from the granules over a period of up to six months.

Liquid Fertilizers in liquid form are fast acting, as they are immediately available to the plant through the roots.

Foliar This is a method of feeding the plant directly through the leaves, using a liquid feed.

Compost for containers

Garden soil can be used for planting containers providing the plants are short term, such as annuals or pansies, and are replaced after a few months. But there are many disadvantages to using soil in pots, not least in that it will be full of weed seeds just waiting to germinate and choke the plants. There will probably be some pests such as chafer grubs, vine weevils and leatherjackets, and spores of various fungal diseases. Garden centres and stores are well stocked with a range of proprietary composts to suit every plant's needs, including soil-based kinds whose soil has been sterilized, and soil-less types using peat, coir (coconut fibre) or other additives to provide a suitable growing medium.

The one great advantage of soil-based compost is that it is more retentive of moisture and so less likely to shrink away from the edge of the pot as it dries out, making rewatering easy. Its disadvantage compared to soilless compost is that it is heavier and a large container recently watered is not easily moved.

There are various specialist composts too, such as ericaceous composts for lime-hating plants and orchid mixes that provide a really open, free-draining material. Composts with built-in resistance to some pests are proving popular and every type of compost contains a fertilizer whose composition is consistent in every bag. There are composts containing slow-release fertilizer that gradually supplies nutrients to the plant roots over a period of anything from 6 months or even up to 14 months for shrubs in pots, but most others are exhausted of nutrients after about six weeks. Plants in pots need regular feeding during the growing period and should eventually be repotted into larger containers with fresh compost.

Succulent perennials require an open, free-draining compost low in fertilizer. The pot must have good drainage holes to prevent waterlogging.

drainage

Water-logged soils will only sustain a limited range of plants that have adapted themselves to the conditions. All the air spaces in water-logged soil are filled with water, preventing the roots from collecting oxygen and causing fine roots and soft stems to rot. To improve the quality of the soil it is necessary to lower the level of the water to allow the topsoil to dry out. There are several methods worth trying. Digging coarse sand or grit into the top 20 cm (8 in) will open up the soil, so that water can drain through to the lower levels. Warm weather will help some water to evaporate, but draining the excess off should be a priority. Use as little heavy machinery as possible – the weight will compact the soil and make matters even worse.

If you have a patch that is wet all year while the rest of the garden is only moist after rainfall, try to investigate the cause of the problem. It might be that there is a burst water main or that rainwater from the roof of the house is piped for a short distance and then allowed to seep away. Or there may be a natural spring close to the surface. The waterlogged area may be lower lying than the rest of the garden and the surface soil may have become compacted, preventing the water from percolating down. Instead it may lie on the surface of the depression and become stagnant.

If this is the case, digging with a four-pronged garden fork to break up the compaction and allow the water to seep away often cures the problem. Where there are large areas to be drained, you need to look for a suitable outlet, such as a boundary ditch or hedge line, at a lower level to drain the water to. Digging back from the outlet to the area to be drained, form a trench about 40 cm (16 in) deep, that slopes towards the outlet. Once the water starts to flow, insert a 10 cm (4 in) diameter plastic pipe with slits to collect the water and carry it away. Ensure that you lay the pipe with a uniform fall or slope, so that water won't lie in the pipe. Cover the pipe with clean, washed 13 mm (½ in) gravel to stop soil working its way into the slits and causing a blockage. The pipe and the stones can then be covered with soil, but take care that this soil does not become compacted, as that would prevent the water draining down into the pipe.

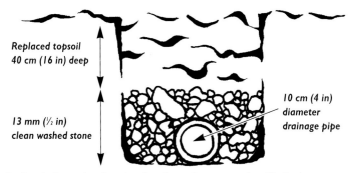

Replaced topsoil 40 cm (16 in) deep

13 mm (½ in) clean washed stone

10 cm (4 in) diameter drainage pipe

Laying drainage pipes is not as daunting as it may sound, and is the best way to deal with water-logged soil. The important factors to remember are keeping the slope uniform so that water doesn't lie in the pipe; and preventing anything from clogging up the drainage slits.

Getting started

Even if your soil needs improving and is going to take time to cultivate, it is still possible to have the fun and enjoyment of getting started straight away by preparing just a small area for planting. Alternatively, you can build raised beds using railway sleepers, bricks or concrete blocks to form walls 25–30 cm (10–12 in) high and fill these with good-quality topsoil that will allow you to grow flowers or fruit and vegetables. Check the quality with the soil supplier, insisting that it is free of weed roots and serious pests such as vine weevil and leatherjackets. If you are constructing more than one raised bed, space them 90 cm (36 in) apart with a path between. Even if you have access from both sides the bed should not be wider than 120 cm (48 in), allowing you to stretch easily to the centre.

Digging: the rights and wrongs

Right　　　　**Wrong**

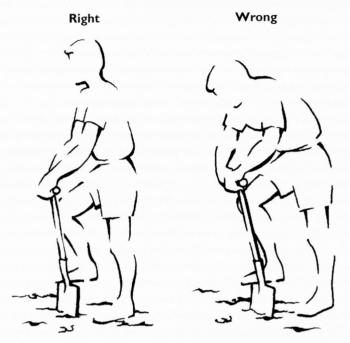

Digging needn't be hard work. With the right technique and a spade that suits you, you can turn the soil over with a minimum of effort and without backache.

Choose a spade to suit your height. When you stand upright with your foot on the lug of the blade, the handle of the shaft should be at waist height; for lifting and turning the soil your other hand should be halfway down the shaft.

Keep your back straight; the handle of the shaft should be at waist height.

A sharp blade will penetrate the soil more easily. Push the blade straight down into the ground. If you hold it at an angle you will cultivate less depth of soil, so getting a planting hole the right depth will take more effort. Keep your back straight as you turn the blade. Move your arms and bend your knees, not your back. Until you get used to the movements, your arms and legs may be sore after a digging session, but that is nothing a hot bath won't put right. A sore back, on the other hand, can be a real long-term problem and there is no need to cause it by digging badly.

Right　　　　**Wrong**

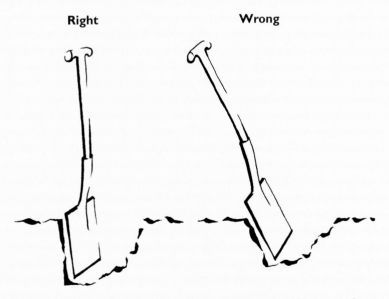

Push the blade straight down into the ground. If you hold it at an angle you will cultivate less depth of soil.

Stone slabs make a handsome path down to a woodland garden. The beds around the shrubs and perennials are mulched with cedar bark.

down to earth

Plants in the garden will do better if they don't have to look after themselves and are given a little tender loving care. Spend five minutes each day looking around your garden to see that all the plants are enjoying your hospitality. The exercise will do you no harm and you will get to know your plants.

tools for the job

One of the first priorities is to purchase some tools to garden with and this needs a clear head and a lot of restraint. There are racks and racks of every sort of tool imaginable, and lots more that you couldn't imagine, on sale in garden centres, but in truth very few of them are necessary or even useful. Indispensable tools include:

- spade
- fork
- rake
- stiff brush
- hand fork

- digging trowel
- watering can
- wheelbarrow
- hosepipe
- secateurs

Oh, there are lots more you can buy later on, but by then you will have an idea of what suits you and the work you have to do. Hoeing is practical only in dry climates – living in Northern Ireland, I don't own a hoe.

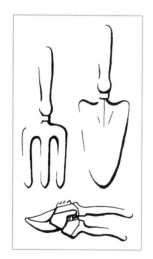

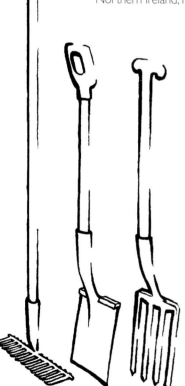

Buy the best tools you can afford and they may last you a lifetime. Choose the size to suit you, so that you don't have to strain your back to use them. Hand tools should feel comfortable.

Tip for tools

Look after your tools and treat them with respect. Don't leave them out in the garden from one day to the next as sun, rain and frost will all cause them to deteriorate. Clean the soil off them before storing. Oil any moving parts on a regular basis and sharpen the blades of hooks and secateurs so that they make a clean cut. Hoes and spades become blunt very quickly, especially in stony soil and the job is a lot easier if you keep them sharp, either by hand or on a grind stone.

It is important that the tools are strong and of top quality, since cheap tools seldom last for more than a few seasons. The best advice is to spend as much as you can afford. Buy tools that are the right shape for you and that you feel comfortable with, making sure that you don't have to bend over when you are using them. An aching back is as likely to be the result of using tools that are too small for you, as of the amount of work that you do.

A good spade will have a broad blade of quality steel with a turned-over lug on either side to take foot pressure without hurting the sole of your foot. The shaft will be long enough to suit your height and be made of splinter-free hardwood with a T- or D-shaped handle. The garden fork will be similar with four broad prongs.

I prefer a landscape rake for general work, but it isn't much use for raking the lawn. It is wooden handled with a wide head of alloy teeth well spaced to allow small stones and debris through but retaining larger stones.

A yard brush with stiff bristles is essential for clearing up soil and leaving a good finish.

Hand tools should be stainless steel with handles that are comfortable to prevent blisters. Buying the best you can afford is particularly important with secateurs and if you get it right they will last you a lifetime.

Over the years your garden shed will blend into the garden and acquire a character of its own.

sheds

A garden shed can be the most romantic place in the garden and an attractive feature rather than a tumbledown eyesore. It is an individual sort of thing and hardened male gardeners who wouldn't dream of wearing gloves happily hang net curtains on their shed windows.

Every gardener needs somewhere to keep equipment and that's what sheds are for. Tools would soon deteriorate if left out in the elements; fertilizers can be kept in the dry to stop them absorbing moisture from the air; and if the shed is frost free and vermin proof, bulbs and seeds can be stored.

If chemicals such as weedkillers, pesticides and fungicides are kept in the shed, they will need to be in a metal cabinet with a strong lock. Garden sheds come in many forms, though they are nearly all timber with a window and door. But you can find DIY kits for plastic and metal sheds on the market. A timber shed needs to be treated with a wood preservative, while a coat of wood stain in the spring will freshen it up ready for the summer. Bright paintwork in blues, yellows or reds is the fashion but you may be more traditional and settle for brown or green.

Where to site a shed Ideally, the shed should be tucked in somewhere; it should be accessible – not sitting in the middle of the lawn, but close to where the action is. You may decide to screen the shed with plants and there are plenty of evergreen shrubs such as ceanothus, camellia,

Points to watch out for

- Raised floors will need support to prevent sagging.
- Site the shed so that the door is on the side sheltered from the wind.
- A screening of plants will keep a wooden shed cooler in summer.
- Don't erect the shed on the garden boundary or you will have to ask your neighbours permission to carry out any exterior maintenance work.

viburnum and eleagnus that will do the job. A little extra thought has to be given to the idea of training climbers up and over the shed for camouflage, in that most of them will lose their leaves in winter. Many species are also too vigorous. Avoid fast-growing clematis such as *Clematis montana* and *C. alpina*, and *Fallopia baldschuanica* – easier to remember as Russian vine or mile-a-minute, which aptly describes the speed with which it will take over and cover the shed.

If it is large enough, your shed can double as a potting shed as well as a tool store. A power supply for heat and light would come in handy on a cold wet day when seeds have to be sown and cuttings taken.

Erect the shed on a solid, dry base of concrete, slabs or gravel and if the wooden floor can be raised up on bricks there is less chance of rot.

cultivation

The point of cultivation is to break up the ground and make it more plant friendly, to allow plant roots to penetrate more readily in search of water and nutrients. If the area of ground to be cultivated is not too large, I recommend that you dig it by hand using a spade or garden fork, rather than cultivating it mechanically. Hand digging allows you to spot weed roots and pick them out and dump them. A rotavator just chops them up and leaves each piece to grow into a new weed. Soils that are in suitable condition for cultivating and not too wet are best dug in the late autumn or early winter, turning the soil over and leaving it rough on the surface. Winter frost will break up the lumps, leaving the soil friable, and at the same time the chill will penetrate the soil, killing overwintering pests. Additives such as compost and grit can be applied at this stage, turning them into the soil as it is being dug.

Rotavating is a quick way to cultivate large areas, as the blades break the soil up, levelling it as they go. Heavy soils and those that haven't been worked for a season or more will require a rotavator that has a separate drive to the blades, allowing the wheels to turn independently. The wheels move slowly over the ground while the blades are revolving at speed to break up the soil. Try to cultivate during a dry spell, otherwise the open ground soaks up the rain, becoming sodden and muddy. Trying to cultivate wet, muddy soil will destroy the soil structure and cause compaction, especially when you walk on it, resulting in poor drainage and sour soil that actually smells. By all means remove large stones and debris,

Geraniums, lady's mantle (*Alchemilla*) and forget-me-nots (*Myosotis*) growing wild in a neglected garden and as troublesome as any weed.

but don't try to cart away every last small stone as they keep the soil open and help drainage.

Knowing a weed when you see one Identifying weeds can be tricky. Some plants act like weeds, look like weeds and even grow like weeds but are in fact highly respectable plants. I always think of weeds as undesirable plants that in different circumstances would be planted in the garden. Some weeds are wild flowers. No one would suggest that Monet painted a field of weeds – of course not, it was a landscape of wild poppies. Some weeds disguise themselves with pretty flowers, such as bindweed with its pure white trumpets on twining, climbing stems. Then there is the dandelion, again with an attractive bloom, and what about the buttercup and thistle? Some of the worst weeds have an impressive pedigree – horsetail is hard to get rid of and that is hardly surprising, as it has been around since before the dinosaurs. Another really obnoxious plant is the bishop's weed, also called ground elder or gout weed, which doubles as a medicinal herb claimed to control gout and other ailments. But it has an attractive variegated form which I like to use for ground cover.

The whole identification problem is made worse by birds – they eat berries that pass through their digestive system unharmed and then germinate in your garden. In this way, shrubs such as cotoneaster, leycesteria, pyracantha and daphne suddenly appear. If you don't recognise them in the seedling stage they end up being composted – which is a pity, especially if you are in need of plants to fill any gaps in your beds. The best advice I can give is, if in doubt, leave unknown seedlings until the young plants are large enough to be identified as friend or foe. The illustrations on page 32 and 33 will help you identify the commonest – and the worst – weeds. Some weeds are useful and even desirable in certain parts of the garden: stinging nettles encourage butterflies and yellow rattleweed will help to weaken grass in a wild area by acting as a parasite and allowing the wild flowers to grow away in the weakened grass.

How weeds spread

Weeds can spread very quickly by seed, roots and runners. It is very important that they are killed, dug up or pulled out before they flower and produce seed, which germinates and in turn produces many more young weed plants. Bindweed spreads by white roots which are easily seen in the soil and should be dug out using a fork to reduce the risk of cutting the root. Even a small fragment will regrow. Try to remove as much as possible, as it spreads rapidly. Weeds with a deep, fleshy root such as dock should be eased out of the ground without breaking the root, as any piece that remains in the soil will reroot. Creeping buttercup spreads rapidly by surface runners and if left alone will soon cover a large area, killing lawn grass or weaker plants that you probably want to keep.

Methods of elimination

Once you have decided to eliminate the weeds, there are various well tried and tested methods for attempting to remove them. The surest but most labour-intensive way is to dig them out and dump them. Deep digging, using a garden fork to remove all of the root is essential, as each piece of perennial weed root that is left will result in another plant.

- **Hoeing weeds** can be done in two ways, using different types of tool. A draw hoe or swan-neck hoe has a blade that is bent towards you and is used to chop or draw the weeds out of the ground; a push hoe is used to cut the weeds off below ground level or lift small weeds out. When the sun is shining the hoed-off weeds can be left to wither and die, but if rain is expected rake the weeds off or they will reroot into the damp soil. In rainy weather and when the ground is wet stay off the beds and leave the weeding for a better day, as you will only destroy the surface of the soil.

- **Flame guns**, which are hand held and powered by gas, are also effective – the flame is applied to the leaves of the weeds, burning them off. It works better on soft weeds and seedlings; larger weeds and those with a tough root system will regrow after a time.

- **Spraying with a chemical weedkiller** can be very successful, but read the instructions first and wear proper protective clothing. Chemicals such as glyphosate, which travels through the leaf into the stems and down into the root, killing the whole plant, are the most reliable. There are also contact weed killers which work in the same way as the flame thrower, burning the foliage. Total weed killers, that kill everything including the toughest plants are available, but many of them contain chemicals that leave a residue in the soil, preventing anything from growing for up to 12 months.

- **Covering the soil with old carpet, black plastic or landscape fabric** – a permeable membrane with a close weave to allow water and air though but no weeds to grow – can also kill weeds. Even the toughest perennial weeds can't survive if deprived of light for a long period. Mulches, providing they are at least 5 cm (2 in) deep, will help to suppress the less vigorous weeds if spread on the soil surface. Old mushroom compost, wood chippings, bark mulch and even old rotted farmyard manure will act as a mulch (see page 46 for more information).

Composting weeds

Be very careful which weeds you put on to the compost heap. Those that spread by seeds should not be added, as the seeds will remain viable in the compost, growing away quite happily a year later when the compost is worked into the ground. Weeds such as thistle, dock and bindweed that spread by root should have their roots removed and dumped before the stems and leaves are composted.

10 worst perennial weeds

	Description	Spreads by	Control
	Horsetail Upright stems with whorls of green branches and black sheaths on the stems	Quick-spreading underground hairy rhizomes and by spores produced in the spring on the cone-shaped female shoots.	Constant hoeing every time growth appears, especially in the spring, to prevent spores forming, will weaken but not kill this weed. Spraying with glyphosate whenever the growth reaches 15 cm (6 in), with the last application in early autumn, will offer reasonable control.
	Japanese knotweed Hollow reddish stems that will reach 3 m (10 ft), with heart-shaped, stiff leaves and clusters of dirty white or pink flowers in autumn.	Quick-spreading underground rhizomes.	Keep cutting the stems at ground level or apply glyphosate at regular intervals as a means of partial control.
	Ground elder Also called bishop's weed and gout weed. It has divided leaves forming spear-shaped, toothed leaflets and flat heads of small white flowers in summer on 60 cm (2 ft) stems.	Shallow-rooted rhizomes that spread quickly through the soil and are easily broken, the pieces of root forming new plants.	Dig out, making sure to remove all the roots. Alternatively, spray with glyphosate as it appears for total control.
	Willow-herb There are many willow-herbs but one of the worst is rosebay willow-herb, which has tall stems and short-stalked narrow leaves. The flowers are purple-pink in long spikes and appear from early summer to early autumn.	Creeping rhizomes and wind-blown seed that may be seen in great silky clouds blowing from waste ground in autumn.	Pull out mature plants before they set seed, removing as much root as possible. Hoe or spray the seedlings with glyphosate.
	Bindweed Also known as convolvulus, a fast-growing climber twisting its stems anti-clockwise. It has heart-shaped leaves and funnel-shaped flowers in summer and autumn.	Brittle roots that break easily as the plant is being dug out. The smallest piece will reroot and produce another plant.	Remove the weeds by the root and burn them. If you can apply glyphosate without getting it on the foliage of other plants, it will have some effect.

	Description	Spreads by	Control
	Dock Plants have a thick, carrot-like tap root; tall, branched stem with large blunt leaves and spikes of tiny red-green flowers in spikes from summer to autumn.	Seed or pieces of root.	Dig out, taking care to remove all the root. Spray with glyphosate when the young, strongly growing foliage is present.
	Couch Other common names are scutch and twitch. A broad-leaved grass with spreading roots.	Rhizomes, which spread quickly to form a mat with growth buds all along the stem. The smallest piece of root will regrow.	Dig out, removing all the roots. Close cutting or spraying with glyphosate as the foliage appears will keep couch under control and, in time, will kill it.
	Nettle Tall straight stems with heart-shaped toothed leaves, often covered with stinging hairs. Greenish flowers hang in tassle-like clusters from early summer to early autumn. Yellow roots.	Root and seed. Another quick spreader.	Easily hoed out at the seedling stage or dug out as large clumps – make sure you remove all the roots. Spray with glyphosate when growing strongly.
	Buttercup Deeply divided leaves and shiny deep yellow flowers in late spring and early summer.	Vigorous rooting runners, each producing many plants. Also spreads from seed.	Hand weeding or glyphosate if there are no other plants close by. A selective broad-leaved weedkiller may be used to kill unwanted buttercups in a lawn.
	Dandelion A rosette of long, toothed leaves and yellow daisy-like flower. Flowers most of the year, peaking in late spring. The flowers are followed by circular heads of seeds, each with a parachute of feathery hairs.	Pieces of the fleshy tap root, or seed blown on the wind.	Dig the plant out before it sets seed, taking care to remove all the root. Spray wtih a broad-leaved weedkiller or use glyphosate, which should kill it in one application.

A raised mixed bed overlooking the sea, with pink, low-growing pelargoniums and salt-tolerant shrubs. Sitting on the wall brings you close to the plants.

making beds

I don't know how they became known as beds, but it is a name that covers all plantings be they of flowers, fruit, vegetables or shrubs. They can be any shape or size you like and surrounded by paths or grass.

Don't be too ambitious to start with. It is better to make a small bed and then enlarge it, than to go in at the deep end and decide later to make the area smaller. Decide on the general location of the bed and use the garden hose to mark the outline. Look at it from all parts of the garden to see that it is a pleasant shape and then view it from the house. If you have a two-storey house look at it from upstairs as well as down, as it will take on a completely different form when looked on from above. Check that the proportions are right compared to everything else and, if the bed has a curved outline make sure that the bends are not too severe, as they could be difficult to cut with a mower.

Carving a bed from grass If you are making a bed from a lawn, the grass will need either to be killed by chemical weed control or to be removed by digging it into the ground, making sure that the grass is buried in the bottom of the bed. Where there is a good depth of topsoil – at least 20 cm (8 in) – the grass sod can be skimmed off the surface with a spade and stacked out of the way, grass side down. It will rot down to form a humus-rich pile of soil. Start from within the proposed bed to avoid damaging the surface of the remaining lawn and when wheeling debris away, don't use the same route over the grass each time or you will damage it. Edge the bed by leaving the soil surface 5 cm (2 in) below the grass – providing the edge isn't broken or flattened by feet it will be acceptable. Stones, bricks on edge and tiles can be used to form an edge but where used to separate the lawn from the bed, they should be flush with the lawn surface, otherwise the grass along the outer side of the perimeter will be difficult to cut.

Where there is no grass, the ground can be dug over and the stones and debris removed to a dump or a skip. Alternatively, stones can be recycled to form a firm base for a path or patio. Remove weed roots as you dig and make sure that the spade or fork goes in to the full depth of the blade or prongs, turning the soil over. Break up large, heavy lumps of soil with the spade and, when the soil dries out, rake it over to provide a fine tilth on the surface ready to receive seeds or plants.

Raised beds There are many advantages to forming raised beds in which the soil is artificially lifted above the surrounding ground. A 90 cm (36 in) wide bed may be raised by simply pushing up the soil to either side to form a mound, which provides better drainage for vegetables or more air circulation, for example, to reduce the risk of fungal diseases in strawberry plants. The effect is like the furrows and ridges in a ploughed field.

If you want a contained bed, surrounding walls may be formed of brick or timber, including railway sleepers, and the bed filled in with layers of compost, farmyard manure, leaf mould and topsoil. This not only avoids poor soil drainage but allows you to grow plants even when the garden soil is unsuitable. Importing acidic soil will allow you to grow acid-loving plants such as rhododendron in a garden that is naturally limy. Gardeners who have difficulty bending to weed and plant, or those who work from a wheelchair, will find that raised beds are the answer.

Another type of bed is the seed bed, which is located in a sheltered position, so that soil warms up quickly to get the seeds off to a good start and is easily worked to form a fine surface for sowing seeds.

Fork over the base of the bed for drainage. Form sides of timber or brick.

Add layers of compost and farmyard manure and cover with topsoil.

Grow plants suited to the soil in the bed.

planting

There are two ways that you can plant, the right way and the wrong way. The latter, which is not noted for its success rate and is not recommended, is to dig a hole, stick the roots in and cover them up. The right way is to become a gardener and do the job correctly, giving the plant the best chance for success.

When to plant Plants that are growing in a container such as a clay or plastic pot or a black polythene bag can be planted in the garden at any time of the year providing the soil that they are being planted into is in a suitable condition. The roots should be disturbed as little as possible when planting, ideally without removing any of the soil around them.

Where plants have been purchased with bare roots, without any compost or container, it is essential that they are planted as soon as possible to prevent the roots from drying out. Bare-rooted plants are available only from late autumn through until early spring. If the weather and soil conditions are not ideal for planting out into their final position in the garden due to frost or sodden ground, then the roots of the plants will need to be soaked and heeled into the ground in a sheltered position or under a hedge. Dig a shallow trench and lay the plants at an angle to resist the wind, before back-filling with soil, making sure the roots are well covered. There they will be safe from harm until conditions improve, providing the soil is in contact with the roots and there are no air pockets.

The planting hole When digging a planting hole, always be generous and make it at least two times the size of the root area of the plant or the container that the plant is growing in. Loosen the base and sides of the hole to allow the roots to move easily out into the soil in search of water and nutrients and to take firm hold to secure the plant. If your planting hole is so large that subsoil has been removed during the excavation, the hole should be backfilled with topsoil and the subsoil disposed of. You'll know you have hit subsoil because the earth becomes inhospitable – rock hard with no fibrous material.

Carefully remove the pot from a small plant by holding the plant upside down and easing the container off. Keep the ball of soil around the roots moist, as dry soil will fall away from the the roots and disturb them.

Plants that are pot bound, with their roots congested in the compost and tangled into a tight ball in the shape of the container, need to have the roots carefully teased out in the planting hole. This will encourage them to spread out into the soil in search of moisture and nutrients, and hold the plant steady and upright in the soil.

A shovelful of compost or rotted farmyard manure in the base of the planting hole and a handful of slow-release bone-meal fertilizer mixed into the topsoil will get the plant off to a good start. Backfill the hole, working the soil through the roots to prevent air pockets, which allow the roots to dry out and kill the plant.

Check the roots of bare-rooted trees and shrubs and cut off any broken or damaged pieces, making a clean cut. Always plant at the same depth as the plant was previously growing: you'll be able to tell by looking at the stems. The one notable exception is clematis, which should be planted 10 cm (4 in) deeper than in the pot. This encourages the plant to root up the stem, which seems to reduce the risk of wilt disease, which can kill clematis.

Once planting is completed, use your boot or fist to firm the soil well around the neck of the plant where it enters the soil, to hold it steady and prevent the wind rocking the plant and damaging the roots close to the soil surface. Then scoop the surface of the ground into a shallow depression around the plant, the same size as the planting hole, to allow water to collect in the vicinity of the roots and soak down to them.

Step-by-step shrub planting

1 Dig a hole at least twice as wide and deep as the pot or rootball.

2 Fork the soil in the base of the hole to loosen it, allowing the roots to penetrate the soil and water to drain away. Add a deep layer of rotted farmyard manure and a handful of bonemeal fertilizer.

3 Remove the plant from the pot and gently tease out the roots.

4 Place the rootball in the hole so that it is at least 8 cm (3 in) deeper than it was in the pot. Replace the soil around it by hand. Gently push the soil in around the roots.

5 Once the hole is full, firm it down with your feet, but don't pack it down. The soil level should be slightly below that around it. Water the soil to settle in round the newly planted roots. Protect the new young shoots from slugs and snails using pellets obtainable from your garden centre, or try trapping them in containers of beer (see page 64).

After planting, always water the plant – even if it is raining – to settle the soil around the roots. Continue to water until the plant is established and making new growth. If the plant can't take up water through its roots and loses what it has stored through evaporation in warm weather, the foliage will wither and the plant will die.

Spacing plants out There is a temptation to group plants too closely together in a new bed, to cover as much of the bare soil as possible, forgetting that the plants will all grow sideways as well as upwards. Plants that are crowded will soon grow into one another, causing the foliage to die and the plant to lose shape and become one-sided. The roots will have to compete for water and nutrients, resulting in a loss of vigour.

The correct spacing for plants can be tricky to achieve. The majority of plant labels give this information: if they don't, ask a knowledgeable sales assistant before purchasing. Remember that if the ultimate spread of the plant is 2 m (6 ft 6 in), that is 1 m (3 ft 3 in) on either side of the plant. If the plant beside it has the same spread, then there should be at least 2 m (6 ft 6 in) space between the two plants. You can fill the gaps between the permanent plantings using short-lived plants such as annuals, bulbs and biennials. These can be sacrificed as the main plants grow into the space, or in the case of longer-lasting perennials, they can be transplanted to fill other short-term gaps.

Herbs can be close planted, then thinned out as they mature.

Transplanting

Digging up a plant and replanting it in a different position is sometimes necessary and the secret is not to let the plant know that it has been moved. Deciduous plants are best transplanted when they are dormant and without foliage. The exceptions are small birches, which should be moved as the leaves are falling, or when the leaf buds are swelling in spring. Move evergreen plants in late autumn or early spring when there is some heat in the ground; then they will quickly make new roots. In every case it is essential that the plant is well watered immediately to settle the soil round the roots.

Small plants are easily lifted with little risk but larger ones need special treatment to make sure they aren't set

Rules for transplanting

- Transplant deciduous plants when they are dormant (i.e. when they have lost their leaves)
- Transplant evergreens in spring or autumn when the soil is warm.
- Prepare the new planting hole before lifting the plant.
- Incorporate some compost and bone meal into the soil being returned to the planting hole.
- Lift the plant when the soil is moist, with as large a ball of soil as necessary to cover the roots.
- Wrap large root balls in hessian or plastic sheeting before moving the plant, to help keep the soil around the roots.
- Retain as many roots as possible, especially the small fibrous roots that collect water and nutrients. If roots are broken, prune them back, making a clean cut to reduce the risk of fungal diseases entering the wound.
- Firm the soil around the roots, making sure that there are no air pockets.
- Water, water and water the soil. Damp the foliage over to stop the leaves transpiring. Then the roots won't have to work so hard to replace lost water to prevent wilting.
- Support the plant with a stake to prevent it rocking in the wind.

back by damaged roots, lack of water or drying winds, which remove the moisture from the foliage. Covering with a tent of polythene or horticultural fleece will reduce water loss through the leaves by raising humidity and protecting the plant from biting cold winds that dry the leaf surface.

There are some plants that don't transplant well – you are unlikely to succeed in shifting pittosporum, broom, elaeagnus, daphne, ceanothus, hawthorn or beech. Lilac, eucalyptus and pyracantha dislike being moved after they have been in the ground a year. Peonies sulk for years, producing lots of leaves but absolutely refusing to flower.

**Leaving space between the new plants gives them room to expand.
1. Lupins will spread to about 45 x 45 cm (18 x 18 in) and will also self-seed freely.
2. *Stachys byzantina* makes excellent ground cover and spreads to about 90 x 90 cm (3 x 3 ft).
3. *Dianthus* will achieve a spread of about 90 x 60 cm (3 x 2 ft).**

staking, training and tying

It is the roots that keep the plant upright in the soil and prevent it blowing over in a strong wind. Until the plant has had time to send roots out in all directions it is easily knocked over. The larger the plant the more subject it is to wind; small plants usually need only to have the soil firmed around the root area. Large shrubs and trees, especially those that are evergreen with leaves to catch the winter wind, need to be supported with a wooden stake or bamboo cane to prevent them moving until the roots have spread out. The period of support depends upon the size of the plant, the amount of exposure and the speed of growth, but it won't be less than one year.

What size stake? It is a mistake to use tall stakes that hold a tree so firmly that it doesn't make the effort to send its roots far and wide. A short stake that holds only the lower portion of the stem, allowing the top to sway, will support the roots and encourage the tree to thicken its stem so that it is able to withstand wind. Timber stakes should be treated with preservative to extend their lives. Round stakes with a point are easier to drive into the ground than pointed square stakes, which twist if they hit large stones.

Drive the stake into the prepared hole before planting, to avoid damaging the roots. Place the plant in front of the stake to screen it and spread the roots out in the hole, allowing them to go in every direction.

The soil should be returned to the planting hole, filling it in around the roots so that there are no large air pockets and firming it in as you go. Leave the surface slightly 'dished' to retain water long enough for it to soak in around the roots. Continue to water the root area as often as necessary to stop the soil drying out.

Using tree ties The plant should be firmly secured to the stake using a proper tie and pad. This is placed around the main stem of the plant and fastened to the support

1. Drive the stake into the hole and the solid soil before inserting the tree, to avoid damaging the roots.

2. Position the stem close to but not touching the stake. Train the roots around the stake.

3. & 4. Support the tree with a tie and pad, making sure to nail the pad to the stake and not the trunk.

with a buckle. If it is a large stake, the tie can be nailed to the stake. A rubber buffer or pad can be placed between the stake and the stem to prevent them rubbing. Bulky shrubs with more than one stem can be held in place with an old pair of tights, the legs woven through the branches and tied to the stake. The ties need to be checked in spring and again in autumn to make sure that they are not cutting into the bark, causing damage and restricting the stem.

Other means of support

• Climbing plants including rambling and climbing roses also require support and something to cling to and scramble over. Trellis or timber laths can be fixed with masonry nails to walls with a 5 cm (2 in) wooden spacer to leave a gap between the wall and the support to allow space for the plant shoots to twine themselves around the timber. Where stems are being tied to a support you should use a soft garden twine or raffia to prevent damaging the shoot. Keep the loop loose enough to allow the stem to thicken up without being constricted.

• Galvanized training wire, which won't rust, can be fixed to the wall and spaced horizontally 30 cm (12 in) apart to train shoots of wisteria along or to tie in the branches of fruit trees to form a framework. Trained trees of apple, pear and peach – often called espaliers – on a sunny wall will reward you with good crops. Masonry nails with strips of soft lead attached (sold as lead-headed nails) are good for training stems into position, using the lead to hold the stem. As the branches thicken, the lead strips unbend without damaging the bark.

• Netting wire or plastic mesh can be used to support vigorous climbers such as honeysuckle, clematis and jasmine and tall varieties of sweet pea, which will use their tendrils to twine around and provide a good grip.

• Peas and beans are best supported on pea sticks. These are twiggy hedge prunings about 90 cm (36 in) long inserted into the seed bed along the rows of peas. They support the plants as they climb, keeping the pods off the ground and making picking easy.

Apple variety 'Orléans Reinette' against a warm, sunny wall. This shape, known as an espalier, is achieved by training the branches across wire or stakes so that they grow horizontally.

• Most herbaceous perennials need to be supported, especially tall plants such as campanula, verbascum and delphinium. There are lots of patented frames and wire supports on the market but a word of caution: when thin stakes or bamboo canes are being used, cover the tops with corks or small plastic pots to prevent eye damage when bending over to work in the bed.

Arches and pergolas
There are many other forms of framework used to support plants. Metal and timber arches at entrances and over paths look charming, but before ordering or purchasing check that, when they are covered with climbers, there will still be space to walk through. Obelisks covered with scented sweet peas will fit into the smallest garden and a timber pergola draped in vines, complete with grapes, and shading a patio, are just two other ways of supporting your plants.

Overleaf: an obelisk supports sweet peas in this scented garden.

watering

Watering the garden is not something that only needs to be done in areas with high temperatures and low rainfall or when there is an occasional drought. We have to water the garden whenever plants need moisture at their roots. Roots of plants growing in a free-draining soil may have difficulty finding water after a few days without rain, especially if the sun is warming the soil and causing evaporation. Anything that has been recently planted, including bedding plants, vegetables, perennials and soft fruit bushes, will all be prone to wilting if there is a water shortage before the plant can get established and the roots are unable to find water. Trees and shrubs can still be vunerable a full year after planting, as a lot of water is needed by larger plants.

Hostas enjoy a moisture-retentive soil and will flourish in the dampest conditions.

Shallow-rooted plants such as rhododendron, mock orange, hydrangea and skimmia are particularly prone to wilting if there is a drought, as all their roots are close to the surface of the ground which is the first to dry out. Other plants are better designed for prolonged periods without rain: they may have roots that go deep in search of water, or have thick leaves and fleshy roots to store water. As a general rule, silver or grey-leaved plants can tolerate dry conditions.

When to water The secret is not to wait until there is a drought, but to water as soon as the soil starts to become dry. Containers such as hanging baskets and pots don't hold much compost and as a result they dry out very quickly. If the compost becomes dry, it shrinks away from the edge of the container and the water runs through before it can soak into the compost. Watering every other day should prevent drying out but, if necessary, the container may be plunged into water for 30 minutes and allowed to become saturated, then set out to drain all the surplus water off.

The ideal times to water are early in the morning and in the cool of the evening. During the day, the sun causes the water to evaporate too quickly.

How much to give Little and often is a bad method: it results in the top few centimeters becoming damp and the soil below this level remaining dry. This encourages the roots to stay in the top crust rather than moving through the soil. If the surface is constantly damp, weed seeds will germinate and thrive. It is better to concentrate on one area of the garden at a time and give it a real soaking that will get down into the lower levels of the ground, where the roots can make use of it. In a large garden, it will be necessary for you to water only those plants that are most in need – there should be lots of plants that are well established and can survive short periods of drought.

Take care when watering seedlings not to wash them out of the soil.

There are areas of the garden that can be dry even when it is raining. One such area is along the base of the house wall, where the rain doesn't fall and any moisture is absorbed into the porous bricks. Areas along the edge of paths and patios, where there is a depth of hardcore to drain away the water, should be given extra attention with the hose.

Form a depression in the soil covering the area of the roots. This will contain the water until it soaks into the soil.

How to apply water Small gardens and containers may be watered using a watering can. Either pour from the open spout to provide a gush of water or use with a sprinkler, called a rose, on the end of the spout to provide fine droplets like rain to gently wet small plants and seedlings. A hose will save carrying water in the watering can and the pressure can be controlled to give a spray or a jet, by using your thumb or a special nozzle. Hose sprinkler attachements are useful for larger areas, where they can be turned on and left to spray away until the soil is well soaked. It takes a sprinkler a long time to wet the soil to a depth of 15 cm (6 in); you will need to check by digging down to see how deep the water has penetrated.

Where to water There's no need to water where there are no roots. In the case of seedlings, it is only necessary to water along the row close in to the young plants. With large plants, the roots will have spread far and wide and it will be necessary to apply water all over the area covered by the canopy of the tree or shrub. If the surface soil is hard and dry, the water will run off before it can soak in. One way to keep the water in the right area is to form a depression or dish around the area of the roots or to form a rim of soil around the perimeter of the root area and fill the inner zone with water that can only escape down into the soil.

Saving water Water is expensive and it makes sense to catch rainwater and store it for use in the garden. A water butt attached to a downpipe from the roof guttering will provide water when it is most needed. If an old pair of tights or muslin is tied over the end of the downpipe, all the leaves and debris will be trapped before they get into the butt.

Grey water, which is a fancy term for used household water but excluding sewage, can be stored and used in the garden, but it won't keep for more than a few days before it starts to smell and it can't be used on edible crops of fruit or vegetables.

The roots will occupy the same spread as the canopy of the plant, so water all the area under the tree, not just the bit closest to the trunk.

mulching

A mulch is a layer of material on the soil surface, usually around plants, that reduces garden maintenance and is of benefit to the plants. Mulching helps to suppress weeds, improves soil structure, encourages plants to make good growth and enhances the appearance of the bed.

• If a mulch is applied to moist soil, it will help to prevent evaporation and keep the soil cool in summer.
• In winter a deep mulch will act like a blanket, keeping the soil warmer and preventing it freezing, so that planting can take place.
• While no mulch on its own is effective against strongly growing perennial weeds, it will stop weeds from germinating in the soil underneath and any weeds that do grow in the loose mulch are easily removed.
• As organic mulches such as farmyard manure rot down, they add humus and some nutrients to the soil.

Types of mulch There are three types of mulch: organic or humus mulches; inorganic mulches such as gravel; and suppressants such as carpet and landscape fabric.

Organic mulches include rotted farmyard manures, leaf mould, garden compost, spent mushroom compost, bark mulch and grass clippings. If these mulches are applied in a layer at least 5 cm (2 in) thick, they will do a good job. As they decompose they use up nitrogen-fixing bacteria and it is worthwhile increasing the rate of nitrogen fertilizer to compensate. Bark mulch, if used fresh, can contain diseases and is best if decomposed before applying. Grass clippings should only be used as a light mulch; a thick layer will turn into a slimy mess.

There is a selection of hard materials that can be used for mulching. Gravels are available in a range of colours and grades; horticultural grit is a coarse grade of sand; pea gravel is larger; then there are round smooth river stones up to 15 cm (6 in) in size. Gravel warms up quickly, giving off its heat. The paler gravels reflect the light and make a good surface mulch for hot beds for sun-loving plants.

Weed suppressants include old carpet, polythene, woven polypropylene and newspaper. None of them is attractive, but if they are left in place for a year the weeds will be killed through lack of light. With the exception of polythene sheeting, they all allow water to penetrate to the soil below. Add a topping of bark and no one will know they are there, yet you will have effective weed control.

When to mulch A mulch acts as a blanket, preserving the soil in the same condition as when it is applied. If the soil is cold and wet, it will remain that way and the same goes for hot and dry conditions. The best time to mulch is when the soil is moist and warm, providing ideal conditions for growth – spring is the traditional season for mulching.

How to mulch If there are annual weeds growing on the bed, hoe them off or spray with glyphosate weedkiller. If you use weedkiller, don't apply the mulch for 10 days until the weeds turn yellow. Rake the soil over to remove stones and debris and give a feed of a balanced fertilizer at 30 g per sq m (1 oz per sq yd). Spread the mulch evenly all over the bed, at least 5 cm (2 in) deep, keeping it away from the stems of the plants, as it could cause soft stems to rot. Where supplies are scarce or expensive, apply the mulch as no more than a collar around each plant, covering the root zone. Weeds will grow where there is no covering, but the plants will still get the benefit of the mulch.

Depending what type of organic mulch has been used, top it up as it rots down. This is usually done each spring, applying the new layer directly on top of the old mulch.

A deep mulch helps to retain moisture in the soil and will reduce the need to weed. *Bergenia* (1), the New Zealand flax *Phormium tenax* (2), *Gunnera manicata* (3) and moisture-loving ferns (4) will all benefit from this treatment.

pruning

There is no great mystery to pruning. Common sense is the main requisite, followed by clean, sharp tools. To prune is simply to cut off branches that are not wanted. This can be for a variety of reasons such as overcrowding, branches crossing each other and rubbing, or diseased stems – for example, canker on apple branches. Some plants produce their flowers or fruit on new growths and are cut to encourage more young shoots. There are plants that need to be cut hard each year, removing most of the growth made during the previous year and these include buddleia (butterfly bush), ribes (flowering currant) and syringa (lilac). Equally, there are some plants that require little or no regular pruning and these include shrubs such as daphne, hebe and pieris.

Pruning for shape – topiary (see page 51) – is on the increase and evergreen plants clipped into the shape of objects and animals are fun to do. Fruit trees are trained and pruned for maximum crop against a wall and fan, cordon and espalier shapes are all popular.

Pruning is also necessary to remove unwanted material, such as suckers of the parent plant growing from below the graft and weakening the plant. Evergreen variegated plants sometimes produce a rogue shoot that is the original green without any variegation. If this is not removed it will grow more quickly, taking over the plant and eventually smothering out the variegation.

Pruning the branches out of the centre of a thorny gooseberry plant makes life a lot easier when it comes to picking the crop.

Diseased branches need to be cut out well below the diseased part and burnt, as in the case of rose black spot and apple canker.

Pruning tools A knife, pair of secateurs, small hand saw, shears and a pair of loppers are sufficient for most jobs and I would strongly recommend that you buy the best you can afford. They will need to be kept sharp and good steel takes and keeps a good edge and that sort of quality costs money.

Pruning shrubs Before tackling any shrub, find out when it flowers. Deciduous shrubs fall into three categories for pruning.

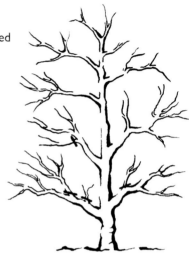

• Winter-flowering deciduous shrubs need very little pruning apart from the removal of diseased branches and those that are growing towards the centre. Young plants will need to be shaped, removing any stems that are causing the plant to be lopsided. The time to prune is immediately after the flowers have faded.

Winter-flowering shrubs: prune only to maintain shape or to remove dead or diseased wood

• Spring- and early summer-flowering deciduous shrubs are pruned as soon as flowering is finished. First remove any diseased or thin shoots, then cut all the branches that flowered to within a few buds of the base and leave the new shoots to flower next year.

Spring and early summer-flowering shrubs: prune immediately after flowering. By mid to late autumn, the young shoots will have grown vigorously and produced new shoots on which next year's flowers are borne.

Late summer flowering shrubs should be pruned in early spring. In the first year cut out only damaged or weak shoots.

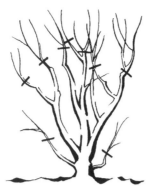

In the second year, cut back the last season's growth by a half, cutting just above strong outward-pointing buds.

In subsequent years, cut back to within one or two buds of the previous year's growth.

• Late summer-flowering shrubs are pruned in late spring when any risk of frost has passed. Again, remove diseased and thin shoots and prune out last year's flowering shoots, allowing the new growths to grow away and flower later in the year.

Deciduous shrubs which have been neglected and are overgrown can be pruned hard, removing the old shoots to the base to encourage new growth. If all the branches are cut there will be no flowers that year and an alternative is to cut down half each year, leaving the other half to flower.

There are some deciduous shrubs that are grown for their coloured stems such as dogwood (*Cornus alba*) and the best colour is produced on young shoots. The plant should be cut to ground level each spring and allowed to grow strongly all summer, colouring up in early winter.

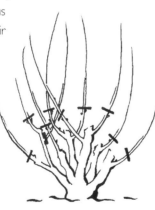

To promote colourful stems, cut back hard in early spring.

Pruning evergreen shrubs
To avoid any risk of frost damage to tender new shoots, prune evergreens in early summer. Remove diseased, thin and spindly shoots and, if the plant needs to be thinned out, remove branches from various parts to prevent it becoming one-sided. Evergreens with large leaves such as laurel should be cut with secateurs rather than shears to avoid making the plant look untidy with leaves cut in half.

Pruning trees
You can prune young trees so that they have good shape and the main branches are well apart, ensuring a balanced tree later in its life. Branches that are low to the ground and those crossing into the centre of the tree can be removed. Where a tree forks and the angle where the branches join is very narrow, remove one of the branches to reduce the risk of them splitting in a storm. When you are removing a large heavy branch, do it in stages to reduce the weight and prevent the limb tearing off and damaging the main trunk. Always make a saw cut part way in, on the underside of the branch, before cutting from the top. This stops the bark tearing off beyond the cut.

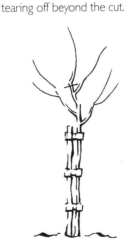

Prune young trees in mid-autumn, cutting each branching stem to within 30–45 cm (12–18 in) of the main stem.

Once the tree is about five years old, prune only to maintain the desired shape.

Fun with topiary: a woman gardener (left) in box, with box hedging containing the herbs; a crocodile (above) formed from *Lonicera nitida* in a spring garden.

Pruning Hedges Pruning promotes growth and this can be used to your advantage with hedges. When you cut a shoot it will send out two or three new shoots and the plant becomes thicker and more dense. By regularly clipping a hedge, it thickens out with no gaps. Old hedges that are bare at the base can be cut hard, encouraging new shoots from the base. These, themselves, can then be clipped to thicken them up and cover the bareness.

Topiary Topiary is the art of shaping plants into objects. It is a form of hedge cutting and can be practised on a great variety of plants. Choose a simple shape to start with: I would hate you to cut the head off the peacock just as you have got the tail exactly right. Ball or cone shapes are fairly easy to do and a matched pair can look good at the top of steps or either side of an entrance. Trim the shoots evenly and regularly with clippers or secateurs, making sure that the plant doesn't lack water or nutrients. More complicated objects are best grown within a wire outline of the desired shape and clipped to build up the bulk. The final shaping is refined as the growths reach the wire outline. Even a moderate fall of snow can play havoc with topiary. The weight bends the branches, opening the plant and spoiling the shape, so brush it off as soon as it falls.

Plants suitable for topiary

Buxus sempervirens (box)
Ligustrum ovalifolium (privet)
Lonicera nitida (shrubby honeysuckle)
Taxus baccata (yew)
Thuja occidentalis (arbor vitae)

Pruning other plants There is no reason to worry about pruning either roses or clematis. Some experts make it sound difficult and complicated but that is only because there are so many different types of each. Once you know the type of rose – for example, a climber or a shrub rose – the pruning is no more difficult than for any other plant. The pruning of each is covered under clematis and roses on pages 160 and 163 respectively.

propagation

Seeds or plants There are advantages and disadvantages in growing from seed rather than buying plants and you would be a poor gardener if you did not use both methods to fill the garden. With seed sowing there is the satisfaction of producing your own plants from start to finish and, in the case of annuals, the time from sowing to flowering can be as little as eight weeks. Then there is the cost factor, where a packet of seed is a fraction of the price of one plant and will result in lots of plants. The cost disappears altogether if you collect seed of your own plants that will reproduce similar to the parent: species delphiniums (rather than cultivars) will do this, as will some marigolds (calendula) and honesty (lunaria), for example. On the other hand if you save your own seed of a named variety of sweet pea that is all the same colour and sow it you will produce sweet pea plants in a whole range of colours.

There is a bigger range of varieties available in seeds than there is of plants that are carried by most garden centres. But buying plants is also rewarding in that you immediately have a plant that may even be in flower already and you will have avoided any possible problems of germination and growing on and caring for the young plant until it is ready to plant out.

Seedlings 'pricked out' and spaced in compost. The healthiest specimens have been selected and given plenty of room to grow.

Some plants are not worth growing from seed, for example, hebe, a shrub that is easy to grow quickly from a cutting. Others such as rhododendron, take years to produce flowers when grown from seed and after all that time may not be the same as the parent – your original seedling may turn out to be a useless plant with poor flower colour and a bad habit of growth.

Growing from seed There are two methods of seed sowing that interest the 'down-to-earth' gardener: sowing outside directly into the soil and sowing seeds in a glasshouse or on the kitchen windowsill in trays or pots of compost.

Direct sowing in the garden soil A perfectly acceptable way of growing plants – after all, it's nature's way. The seeds can be sown in rows and then transplanted to their permanent positions when they are big enough to handle. Or they can be broadcast sown by scattering the seed into the soil where they are to flower and this method is often used for displays of annual flowers for summer colour.

Biennials such as wallflowers and perennials such as hollyhocks are often sown in early summer in rows outdoors and the seedlings transplanted to their permanent positions in the autumn.

Seed is available in a range of options to suit your needs.
- The most popular is still loose seed in a sealed packet.
- If you find fine seed flows between your fingers too quickly, resulting in a forest of seedlings all jammed together, then you should try pelleted seed where each seed is coated to form a little pellet not unlike a sweet pea seed and just as easy to handle.
- Another foolproof method is a line of seeds pre-spaced in a strip of 'tape' which dissolves when the seeds are in the ground and watered.

Tips for successful sowing outside

- Buy hardy varieties of seed that are recommended for growing outdoors

- Before opening the seed packet, make a label written with a waterproof pen on a plastic strip, stating the variety and the date of sowing and insert it at the end of the row before you sow.

- Check the packet as to the depth to sow the seed: it can vary from surface sowing with a mere dusting of horticultural sand to cover the seed, to 5 cm (2 in) deep in the case of broad beans.

- If the packet states that spring is the time to sow seed outdoors, don't read that literally as the first day of the spring. What it means is when the soil has warmed up and is moist but not wet and any risk of frost has passed. Then is the the time to cultivate the soil and rake the surface to remove any stones.

- The surface of the soil must be firm, dry and fine with no lumps. Remember, the tiny shoot that emerges from the seed has to get to the surface and the daylight as quickly as possible. A lump of soil or a stone will prevent that happening and the seedling will die.

Young transplanted cabbage plants covered with netting to prevent birds – especially pigeons – eating them. The fruit cage in the background also protects crops from hungry birds. This sort of protection is useful if you have a cat, or if your plants are likely to be attacked by rabbits or other wildlife.

- When sowing in rows, use a length of string and two short sticks – a gardener's 'line' – to mark the row. Form the drill at the depth recommended by pulling the end of a rake or the corner of a hoe along the line. If the soil has been properly prepared, there will be no lumps or large stones in the drill.

- Sow the seed thinly to allow each seedling space to grow without competition.

- Once the seed has been sown in the drill, cover it to the correct depth with fine soil or horticultural sand if specified, and gently firm with your foot. Water the rows of seeds with a fine rose on the end of the watering can or hose.

- Some varieties of seed such as lettuce or marigolds (*Calendula*) will be germinated and showing after a week or ten days, while other types such as parsley or sweet williams can take much longer – up to nine weeks – so resist the temptation to scrape the soil away to see what is happening.

- Have faith, most seeds manage to grow even if the conditions are not perfect.

- Transplant the seedlings by easing them out of the soil using a hand fork and taking care not to damage the roots. Hold the seedling by the leaves and not by the stem, which is easily bruised, allowing fungus disease into the wound and killing the plant. Replant at the spacing recommended on the seed packet and at the same depth as the seedling was growing before. If you have plants to spare, you can thin out and throw away the surplus, leaving the rest in situ at the correct spacing.

Tips for successful sowing indoors

Seed sown in a glasshouse or on the kitchen windowsill in seed trays or even used yoghurt pots with drainage holes in the base, filled with a special seed compost, will germinate more quickly than outside in the cold. The seedlings must then be 'hardened off' before they can be planted out. This is done by leaving the plants out during the day and bringing them in at night until they become acclimatized to the outside temperature.

• Sow the seed at the right time, depth and temperature as recommended on the seed packet. The compost should be fine with no coarse material and low in nitrogenous fertilizer, as you want sturdy plants rather than soft lush growth.

• Water the seed compost after sowing using a fine rose on the watering can. Thoroughly wet the compost rather than just dampening the surface.

• Cover the compost with newspaper to keep it warm and dark until the seeds germinate. Remove it before the seedlings become leggy from lack of light.

Pots and trays of seedlings on a glasshouse bench, all well labelled and growing away. Once the seedlings are sturdy enough to handle they can be transplanted into larger containers and eventually moved outside.

• Thin the seedlings out into trays or pots as soon as they are large enough to handle, to give each plant the space it needs and prevent overcrowding. You will need to toughen up the seedlings to prepare them for the colder weather outside. Start by giving them lots of ventilation and then setting them outside during warm days, but bringing them in each evening. When you finally plant them out, take precautions against a really cold night by keeping a cover of horticultural fleece handy.

Any surplus seedlings can be grown on in pots or given to friends or, as a last resort, composted.

• Hold seedlings by the leaves, not by the stems, which bruise easily, allowing disease to enter. Damping off is a fungus disease that seedlings are prone to and can be caused by overcrowding, unsterilized soil, damp conditions and damaged plants. Seedlings rot at the stem base, then keel over and die. Watering the seedlings with a solution of Cheshunt compound (a fungicide) will prevent damping off.

• Don't allow the compost to dry out as it is hard to wet again and it doesn't take much of a check in growth for the plants to die.

What terms mean

Hardening off Gradually getting plants acclimatized to lower temperatures so that they don't suddenly recieve a severe setback when they are planted out.

Thinning out Reducing the number of plants in a container or outside bed to allow the remaining seedlings space to develop.

Pricking out Transferring seedlings to space them out and give them room to grow.

Dibble To form a hole in the compost or soil using a tool called a dibbler, to plant seedlings or sow large seeds.

Broadcast To sow seed at random, scattering it over the soil, for example sowing grass seed for a lawn.

Drill A narrow V-shaped depression made in the soil to sow seed in, or the actual row of seedlings that has germinated.

Opposite: **A clean glasshouse with concrete floor, good ventilation, lots of light and sturdy staging provides the ideal conditions for growing cacti from seed. They can be slow to germinate, but are worth the wait.**

dividing plants

This is one of the important methods of propagating and a way for the most inexperienced gardener to increase plants with as good as 100 per cent success. The types of plants that lend themselves to division are those that form mats, tufts or clumps, and include many perennials, alpines, water plants and even some suckering shrubs such as kerria. Some plants dislike being disturbed and these include the peony and Christmas rose and those plants with thick main roots but few fibrous roots, such as the oriental poppy and lupin.

As well as increasing the number of plants, dividing is a good way of rejuvenating an old clump, by retaining and planting the young rooted pieces from the outer edge and discarding the older woody centre. Division is carried out in either the autumn or in the spring. I prefer the spring when the plants are just starting to grow, the weather is improving and they have the whole summer to produce a large plant before they die down for the winter.

How to divide a plant Dig up the clump when the foliage is starting to grow, taking care not to damage the roots. Remove any surplus soil. Clumps with fibrous roots that are not matted together may be teased apart, separating them into small pieces of plant complete with roots. You can prise apart dense clumps using garden forks or, in some cases, solid masses of hostas can be cut with a knife or a spade. Any plants that have become infested with perennial weeds should not be used: it is difficult to separate the roots and if one piece of weed root is missed, it can grow away protected by the plant.

Replant the new plants as quickly as possible to prevent their growth being checked by a long spell out of the soil. Plant them in well-cultivated soil, free of weeds and dressed with some bone meal. Water the plants in, to settle the soil around the roots.

Growing from cuttings Taking and rooting plants from cuttings is the most satisfactory gardening job of all. There is real pleasure when you ease a piece of plant out of the compost and see the mass of roots. It is particularly satisfying to be able to root plants that are listed as difficult. Years later you will still remember the plant you rooted and where it came from before it ended up in your garden. There is a story behind every plant you manage to propagate in this way.

There are lots of ways of rooting cuttings that will become plants identical to their parents. The easiest foolproof methods are from softwood cuttings in summer and from hardwood cuttings in winter.

Softwood cuttings Softwood means exactly that; you use the current year's shoots that are soft but not floppy. You cut them about 5-10 cm (2-4 in) long in late spring and early summer, before the stem becomes hard and woody, and root them in a container of compost, covering them with clear polythene to prevent them wilting. When they are rooted, which can be in as short a time as six weeks, they can be repotted or planted out in the garden. This is a quick, cheap way to increase a whole range of shrubs, perennials and alpines, especially if you have a good source of cuttings. Friends with gardens are usually only too pleased to offer pieces and if you ask your local parks manager, he will probably cut you a few suitable stems. The one thing that you must not do, of course, is to take cuttings without permission when on a garden visit.

Honeysuckle (Lonicera) is easy to propagate from softwood cuttings in summer, as well as from hardwood cuttings in winter.

Tips for successful softwood cuttings

- Take the cuttings, using a sharp knife or secateurs, from healthy plants which are young and growing strongly. Check carefully that there are no pests on the foliage or stems and that the plant is disease free. If there is any distortion of the stems or foliage, or if the leaves are mottled there is probably a virus in the plant and no cuttings should be taken.

- The prepared cutting should be about 5-10cm (2–4 in) long, with the stem cut just below a leaf or a pair of leaves. Remove the lowest two leaves by pulling them off or cutting them close to the stem with a sharp knife. If the remaining leaves are large – for example, laurel and hydrangea – they can be cut in half to reduce the loss of moisture through transpiration.

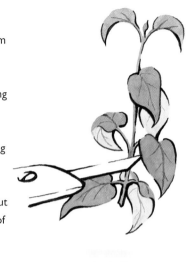

- As soon as the cutting has been removed from the plant, place it in a polythene bag or bucket of water to prevent it from wilting until you are ready to propagate.

- Alternatively, a suitable side shoot can be pulled away from the main stem with a heel attached, which is a small strip of the older wood from the main stem. Trim the bark back to leave a heel of 10 mm (just under ½ in).

- The tip of the cutting, which will be thin with tiny unfurling leaves, should be removed by nipping it out using your finger nails. Plants that flower on young growth, such as hebes and fuchsias, may have flower buds at the tip of the cutting and you should nip them out along with the tip.

• Dip the base of the cutting in hormone rooting powder or liquid, covering the lower 6 mm (¼ in) of the cutting, before inserting it in the compost. Most cuttings will root easily without the benefit of hormone treatment, but it will speed up the rooting and assist difficult species such as rhododendron and hollies to produce roots. It also contains a fungicide to protect against soil-borne diseases that can easily kill the young plant before it has the strength to fight the attack.

10 easy-to-root plants by softwood cuttings

Choisya	Hydrangea
Deutzia	Lavender
Escallonia	Olearia
Fuchia	Philadelphus
Hebe	Weigela

Deutzia gracilis, in the foreground, and *Deutzia x rosea*, both easy to root from softwood cuttings.

• The rooting compost should be equal parts peat and coarse grit without any fertilizer. You can root a small quantity of cuttings around the edge of a single clay or plastic pot, or in a seed tray. Check that the container has drainage holes and that they are not blocked.

• The compost should be moist and a hole made for the cutting using your finger or a blunt stick. Insert the cuttings 5 cm (2 in) apart but don't firm them in. Instead, water the cuttings with a fine rose on the watering can to settle the compost around the stems. Cover them with clear polythene, without letting it touch the foliage, to prevent moisture loss by transpiration until the cuttings are rooted and can take up water.

Hardwood cuttings Rooting hardwood cuttings is a simple, cheap and effective way of propagating. You won't even have to provide protection from the elements.

Hardwood cuttings are taken in late autumn and winter when the stems of that year's growth have hardened up and, if the plant is deciduous, all the leaves are off. This method of propagation is used for shrubs and some trees. The cuttings are taken about 30 cm (12 in) long and are inserted in the open ground in a sheltered part of the garden. The cuttings take longer to root than softwood cuttings, producing well-rooted young plants after a year – ready for planting out in their final position in the garden or potting up.

Tips for successful hardwood cuttings

Propagate from healthy plants that are not showing any stem or leaf distortion or mottling and are free from pests.

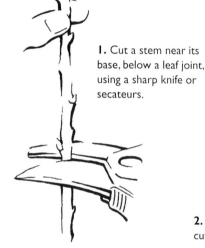

1. Cut a stem near its base, below a leaf joint, using a sharp knife or secateurs.

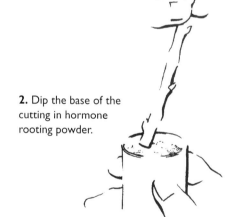

2. Dip the base of the cutting in hormone rooting powder.

3. Remove the top of the shoot above a leaf to encourage the rooted cutting to form side shoots for a well-branched plant.

10 easy-to-root plants by hardwood cuttings

Blackcurrant	Honeysuckle
Buddleia	Privet
Dogwood	Poplar
Escallonia	Rose
Forsythia	Willow

Cornus alba (dogwood), grown for its brilliant autumn colour and red winter bark, is easy to root by hardwood cuttings.

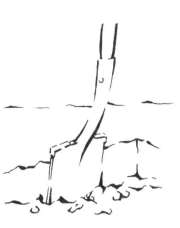

2. & 3. Bury the cuttings in the soil to half of their depth and water them in.

1. Insert the cuttings in a sheltered weed-free site such as under a hedge, in a 15 cm (6 in) deep trench with a 2.5 cm (1in) layer of coarse washed grit in the base to help drainage.

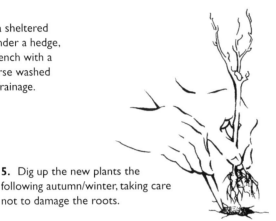

5. Dig up the new plants the following autumn/winter, taking care not to damage the roots.

4. Firm the cuttings in with your boot. Water regularly during the growing season, providing sufficient water to ensure that it is reaching the base of the cuttings where the roots are forming.

Semi-ripe cuttings, sometimes referred to as semi-hardwood, are rooted between mid-summer and autumn, using cuttings from the current season's growth when the base of the cutting is becoming woody but the top of it is still soft. Prepare and root as for softwood cuttings.

Eye cuttings are used to propagate hardwoods when plant material is scarce. The stem should be fully ripened wood after the leaves have fallen, and as thick as your little finger. Cut with sharp secateurs 2.5 cm (1 in) on either side of a plump bud. Dip the lower end into hormone rooting powder and insert it into seed or cuttings compost with extra grit or coarse sand added for drainage. Keep the bud level with the surface of the compost. Alternatively, slice away a strip of bark from the length of stem opposite the bud and coat the bare stem with hormone rooting powder. Lay the cutting horizontally in the compost with the bud exposed and it will root along the length of the cutting.

Stem sections increase stock of thick-stemmed house plants such as dracaenas, dumb cane, sugar cane and cordyline. Select a healthy stem and cut it into lengths with at least two nodes or rings where the leaf is produced. The cutting can be as small as 5 cm (2 in) and you can insert it vertically (right way up) or horizontally in moist compost with the nodes showing. Water the cuttings and keep them in a warm humid area. The new leaves will appear at the nodes and the rooted plant can be potted up.

Pipings are taken in late summer from carnations and garden pinks. Gently pull the tip out from the main stem above a leaf node and remove the lower leaves to leave the cutting with four pairs of leaves. Dip these 'pipings' into hormone rooting powder and insert them around the edge of a pot of free-draining gritty compost. Screen the cuttings from strong sunlight and don't allow the compost to dry out. You will have young rooted plants within the month.

pests and diseases

You will soon find that pests and diseases are completely natural in the garden and hopefully you will be able to live with them without declaring all-out war. There is a need to be constantly vigilant for a serious attack but quite often a few creepy crawlies or diseased spots are of no consequence. Mind you, I suppose that the Great Famine of Ireland, partly caused by blight on potatoes, started as a few spots on a leaf or two.

Diseases such as black spot defoliate the plant, while viruses distort the leaves and stunt the plant. Canker can kill even a mature tree by completely ringing the bark and preventing the flow of water and nutrients. Fruit trees are particularly vulnerable.

Blight isn't confined to potatoes – tomatoes may develop the same symptoms.

Good hygiene both outside and under cover in a glasshouse or poly tunnel will go a long way toward preventing diseases. Removing decaying material will reduce the spread of botrytis or grey mould and some of the mildews, and a movement of air will reduce the high humidity that helps spread fungal spores.

Not all insects are pests, indeed many garden visitors are on our side, helping to eliminate the trouble-makers and keep a balance. Ladybirds and their larvae, plus the larvae of hoverflies and lacewings eat

This aphid attack on a honeysuckle flower is both unsightly and potentially damaging to the plant's growth.

enormous quantities of aphids (greenfly). Spiders are to be welcomed in the garden as they eat all sorts of pest insects.

Frogs and toads help to keep the population of slugs and snails at acceptable levels, while many small birds eat aphids. When chemicals are used to kill pests, they also destroy the natural predators that, over time, could multiply to a level where the chemicals would not be needed.

Sometimes you can't leave everything to nature. Some pests can cause enormous damage. Those that suck the sap of the plant, such as greenfly, whitefly and blackfly, cause the leaves to become distorted and they also spread diseases, including viruses. They exude a sticky honeydew, which becomes mouldy, turning black and disfiguring the leaves.

Earwigs are a pest of the summer and autumn when they damage the blooms of chrysanthemums and dahlias. Then there are the caterpillars of the cabbage white butterfly that munch their way through leaves at an alarming rate, but it is the pests in the ground that I dislike most. Vine weevils, leather jackets and chafer grubs all do enormous damage to the roots of plants while alien flat worms eliminate the benefical earth worm.

Larger pests include moles (did you know that there are no moles in Ireland?), mice, rats and other vermin, plus pigeons that can cause annoyance in the garden by devouring transplanted green vegetable seedlings.

Earwig

Easily recognized by the pincers at the rear of the body, earwigs are shiny brown and up to 15 mm (over ½ in) long.

Attacks The foliage and flowers of many plants, leaving a ragged hole. Chrysanthemums and dahlias are particularly prone to attack and their flowers may be destroyed.

Prevention Earwigs like to hide in the dark during the day and one way to trap them is to hang an upside-down flowerpot filled with straw on a cane among the plants. Shake the pot over a bag every afternoon to release the pests, then dump the bag.

Control Earwigs feed in the evening and you can catch lots if you patrol with a torch. Insecticides are best applied in the early evening all over the plants, taking care that the chemical doesn't mark the flowers.

Gooseberry sawfly

There are three different gooseberry sawflies, but it is their caterpillars that do the damage. All three larvae grow to 20 mm (¾ in) long and are pale green; two of them are marked with black spots.

Attacks The foliage of the gooseberry plant just as the fruit is ripening, quickly stripping off the leaves to leave only the main vein and the leaf stalk. Red and white currants are also attacked.

Prevention None.

Control Inspect the plants daily from mid-spring, especially under the leaves where the eggs are laid. Remove the caterpillars by hand or spray with pyrethrum.

Carrot fly

It is the maggot (larva) of the carrot fly which causes the damage. The creamy yellow grub is up to 10 mm (almost ½ in) long and up to three generations may be born between late spring and autumn in the same year.

Attacks Carrots are the main host, but celery, parsnip and parsley are also subject to attack. The fly lays its eggs close to the plant and the maggot tunnels into the root. Tunnels close to the surface show as brown lines on the root. Other rots enter the wounds and the root becomes useless. Parsley foliage turns yellow and the plant may die.

Prevention The fly is attracted by the smell of the foliage, so sow sparsely to avoid having to thin the seedlings, which is what causes the distinctive smell. The fly is low-flying, so if a barrier such as a horticultual fleece 30 cm (12 in) high is erected round the crop the fly will be unable to get through to lay its eggs. Sow after the first generation of maggots has emerged n late spring and crops harvested before late autumn will miss the second generation.

Control Varieties of carrot that are less subject to damage include 'Flyaway' and 'Systan'. There are dusts available that can be applied to the seed drill at sowing time.

Aphids

Aphids are more commonly known as greenfly, although they may be brown, black, yellow, pink or grey in colour and are usually 2–3 mm (½2-⅛ in) in length. As they grow they cast their skins and may be mistaken for other insects.

Attacks There are few plants that aphids don't feed on, but they are common on beech, lime and cherry trees, roses, honeysuckle, beans and lettuce. They suck the sap, weakening the plant and causing stunted growth. As they feed they exude a sticky honeydew on to the lower leaves, which becomes mouldy and black, resembling soot. Virus disease (see page 68) is spread by aphids.

Prevention There is no successful way to prevent aphids in the garden.

Control Insecticides, including systemic chemicals that are absorbed by the plant and kill the aphids when they suck the sap are effective, but it is necessary to change the chemical regularly, as the aphids will, in time, build up immunity to most products. Organic treatments include pyrethrum and soaps. There are beneficial insects such as the hover fly and the ladybird that devour aphids and help to keep them under control.

Caterpillars

These are the larval stage of moths and butterflies and are usually long and thin with an obvious head, three pairs of legs at the front and two to five pairs on their abdomen. They come in all colours and quantities of hair depending on the type.

Attack Most of the well-known pest caterpillars, such as the larvae of the large and small cabbage white butterfly, feed on leaves. Others, including cut worms, feed on roots and codling moth larvae feed on fruit.

Prevention Pheromone traps may be used to trap the male codling moth, preventing mating and reducing the number of maggots attacking the apple crop. Picking off the caterpillars when

you see them is a help and, since some feed at night, a patrol in the evening with a torch will catch a lot. Planting nasturtiums close to cabbages will divert the butterflies and, as the young caterpillars appear on the leaves, they can be picked off, leaf and all, and dumped or flattened with a heavy boot.

Control Pyrethrum may be used as an organic spray. Alternatively, try the biological control *Bacillus thuringiensis*.

Leatherjacket

These grey-brown tubular larvae without legs or obvious head grow up to 4 cm (1½ in), and are found in the soil. They are the larvae of the cranefly (daddy-long-legs) which lays its eggs in late summer, usually in long grass.

Attacks New lawns, causing serious damage by eating the grass roots and causing the plants to turn yellow. They will also eat the roots of vegetables, strawberries and seedlings.

Prevention The easiest way to get rid of them in a lawn is to irrigate the grass and then cover it overnight with black polythene. The leatherjackets will come to the surface and can be cleared up in the morning or left for the birds for breakfast.

Control Insecticides such as lindane dust are effective only against the young larvae. If the soil is damp and above 14°C (58°F), nematodes (*Steinernema*) are effective against all larval stages.

Slugs and snails

These are similar enough to be lumped together, although snails have shells and so prefer a limy soil, which supplies the calcium to make their home. Slugs mainly live below ground. Both secrete a slimy mucus which dries to a silvery trail to show where they have been. Providing the temperature stays above 5°C (40°F), slugs will feed all winter.

Attack Leaves, flowers and stems, destroying the foliage of many plants, notably hostas. They also attack tender spring shoots, seedlings and fruit, including tomatoes.

Prevention It is not possible to eradicate slugs and snails from the garden and the best form of prevention is to stop them getting to the plants. A layer of coarse grit spread over the soil surface will deter them from crawling on their bare tummies. A strip of copper wire around the rim of pots and trays of seedlings is effective, as slugs and snails won't crawl over the copper. Good hygiene helps – removing debris and leaves will leave them with nowhere to hide during the day.

Control Slugs and snails are very active at night and can be picked off by torch-light. Poisoned pellets are effective in dry weather but some are dangerous to dogs and cats and need to be used with care. Trap them by placing small containers of beer at ground level – the slugs and snails fall in and drown. Try biological control using the nematode *Phasmarrhabditis* in spring and autumn when the temperature is above 5°C (40°F), but it is not very effective against snails living above ground.

Whitefly

Glasshouse whitefly are sap-feeding insects 2 mm (1/12 in) in size with white wings. When disturbed they will fly around. The nymphs are green-white and immobile and are found on the underside of leaves.

Attacks Under glass whitefly is a real pest of crops and houseplants. Both the fly and the nymph excrete a sticky honeydew on to the leaves and this becomes mouldy, turning black. Tomatoes and fuchsias are particularly prone to attack.

Prevention There is no real prevention.

Control The parasitic wasp *Encarsia formosa* is the best form of biological control, providing it is introduced into the glasshouse before large numbers of whitefly emerge. Insecticides other than soap will kill *Encarsia,* and whitefly quickly build up resistance to most insecticides anyway. As an alternative, hang sticky yellow traps early in the season to catch whitefly before they mutiply.

Red spider mite

There are three common types of spider mite – fruit, conifer and glasshouse – but it is the latter that is the most troublesome. The mites are tiny – less than 1 mm (¹⁄₂₅ in) with four pairs of legs – and, without a magnifying glass, they look like pepper on the back of the leaf. They colour up in the autumn from pale green to orange-red, producing a fine web from leaf to leaf.

Attacks Most glasshouse ornamentals and food crops, especially fuchsias, peaches and citrus plants. During hot summers the mites will move out of doors, attacking strawberries, roses and beans. Leaves dry up and fall off.

Prevention There is no good method of prevention, but if weather conditions permit, regular spraying and misting over with water will help deter them. The mites seem to collect near a draught and if doors and windows are sealed they seem to build up more slowly.

Control Red spider mites quickly build up resistance to insecticides and it is necessary to change to a different chemical after a few applications. Spray every 7-10 days for a few weeks to provide a good control. Biological treatment with the mite *Phytoseiulus persimilis* will be effective if the infestation is light.

Vine weevil

Larvae are creamy white with a brown head, curved, legless, about 10 mm (just under ½ in) long and live in the soil. The adults are a dull black with antennae bent in the middle. All weevils are female and lay hundreds of eggs in a season.

Attacks Larvae feed on the roots of houseplants and outdoor plants, including rhododendron and primula, causing wilting and even death. They tunnel into the corms of begonias and cyclamens. The adult weevil is more noticeable between spring and autumn, feeding at night and eating irregular notches into the leaf margins of euonymus, rhododendron, pieris and hydrangea.

Prevention None.

Control Insecticides mixed into potting composts offer some control. Biological control using nematodes is effective if watered on to warm, moist potting compost in late summer. In open ground the temperature has to be over 15°C (60°F) for this to be effective. In wet or heavy soil the nematodes die, so the treatment has to be repeated every year.

Damping off

This fungal disease is a killer of seedlings – an entire tray of emerging plants may be lost within a few days of infection. The seedling stems are infected at ground level and quickly die, followed by others close by.

Attacks All seedlings are vulnerable.

Prevention Good hygiene is the best form of protection: make sure that pots and trays are sterilized and used sterilized soil for growing seeds. Seeds sown thinly in the container are less likely to be attacked. Use mains water for watering the seedlings, rather than rainwater, as it is less likely to contain bacteria or bugs.

Control Burn infected plants and thin trays of seedlings to allow a good movement of air. The compost may be drenched with a copper-based chemical when the seed is sown.

Canker

Usually seen on the bark of trees, where it causes raised and cracked areas. With some cankers, bark wounds ooze a sticky gum. When the canker spreads to encircle a branch it prevents movement of water and nutrients and the growth above the damage dies.

Attacks Fruit trees, especially apple and pear. Cherry and plum also suffer from bacterial canker and poplars often die from an unchecked attack.

Prevention The fungus spores are easily moved about and there is no effective form of prevention.

Control Improve the growing conditions of your plants, as it is those under stress that are most prone to infection. Remove affected branches as soon as the disease is noticed and paint the stem wounds with a sealant to keep the canker spores from infecting the clean wood.

Rose black spot

Black spot is a fungal disease first noticed as small black areas on the foliage which quickly enlarge, turning the leaves yellow and causing them to drop early. Purple-black spots will also appear on the stems.

Attacks Most species and varieties of rose are prone to black spot, though some varieties such as the Flower Carpet series are less susceptible.

Check with your local garden centre for the latest developments.

Prevention None.

Control Good hygiene is essential, so remove as many infected leaves as possible, pruning out diseased stems and burning them. In autumn rake up all the leaves to prevent spores from overwintering. Commence spraying with a recommended fungicide in early spring before the leaves appear and continue at fortnightly intervals all summer. At the end of the season give a final spray over the surface of the soil to reduce the number of overwintering fungus spores.

Potato blight

First noticed as brown patches on the edges of leaves; the patches quickly grow in size and the leaves wither. The potato stems develop black patches and collapse. The potato tubers develop sunken patches with a red-brown discoloration on the inside.

Attacks Potatoes are prone to serious damage, but tomatoes also suffer, the symptoms being exactly the same as for potatoes.

Prevention Some varieties of potato, including 'Cara', 'Record', 'Valor' and 'Maris Peer' show considerable resistance to blight infection.

Control If the stems of the crop are badly infected, cut off the foliage as soon as it starts to wither and remove and burn to prevent the fungus spores washing down to the tubers. Piling the soil up over the tubers will have the same effect. Spray foliage as a prevention rather than as a cure, using a copper-based chemical such as Bordeaux mixture.

Botrytis

A fungus commonly called grey mould and seen as a grey, grey-brown or dirty white furry growth on infected parts of plants. Initial infection is usually through wounds and damaged parts of the plants.

Attacks Most plants and will damage any part that is above soil level, including fruit and flowers.

Prevention None. The fungus is so common that the spores are almost always in the air and are spread by water splash and rainfall.

Control Remove any dead material and debris from around plants, especially in an enclosed area such as a glasshouse. Infected plants should be removed; if damage is noticed early

enough, the infected part should be cut back to healthy growth. Spray with a fungicide to kill the spores.

Honey fungus

Also known as bootlace fungus, because the fungal strands, found under the bark, look like bootlaces. The roots and base of the trunk of infected plants develop a dirty white mycelium (sheet of fungus). Honey-coloured clumps of toadstools may appear in late autumn at the base of infected trees.

Attacks Most woody plants, including climbers and herbaceous plants, although a few species seem to be able to resist it. These include bamboo, beech, yew, box, oak, clematis, elaeagnus, pieris and rhus.

Prevention Small areas may be isolated by digging a trench 60 cm (24 in) deep and lining it with a barrier such as polythene. Ensure that the barrier finishes above the surface of the soil. The 'roots' of honey fungus travel about 90 cm (36 in) per year. Since the fungus can live on dead material as well as killing living plants, it is important that old roots and dead stumps are removed. Plants that suddenly die should be burned. Don't replant a woody plant in the same area and, if you have had an attack, try to use plants that are known to have some resistance to the disease.

Control There are various chemicals on the market that offer control of honey fungus, but I don't know of any that is 100 per cent successful.

Clubroot

This disease is caused by a soil-borne slime mould. It can persist in the soil for more than 20 years and causes the roots of susceptible plants to swell and become distorted.

Attacks All the members of the *Brassica* family such as cabbages, cauliflower and kale, and some ornamentals including stock, wallflower and candytuft. Heavy, wet, acidic soils are most prone to clubroot.

Prevention Don't purchase *Brassica* plants in case they are infected – grow them from seed instead. Always clean your boots before working in the vegetable garden. Imported soil and manure may introduce the disease.

Control Burn infected plants and remove as much soil as possible from around the roots and dump it. Drain heavy soils and apply lime regularly. Raise your own plants in sterilized soil or soilless compost. Remove weeds as they appear, especially those likely to carry the disease, which include charlock and shepherd's purse. Some vegetables have resistant varieties that are worth trying – find out what your supplier or local garden centre stocks.

Downy mildew

The surface of the leaf develops yellow patches and a grey-white fuzzy fungus appears on the underside. Badly affected leaves will die.

Attacks A wide range of plants, especially young plants and those growing in a moist atmosphere. Cineraria, geraniums, pansies, roses, onions, grapes and lettuce are particularly prone to damage.

Prevention Good air circulation is the best way of avoiding this fungus. Under glass, open both the top and the bottom ventilators to encourage air movement. Outside, keep crops weed free and well spaced.

Control Remove any infected leaves as soon as they appear and spray with a suitable fungicide.

Peach leaf curl

When affected leaves appear in spring they are puckered and blistered, turning purple or bright red before the white fungus spores become visible. The leaves fall off and are followed by a second flush of foliage, which is usually free of disease.

Attacks Peaches and nectarines are the most susceptible plants.

Prevention The spores are carried by wind and rain so, for plants growing outside, forming a canopy over the plant in winter and late spring will keep the spores off and prevent damage.

Control Remove infected leaves as soon as they appear, before spores form. Water and feed the plant well, as damage is worse in weak plants. Unless the plant is infected every winter the disease won't do much harm. Spray with a copper-based fungicide in late winter before flower buds open, and again in early autumn before leaf drop.

Virus

There are many different types of plant virus; some are quite mild, while others are killers. The most noticeable symptoms of a virus attack are stunting of the plant, distortion and marking of its leaves, and poor crops of fruit and vegetables.

Attacks An enormous range of plants are stunted by virus.

Prevention Sap-feeding insects spread the disease from plant to plant. If you are doing jobs such as disbudding chrysanthemums, you may also be helping the disease to spread: wash your hands regularly if you are dealing with large numbers of plants. Dig out and dump any suspect plants

Control Always wash your hands before you start to work on a new batch of plants. Dig out any that have the disease and burn the whole plant, root and all.

Safety first with chemicals

• Never decant chemicals into a different container, especially not a drinks bottle.

• Keep all chemicals locked up out of the reach of children.

• Store chemicals in a cool, dry, dark place and never in the glasshouse.

• Read the directions on the container and use the correct dosage.

• Wear the proper protective clothing recommended, including gloves and goggles.

• Don't apply chemicals when the temperatures are high or in bright sunlight. Spray in the evening when the bees are in their hive.

• Diluted spray should not be kept as it deteriorates.

• If chemicals get on your skin, wash thoroughly with cold water.

Welcome guests It is possible to wage biological war on a whole range of pests using parasitic insects and predators to attack slugs, vine weevils and whitefly. For example, there are parasitic nematodes (a type of minute worm), which can be mixed with water and applied to the soil to attack vine weevils and slugs, but they are only effective when the soil is moist and the temperature is above 12 °C.

Some pests can be controlled by hand – your hand. Aphids can be removed by rubbing your fingers over buds and shoots, and caterpillars, slugs and snails can be picked off the leaves. A garden visit at night with a torch will spotlight lots of creepy crawlies that can be caught and disposed of.

Saucers of beer and orange or grapefruit skins will attract slugs and snails and, once trapped, they can be disposed of without resorting to chemical pellets.

Organic growers have success with companion crop growing, where one plant will give protection to a different species growing close by. Carrot fly is attracted to carrots by the scent of the foliage, but if lavender is grown in the next row, the carrot scent is disguised and the fly can't find the spot to lay its eggs.

You can also use sacrificial plants. Aphids love the herb basil and if it is planted close to other plants that normally suffer from aphid attack, they will all colonize the basil instead. When the plants are smothered, they can be pulled up and burnt. In the same way, red spider mites love broad beans and a few planted close to a peach tree will leave it free to crop at the expense of the beans. Tobacco plants will play host to whitefly, leaving the tomatoes to get on with producing fruit.

Tagetes minuta, the Mexican marigold will reduce the harmful nematodes in the soil, while *Tagetes sinuata* will protect potatoes from eelworms. In both cases, substances secreted by the roots are thought to do the trick.

It is advantageous to avoid using chemicals as a means of eliminating pests and diseases, but I would not suggest that you should never use them. Occasionally they can provide the most efficient method of control and if their use is

Edible marigolds (*Calendula*) growing alongside vegetables in the kitchen garden. Advocates of companion planting have found that these marigolds attract hoverflies, which are beneficial in eliminating aphids.

confined to ornamental rather than edible crops, you will be in control of the situation.

Always read instructions and follow dilution rates exactly. There is nothing to gain by exceeding the dosage and you could lose plants or at least waste your money. Don't spray on a windy day as there is a risk of tiny droplets of diluted chemical being carried on the wind to other plants – soft fruit for example. Alternatively, a watering can, kept solely for pesticides and fungicides, can be used with a fine rose on the outlet. Where pests or diseases are localized and only a small area requires treating, try a ready-to-use dispenser.

compost

With some gardeners the making of compost is a religion and, like wine makers, they have good years and great years. The idea is to turn all the weeds, grass cuttings, leaves and other debris into usable compost that can be returned to the garden soil to add humus.

The finished product can be used in many ways but is a great bulky additive to the soil, opening up heavy soils to encourage drainage while at the same time making light, free-draining soils more retentive of moisture. Used as a deep mulch on the soil surface, it will reduce weed germination and prevent water evaporating in warm weather. The worms will draw the compost down into the soil.

Now let me give you a word of caution: making compost sounds easy and experts will tell you exactly how easy it is to make perfect compost. And it's true that when compost is made properly it is a wonderful material and of enormous benefit to the garden but, to be made correctly, a few rules have to be followed.

What is required is an area screened behind tall shrubs where you can make and store the compost out of sight. For small amounts of materials, a compost bin will do the job. There are various designs on the market: most resemble a plastic refuse bin with a lid but no base. The waste material is able to heat up quickly and there is no need to turn the compost.

Larger quantities can be composted in a purpose-built compost heap with a length, width and height of 1.2 m (4 ft). The sides can be made of either wooden slats or netting wire with a wooden post at each corner. In a big heap, the compost will warm up more in the centre, so the whole pile should be turned after four months to mix the compost and ensure that it all rots down evenly. Cover the heap with old carpet to help keep the heat in and heavy rain out.

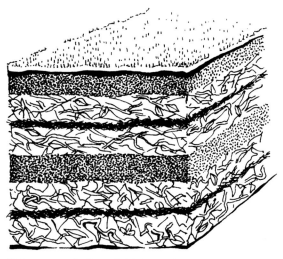

Make compost in 15 cm (6 in) layers of light prunings, leaves and annual weeds, a similar quantity of soil, then a 5 cm (2 in) layer of grass cuttings. Top with old carpet to keep rain off.

What to compost

Suitable materials for composting include annual weeds that haven't formed seed, leafy softwood prunings, old bedding plants, autumn leaves and grass clippings.

Build the materials up in 15 cm (6 in) layers. If they are dry, they can be damped over. To get the heap started add 60 g (2 oz) of a nitrogenous fertilizer per square metre of surface area, as it is the nitrogen-fixing bacteria that rot down the materials. A layer of garden soil 15 cm (6 in) deep in the middle of the heap and as a final cap on the top will add extra bacteria to speed up the process.

Grass cuttings can become slimy and should be used sparingly, the layers no deeper than 5 cm (2 in) and sandwiched between layers of coarser material. Avoid adding perennial weed roots such as docks, thistle and nettles as they will come out of the compost heap alive and ready to grow. Weed seeds will also survive unless the heap builds up to a high temperature as it decomposes. You will know when the compost is ready as the rubbish will have turned into the most wonderful, rich, peat-like humus that will do wonders for your soil. Ideally you should have two compost heaps so that while one is full and rotting down a second can be filled gradually.

Composting autumn leaves Leaf mould can be easily made from the autumn fall of leaves by collecting them using the lawn mower with the blades set high and shredding them straight into the grass box. They can then be bagged into black polythene and damped over before securing the top of the bag and leaving to decompose. Alternatively, the leaves can be composted in layers with the other materials in the normal compost heap or on their own in a frame with more open sides to allow air to circulate. Chicken wire mesh or wooden slats 2 cm (1 in) apart are ideal. The resulting leaf mould should be ready for use within 12 months and is so good it could be mistaken for peat.

Watch out for

• Wildlife will enjoy the warmth and protection of a compost heap. Less welcome will be vermin such as rats and mice, attracted if kitchen waste is being incorporated into the heap.
• Thick layers of grass cuttings will become slimy and should be used sparingly and mixed with rougher material.
• Cuttings from lawns that have been treated with weed-killer should not be added for at least four cuts.
• Hard woody stems and thick hedge prunings won't compost as easily but you can chop them up or shred them before adding in layers to the heap. Any bits that refuse to rot down can be removed as the compost is being used.

A carpet of the autumn leaves of *Acer palmatum* and *Lindera obtusifolia* ready for collection for the compost heap.

Bonfires If you have no interest in making compost, bonfires, where they are permitted, are a great way of disposing of weeds and prunings. The resulting ash is a source of nutrients especially good for fruit trees, but dig it in rather than spreading it on the surface, as it turns into a sticky mess when wet. Never use plastic or old car tyres as an aid to combustion – not only will the air be polluted, but the ashes will have unwanted residues. If burning isn't allowed or you haven't the space for a fire, a shredder will do a good job of reducing the debris to a fine mulch. Providing there are no perennial weed roots or weed seeds, it can be spread on the soil straight away or stockpiled to partially rot before being used.

Watch out for

• Small animals hibernating in the base of the heap of debris for the bonfire. Before you light it, turn the complete heap and move it to another site.
• Before you light the fire, check the direction of the wind to prevent it blowing smoke and sparks towards your house, the neighbour's house or the clothes line.
• Don't leave the fire unattended and have a hose ready, connected to a water tap close by.

Tip for a tidy garden

Since every garden needs a dumping and storage area plus the space for the compost bins why not hide them away out of the public eye. Form an area at the bottom of the garden and screen it with a high hedge or a timber panel fence. Flowering climbers such as honeysuckle, clematis and roses can be trained over the fence on the garden side. Make a discreet entrance so that it can't be viewed from the house and, for ease of tidying up, surface the ground with paving slabs or gravel.

Absence of soil is no reason not to garden. Pelargoniums, lilies, begonias, roses and nemesia are all happy growing in containers.

starting points

Undoubtedly, a large number of first-time gardeners move into new houses with a bare canvas for a garden and are going to have fun deciding what type of garden to go for and what feature to put where. Others will opt for an older house with a garden that is in some sort of condition, be it well maintained or in need of a change, and here you can take a bit of time to decide what you are going to do. Some of the potential gardeners will be young and others won't be so young. There will be couples with young families and those whose children have children of their own, and at least part of the garden has to be for them and their friends when they visit.

Trust me, you are going to enjoy being a gardener and it will show. Leaving out the extremes of a castle with parkland and a tenth-storey flat with a balcony, I have tried to include most of the garden types encountered. Follow these ideas to work with what you've got, looking at the hard landscaping before you start adding any plants.

When starting a garden from scratch, clear the area thoroughly and dispose of all rubbish and debris off site. Retain any larger trees to provide some maturity while you sort out the rest.

new house, vacant plot

It is very easy to despair and want to throw in the towel when faced with a new, raw garden; either bare earth or covered with weeds and a boundary highlighted in concrete posts and wire. A blank canvas and you have never painted before! Let me give you some words of comfort: at least you have nothing to undo, no one else's mistakes to rectify and that will save you time and money.

Clearing up The first job is to find all the gardening gifts that the nice builder has left behind for you. They are usually hidden under the thin layer of topsoil that has been spread like butter over the hard packed clay subsoil. This in turn was flattened with a digger bucket when the ground was a quagmire. There will be all sorts of rubbish and debris including bricks, timber, plywood, roof tiles and an area of weak, semi-hard mortar where the cement mixer was religiously washed out every night.

Remove as much of this debris as possible from the top 25 cm (10 in) of soil and dispose of it off site or in a skip and immediately the whole garden will look better.

Skip-loads of builders' rubbish are a worst-case scenario – many construction firms go out of their way to clear up the site before handover. If the topsoil was stripped and properly stored prior to building there should be at least as much to be replaced as came off the garden, plus an extra few inches that was originally on the drive and the building plot itself. A polite request and even a friendly smile will probably not get you any extra soil, but holding back the final cheque usually guarantees you as much as you need.

What have you got? Your garden may be a bare plot of ground but it can provide you with a lot of information. We have already discussed types of soil and drainage problems. If you look around you can identify areas of shade, what is causing them and the time of day they are shaded. A neighbour's tree may cast a shadow or part of the garden may simply face away from the sun. You can find which direction your garden faces by noting where the sun is at different times of the day.

What is the boundary to your property made of? Post and wire fences don't do much for a garden. Timber fences make better boundaries and it would be great if you happen to have a hedge of some sort.

Perimeter screen With a new garden, screening for shelter and privacy is a priority. This can be achieved by timber fencing, walls or a living screen of trees or shrubs (planting instructions are on page 36). But remember that tall trees or high hedges can shade the garden. If the same type of fence or hedge is used for the entire boundary, the garden can look closed in and monotonous. Ring the changes with different materials and types of hedge.

Marking beds Landscape design cannot be rushed. To give you the time to change your mind and come to a final decision on the location of flower beds, fruit garden and other areas, it is worthwhile sowing the majority of the land with grass, maintaining the lawn until you decide where everything is going to go. You can then mark these out when the grass is established, using a trickle of sand or a hose pipe to shape the bed. New grass is easily killed with glyphosate weedkiller or dug over to form a bed.

A lawn is a good start and allows the garden to be used and enjoyed while you make up your mind on the overall design.

Shaping beds with a hosepipe allows you to keep changing your mind until you find the look you like.

Hyrdrangeas to either side of the entrance soften the edges of the path and draw you in. In a new garden, well-filled containers provide colour while other plants establish themselves.

Up the garden path A path is one of the first features to be constructed in the garden. It allows you to move about the area and transport materials in a wheelbarrow, even in wet conditions. A path should lead somewhere. It can finish at the compost heap or a sun dial, but make sure there is something at the end.

Path surfaces can be varied and materials are often chosen to match a patio surface. A grass path between matching shrub or herbaceous borders is pleasant, providing there is not too much foot traffic and that you can avoid using it after a period of rain, when it will turn into mud.

Pea gravel is another material that works well, but like all gravels, it tends to move and needs to be edged to keep it in place. A path also needs to be edged when it is lower than the ground on either side – pre-cast plinths, bricks, tiles or reproduction Victorian rope edging can be used. For walks through a woodland area, bark chippings can be used to great effect. Slabs, bricks, tiles, paviors and crazy paving all form interesting, practical surfaces for paths.

An informal gravel path winds through a bog garden, directing the pedestrian past the most interesting plants.

Laying a path Paths should be sited where there is a 'desire line' that takes you from A to B. Since every effort should be made to make even a short path interesting, you may go from A to B via C, if C happens to be an interesting bed, unusual plant or some other feature. A path can head off from the patio or house towards the tool shed, the glasshouse or the vegetable garden and while it is effective to run it along the edge of a shrub bed or between double herbaceous borders, it can be designed to cut through a bed using stepping stones, reverting to a path on the other side, which gives added interest. Make the path wide enough to enable you to take a wheelbarrow and, where space allows, for two people to walk together.

Points to remember

• Perennial weeds must be removed as they appear and before they can get established.

• Where the ground level changes, paths that are used for wheelbarrows should slope up to the higher area – avoid using steps.

• If you don't give them a proper base, stepping stones will sink in the lawn and fill with water after rainfall.

• Lawn grass will grow over the edge of the path and will need to be trimmed back, which is why you need to keep the path at the same level as the lawn.

Hard-surface paths should be constructed to a reasonable specification as they will have to stand a lot of wear and carry wheelbarrow traffic.

• Mark out the line of the path with pegs and string, and excavate the top 15 cm (6 in) of soil.

• Then add a 10 cm (4 in) layer of hardcore. You'll need to hire a vibrating hammer to consolidate it.

• Set your chosen path surface in a weak concrete mix on top of the hardcore, keeping the surface level.

• Avoid walking on the path until the concrete has set.

• Gravel paths need a similar hardcore base topped with a layer of coarse gravel, then consolidated before the final finer layer of gravel is laid. Don't make the top layer any deeper than 2 cm (1 in) or it will be difficult to walk on.

• Crushed rock gravel is angular and less likely to move under your feet than round gravel; it comes in a large range of colours and textures depending on where it has been excavated.

Paths and lawns Where the path borders a lawn, the finished path should be at or slightly below the grass level, so that the lawn mower can be driven over the path without damaging the blades. Stepping-stone paths through a lawn should be set at the same level as the grass and should be spaced no more than 30 cm (12 in) apart. The stones can be made from flat pieces of natural rock or man-made tiles or slabs. Space them out on the grass to decide the direction the path is going to take and to work out the ideal, most comfortable spacing. When the route has been decided, the stepping stones may be used as templates. Cut around the perimeter of each one, marking the grass in the shape of the step. Remove the grass sod with a sharp spade and make a hole 15 cm (6 in) deep. Fill with 2-5 cm (1-2 in) grade hardcore. Bed the slabs in a weak concrete mix, keeping the finished surface at the same level as the grass or 1 cm (½ in) lower, so that the lawn mower can cut over the stepping stones.

Tips for new gardeners

• If you are planning to install a boundary fence or plant a hedge, try to share the cost with your neighbour.

• Dig the ground over in the autumn, leaving the rough lumps to be broken down by the winter frost.

• Leyland cypress is a fast-growing evergreen conifer, which is ideal as a screen in parkland or in a large garden where something needs to be blocked out. But if it is not kept well pruned every year it will grow to 25 m (80 ft) high with a spread of 8 m (26 ft). It is not a suitable plant for a small garden or a lazy gardener.

• Man-hole covers are more difficult to conceal in the lawn than in a planted area.

Stepping stones also make an informal path, are easy to walk on if closely spaced and prevent you treading on newly planted plants.

making over an established garden

I have often looked at a garden and thought that I would have done it differently, and I am quite sure that there are lots of gardens I have landscaped that other designers would have changed. That is the marvellous thing about garden design: there is no absolutely right way and if you are happy with what you've got that's fine by me. But if you are unhappy with your garden, or have just moved in and are dissatisfied with certain areas, then by all means plan to change it. Perhaps it is overcrowded, devoid of colour, not suitable for a young family or just not to your taste. The beauty about an established garden is that you can do a gradual make over, changing a bit at a time and yet leaving the bulk of the area usable and not looking like a derelict site.

When long-established plants are being removed, remember that they will have exhausted the soil by using up all the available nutrients. To give the new inhabitants a good start in life, top up the soil with fertilizer and some humus to make it more moisture retentive. About 30 g (1 oz) of general-purpose fertilizer scattered over 1 sq m (1 sq yard) of earth and raked in will do the job. Add well-rotted farmyard manure, old compost or leaf mould at a rate of a wheelbarrow full to 4 sq m to bulk up the soil.

Where plants are spreading over a path, they should be cut back before the path disappears. Mature trees and shrubs may grow larger than you want them to be, and should be dealt with before they get out of hand.

1. As this pine grows, it may create a large area of shade. Get an expert in to cut it back.
2. Sage can be pruned hard without suffering ill effects.
3. This *Helianthemum* (rock rose) can be trimmed so that it doesn't encroach on the path. Of course, if you don't like it, you can simply remove it altogether.

Providing you are not growing ericaceous plants such as rhododendron, azaleas and pieris, all of which like acid soil, then spent mushroom compost, which contains small amounts of lime and so is slightly alkaline, can be added.

New roses for old In areas where old roses have been dug up, don't replant with new roses. The soil will be rose sick, causing new stock to do badly and gradually die. If you want to replace just one or two plants, dig out and change the soil to a depth of 45 cm (18 in) Add fresh loamy soil and plant the new roses into that. On a larger scale, it is better to choose a new site for the rose bed.

Repairing paths Old paths can usually be replaced or resurfaced. Crazy paved paths are easy and relatively inexpensive to repair: relay the old slabs on a weak mortar base and grout the cracks with mortar. Try to ensure they are all of the same thickness for ease of laying and they are on a firm, consolidated base – if it was a well-made path, they will have been. Keep the joints close together to reduce the risk of weed seeds germinating in the cracks.

If you want to reposition a path altogether, you will find that the soil below the foundation of the old path is sterile, sour and suffering from a lack of oxygen. Digging deeply and adding fertilizer and compost will help make the soil usable.

Sprucing up patios Patios and hard surface areas that have become shabby and green with algae will benefit from cleaning with a pressure hose. Don't use detergent or hot water, as both will damage nearby plants. Weak mortar in the cracks may lift out during cleaning and should be replaced as soon as possible. Try not to disturb mat-forming and ground-

cover plants growing in crevices, as their roots will be going far and wide under the hard surface in search of moisture.

Rejuvenating borders   Herbaceous borders which are not well maintained quickly become old and tired looking. But unlike rose beds, they can be dug out and the area cultivated and beefed up with old farmyard manure or compost. Clearing out the bed can be done at any time, but it is easier to identify the perennials when they are growing and you may find some worth propagating. Dig out every piece of weed you can see and leave the bed without plants over the autumn and winter, removing weeds with a garden fork as they appear. Replant in spring as growth is starting. Add a general fertilizer at a rate of 60 g (2 oz) per sq m at planting time.

Moving established plants to a new position   If you have inherited a plant that you like but think is in the wrong place, don't worry. It is possible to move most plants of manageable size, providing you don't damage the roots and the plant doesn't suffer from a loss of water. Full transplanting instructions are on page 38.

An overgrown garden where only the sun can reach the sundial. The buddleia on the left should be pruned hard and you will need to cut back a lot of unwanted plants before you find the original beds and paths. The *Choisya ternata* to the left of the sundial should be worth saving.

Tip

If a large conifer needs removing from a confined space, it is not necessary to dig up the root. Employ a tree surgeon to cut the tree at ground level and leave the root in the ground. It won't regrow, although yew will reshoot from the main trunk, but these thin stems are easily cut back.

an overgrown garden in need of an overhaul

Without constant attention, gardens can quickly become overgrown and quite jungle like, with the strongest-growing plants choking out the remainder. I suppose there is some satisfaction in believing that if it was not for gardeners, the whole world would be in a worse mess.

After some pruning and general thinning out of overgrown plants and the removal of weeds, you will soon see light at the end of the garden – and above and around you as well.

Revealing the underlying structure of a garden

• Paths, particularly gravel ones, can quickly disappear under weeds and a coating of dead leaves. Try to identify the main routes and clear them back, removing all the weeds and seedling plants off the path. Dig out border plants that are too close to the edge, so that the path can be used again. In this way you can be sure that you are not tramping over the original beds, where there may be plants which are worth saving.

• Identify all the bulky large plants. Find out if they have any particular pruning requirements, their speed of growth and season of flowering. Then decide if each one gets the thumbs up or the chop. Some plants will be easily identified from books but it will be necessary to involve an expert for some of the more unusual plants. A landscape contractor or staff from your local garden centre should be able to help.

• Seedling trees of ash and sycamore, which quickly colonize a neglected garden, can be removed in winter or early spring by digging them up with a spade. Give them to those with the space for them or take them straight to the dump or bonfire. If they are not removed when young they will grow into huge trees.

• Perennial and annual weeds can be sprayed with glyphosate weed killer, but take care not to allow the chemical to come in contact with plants you want to keep. Glyphosate should be applied on a calm, dry day, anytime from late spring until late summer, when the weeds are actively growing. The chemical is translocated through the leaves into the roots, killing the weeds from the bottom up. Follow the manufacturer's instructions and wear protective clothing, including gloves, when using chemicals.

• Overgrown gardens are often home to a mat of ivy over the ground, ivy up the tree trunks and ivy covering the paths and walls. It is practically impossible to eliminate it, but constant digging, cutting, pulling and removing will keep it at bay. Repeated applications of glyphosate will have some effect but you need to add a 'sticker' chemical to the mixture, otherwise the spray runs off the shiny leaves. Ask at your local garden centre for advice.

• Brambles very quickly take over a neglected area, as the tips of the shoots root where they touch the ground. The best way to remove them is by digging them out. Where there is a whole patch of brambles and no other plants to worry about, the brambles can be cut close to the ground. When new growth appears in spring, spray with a brushwood weedkiller, which kills all shrubby plants. Nettles may be sprayed with glyphosate or dug out, removing as much of the yellow root as possible.

What to do with trees and shrubs By leaving an upper canopy of mature shrubs and trees, you can form a woodland area in the garden where you can grow all those lovely plants that dislike full sun. Start by identifying the shrubs and trees you have. Some shrubs, such as fuchsia, weigela, lavender and spiraea, are just not worth rejuvenating if they are old and very woody. They are inexpensive to replace and quick growing so, rather than spending a lot of time trying to save your over-mature plants, dig them out and start again.

Examine other ornamental shrubs and trees. Strong shoots that look slightly different to the main plant and are growing from below or at ground level are likely to be suckers. These grow from the roots of the plant that the variety was grafted onto and should be removed before they overpower the tree or shrub. If they are cut at ground level they will grow again. It is best to pull or tear them off where they join the root. Roses, contorted hazel, viburnum and witch hazel are all prone to suckering.

Old fruit trees are almost certain to have diseased branches that must be removed and burnt. The most noticeable and dangerous disease is canker, which will kill large branches and eventually the complete tree. It is easily seen in winter when there are no leaves on the trees; it causes sunken areas of discoloured bark that are cracked, while the surrounding area is swollen. Small infections can be cut out, removing all of the wood that is stained brown, but once the canker circles a branch, it will kill it.

Silver leaf is a serious fungal disease of plums and cherries. The foliage becomes silvery and infected branches do not produce leaves the following year. There is no control,

10 plants that can be pruned hard

Buddleja davidii Prune in spring.

Cornus alba Prune in spring.

Escallonia rubra **var. macrantha** Prune after flowering in late summer.

Forsythia **x** *intermedia* **'Lynwood'** Prune in spring after flowering.

Hebe **'Purple Queen'** Prune when large in early summer.

Hydrangea macrophylla Prune in early summer.

Rosa rugosa Prune in late summer after flowering.

Sambucus nigra **'Marginata'** Prune in late spring.

Ulex europaeus **'Flore Pleno'** Prune every two to three years after flowering.

Viburnum tinus Prune in early spring.

but you can cut the diseased branch off well below the obviously infected part, which will have a brown stain when cut. You may be lucky, but most infected trees gradually die.

Giving old hedges a new lease of life Old overgrown hedges can be rejuvenated by cutting hard into the old timber and watering and feeding regularly to encourage new growth. It will take a few years to make a good screen but may be a better option than removing the whole hedge.

Similarly, hedges that have spread sideways and become too wide can be cut back over a two-year period. Cut them hard on one side the first year and on the opposite side the following year, reducing their width by half. In both cases, cut in late spring to encourage some growth before winter. The cut side will look bare until it grows over, but it is still quicker than starting from scratch. Cut all branches on an angle rather than straight across, to allow water to run off the wound and reduce the risk of rot. Hawthorn, laurel, privet and yew hedges can be cut hard and will produce new shoots from the old wood, but beech and most conifer hedges are reluctant to do so.

Tip

Hiring a shredder to chop up all the prunings and plants that have been removed can not only save a lot of time and space but present you with an ideal mulch for use on shrub beds to reduce weeding. Avoid shredding diseased wood, which should be burnt along with the thicker branches, tree roots and weeds. The resultant wood ash can be spread on the ground in autumn as a source of high-potash fertilizer. Potash will harden up soft growth that has been produced late in the season and would be easily damaged by frost.

Escape through the back gate seems the only option after years of neglect. But two years and a lot of compost later, this simple makeover has led to a garden to be proud of.

1. Only the fuchsia was worth saving.
2. The lawn leads the eye down the garden to a climbing honeysuckle that has taken off over the gate.
3. *Lavandula angustifolia* 'Twickel Purple' and hebes 'Dazzler', 'Purple Shamrock' and 'Quicksilver' enjoy the sun in the central bed.
4. Shrubs, including *Buddleja davidii* 'Black Knight', *Weigela florida* 'Foliis purpureis' and *Spiraea japonica* 'Anthony Waterer' soften the wall.

keeping a well-maintained garden looking good

General garden maintenance involves weeding, feeding, pruning and grass cutting. If you can keep on top of these, the garden will at least look tidy and the plants won't suffer.

Getting to grips with weeding The person who claims not to have weeds lives in a high-rise block of flats, the Sahara desert or perhaps thinks of them as plants to be fed and watered. Weeds and their control are dealt with on pages 30-33, but it is reasonable to assume that in a well-maintained garden, most of the weeds will be annual or 'soft' weeds that are easily controlled. Try to remove them while they are still small, before they produce a deep root system and especially before they start to set seed. If you are doing this by hand, the job will be a lot easier after a shower of rain when the soil is moist.

On the other hand, it is best to hoe weeds when the ground is dry and no rain is expected, allowing them to wither and die. If the soil is moist, weeds should be removed after hoeing to prevent them re-rooting into the damp soil and growing away better than ever.

Feeding – keeping a balance It is quite possible to over-feed plants, causing an imbalance of nutrients. As a result the plant doesn't flower or may have stunted growth or an excess of spindly shoots. Most plants growing in the ground will benefit from a dressing of slow-release fertilizer

such as bone meal in the planting hole at planting time. Thereafter, they are quite content to send their roots out in search of nutrients. Impoverished soils and heavy clay subsoils can be enriched if the plants are not making satisfactory growth.

Pruning mature plants Pruning is covered more fully on pages 48–51, but the point to remember here is that it promotes growth. With older, established shrubs pruning is necessary to keep the plant growing or it will go into decline with less flower and foliage. Buddleia has to be cut hard each spring to encourage new growth which flowers the same year – it can produce branches 2. 4 m (8 ft) long by summer. Lavender needs to be pruned every year to encourage new growth from the base, or the shoots become woody, producing little growth. Pruning will also keep a plant in shape and keep it under control.

Keeping the lawn in good shape I have a love-hate relationship with grass cutting. It is the most boring repetitive chore in the garden and the satisfaction of a good job well done soon wears off, as the grass starts to grow again before the mower is back in the shed. To keep a lawn looking good, you have to cut it once a week from mid-spring until at least mid-autumn, with a couple of cuts during the winter if the weather is suitable.

On the other hand, mowing is a simple operation, requiring little concentration, allowing you to think of more important things. If you are using a walk-behind mower, there is the bonus of a bit of exercise. Regular mowing is less trouble in the long run, as tall grass is hard to cut. If it is wet and long, the machine constantly clogs up with wet grass. Ride-on grass cutters are fun, but not worth buying if you have less than half an acre of lawn all in one piece.

Pruning is necessary to keep many shrubs healthy, but remember that it promotes growth. In a mature garden you may have to move some plants to give the others enough space.
1. *Rosa* 'Sanders White' scrambling over the entrance will need pruning every year.
2. Plants overhanging the path may be cut back, but will probably grow back all the faster.
3. Don't allow other plants to smother the side of the conifer or the foliage will turn brown.

Overcrowded borders Plants may need moving as they grow, to prevent them becoming overcrowded. The time to do this is in the autumn or early spring. High density can be caused by planting too closely in the first instance. Another reason is the filling of every available space with impulse purchases, squeezed into any gap, even if the area has been deliberately left for surrounding plants to fill.

Three ways to a faster cut

• Eliminate all the grass from the base of walls and fences where you need to use a strimmer. Instead, form a hard surface strip about 10 cm (4 in) wide, using bricks or concrete at the same level as the grass to form a mowing edge.

• Avoid obstacles in the lawn such as trees, individual shrubs, seats, bird tables, sun dials and play equipment. Incorporate the plants into a curved bed that can be mown around and set ornaments on a hard surface base, flush with the grass so that that the mower can cut over the edge.

• Design out any tight corners of grass that are awkward to cut by curving the edge of the lawn past the corner and planting up a bed where the grass has been eliminated.

10 cheap gap fillers

Aubrieta Spring-flowering perennial evergreen

Aurinia saxatilis Spring-flowering evergreen sub-shrub

Centranthus ruber Short-lived perennial

Geranium macrorrhizum Evergreen perennial ground cover

Helianthemum apenninum Evergreen mat-forming shrub

Houttuynia cordata **Variegata Group.** Perennial with variegated leaves

Iberis semperflorens Evergreen sub-shrub

Phlox subulata Evergreen perennial

Stachys byzantina Perennial with white-woolly leaves

Thymus vulgaris Evergreen sub-shrub

Always read the label to check the ultimate height and spread before positioning plants. Where large spaces need to be left, these can be temporarily filled with annuals , biennials or perennials. The annuals and biennials can be pulled out and discarded after they have flowered, while the perennials can be dug up and transplanted in the autumn or spring, before they are covered over as the space fills up. Bulbs are great for infilling bare spaces for seasonal display.

A well-planted mature garden will still need weeding, pruning and thinning to keep it looking smart.

a small garden

The only thing wrong with a small garden is that it is always just too small. As a gardener, there is always another plant that you would love to have room for.

Small gardens need to be well designed to get the maximum use of the space available. With a bit of thought, it is surprising how much you can fit into the space and how big you can make your garden appear.

Containers of all shapes and sizes are a must for the small garden. Planted with a range of ever-changing plants, they can provide maximum colour the year round. Annuals in vibrant colours can be followed by winter bulbs and winter-flowering pansies, polyanthus and wallflowers. Patio roses especially the Flower Carpet series will provide summer show and aromatic herbs such as lavender, thyme and sage create a Mediterranean feel.

10 favourite small trees

Acer palmatum **'Bloodgood' (Japanese maple)** Deciduous with deep purple leaves changing to bright red in autumn.

Amelanchier canadensis **(snowy mespilus)** Deciduous with brilliant spring and autumn leaf colour.

Betula pendula **'Youngii' (Young's weeping birch)** Leaves turn yellow in autumn.

Magnolia x soulangeana **'Lennei'** Deciduous with dark purple goblet-shaped flowers.

Malus **'Royalty' (crab apple)** Deciduous, with dark purple leaves turning red in autumn.

Parrotia persica A brilliant tree for autumn colour.

Prunus x subhirtella **'Autumnalis'** Ornamental winter-flowering cherry tree.

Prunus **'Amanogawa'** A cherry with fragrant, pale pink flowers in spring and good autumn leaf colour.

Sorbus sargentiana **(Sargent's rowan)** Deciduous, with large deep green pinnate leaves that turn the most spectacular red and orange in autumn.

Sorbus vilmorinii A small tree with dark red berries that turn pink and finally pure white.

Making the most of a small area: fuchsias frame the patio, where containers and troughs overflowing with geraniums, petunias and nasturtiums add to the colour.

Boundary fences and the walls of the house can be utilized to grow plants vertically, without taking up floor space. As well as the usual climbers such as roses, honeysuckle and clematis, there are excellent shrubs for walls including pyracantha, garrya and camellia. Fruit trees such as apple, pear, cherry, peach and fig can be trained on a wall. They need a sunny wall and need to be pruned in summer as well as winter, to keep them in shape.

Even the smallest of gardens needs to have space for a table and seats where you can sit out and enjoy the view. In winter, use the space for planted containers.

If space allows try to get at least one upright plant with a bit of height to give the garden a three dimensional appearance. There are plenty of small trees suitable for tiny areas (see box, left).

Gardening isn't just about plants: here, the variety of horizontal and vertical hard surfaces provide as much interest as the choice of colours, textures and shapes in the planting.

garden features

The wonderful thing about gardening is that it is much more than just plants and soil. There are all the other aspects and disciplines that make gardening and garden design so interesting. Fencing, patio, decking, paths, shed, pergola and glasshouse – all or some of them have to be allowed for. Then there are seats, sundials, bird baths and barbecues. A water feature, play area or compost heap will take up more space and if they are not all carefully planned and placed, there will be no space in the garden for the plants.

fences and hedges

Timber fences play an important part in the garden, either as a boundary or to subdivide a section such as the vegetable garden. They can be used to provide shelter or guarantee privacy.

• Sawn boards for vertical fences can be 15 cm (6 in) wide and up to 2.4 m (8 ft) high. Fix them on timber runners with 2 cm (1 in) gaps between the boards, supported on posts.

• The more exposed the site and the more solid the fence, the stronger the support needs to be. In extreme cases, concrete posts are the answer. Where less will do, timber posts can be concreted into the ground or special metal stakes driven in and the post attached to the metal base.

• All measurements must be exact or panels and pre-cut timber won't fit. The uprights for the fence must be plumbed with a spirit level or the finished result will be in and out like a dog's hind leg.

A timber fence softened by foliage and flowers. The poppies make a splash of colour.

• Sawn boards may also be formed into panels 2 m (6 ft 6 in) wide and 1–2 m (3 ft–6 ft 6 in) high with boards overlapping horizontally.

• Peeled bark posts can be cut and assembled on site to form rustic trellis fencing for use in cottage gardens to grow climbers up.

Points to watch out for

• On sloping ground, the fence will have to be stepped, keeping the posts vertical.

• Keep the base of the fence clear of the ground to prevent the timber rotting.

• Use galvanized nails to prevent rust.

• Don't use paints, preservatives and stains that are not plant friendly.

• On windy sites, don't use solid fences. A solid barrier will stop the wind filtering through: this causes turbulence on the other side of the fence which is supposedly sheltered.

• Tanalized timber treated with a preservative will last for years. Apply a combined wood stain and preservative every year to make it look like new and prevent timber rot.

Using diplomacy Erecting boundary fencing can be fraught with problems when there are neighbours involved. If your deeds or tenancy agreement do not specify who is responsible for the boundary, the best option is for both of you to share the cost of the fence and maintain it year about. To keep the peace it is desirable that the fence is double sided, so that it looks attractive from each side.

Fencing within a garden In larger gardens, internal dividing fences can be used to good effect to partition fruit and vegetable plots and to screen unsightly cluttered areas. These fences can be planted with climbers or even trained fruit trees. Where it is not necessary to keep domestic animals out or in, open ranch fencing or rustic trellis may be used and softened with plants. This type of fence around a patio will provide shelter and a level of privacy.

Total privacy and shelter are provided by a dense beech hedge with an arched entrance in the corner.

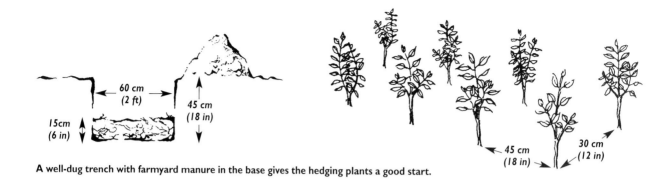

A well-dug trench with farmyard manure in the base gives the hedging plants a good start.

Planting a hedge Hedges are a form of living boundary that provides shelter, screening and security. They can be formal or informal, depending on the style of your garden.

• Before planting, dig a trench 60 cm (24 in) wide and 45 cm (18 in) deep and add a 15 cm (6 in) layer of compost or old farmyard manure to the trench base. Incorporate a handful of bonemeal per square metre in the soil that is to be backfilled around the roots.

• Space hornbeam, beech, privet, hawthorn and rose plants 45 cm (18 in) apart in a row. Then add a second, staggered row of plants, 30cm (12 in) behind the first row. This will produce a tight solid hedge in a short time.

• Hedges of berberis, escallonia, pyracantha, holly and conifers can all be planted in a single row, 45 cm (18 in) apart. Leyland cypress should be planted as a single line, with plants 1.5 m (5 ft) apart, but take note of the warning on page 77.

• Clip all hedge plants hard after planting, removing one-third of the growth, to encourage them to branch and form a dense hedge at the base.

• Apply a general purpose fertilizer once growth starts in the spring and water regularly to keep the soil moist. Keep the base of the hedge weed free to prevent the lower branches becoming choked and losing their leaves.

Pruning times for hedges

Species	Season	Tools
Beech	Early spring and early autumn	Power clippers
Box	Regularly between spring and autumn	Hand shears, if dwarf
Escallonia	Late summer after flowering	Power clippers or secateurs
Forsythia	Spring after flowering	Secateurs
Hawthorn	Early summer after flowering	Power clippers
Holly	Early spring	Power clippers
Hornbeam	Late summer	Power clippers
Laurel	Late spring and early autumn	Secateurs
Leylandii	Late spring and early autumn	Power clippers
Privet	As required between spring and summer	Power clippers or hand shears
Yew	Summer and early autumn	Power clippers

Tip
Use a long-handled brush to knock off any clippings that are lodged in the foliage on top of the hedge. If they are allowed to remain, they will wither and become unsightly.

An informal hedge of evergreen *Cotonoeaster lacteus*. Its white flowers in summer are followed by red fruits which last well into winter.

Formal or informal? Formal hedges are tightly clipped to a precise shape. Ideal hedging plants include beech, hornbeam, yew, griselinia and privet. Informal hedges are allowed to grow more loosely, with general shaping. They are pruned rather than clipped and often include flowering shrubs, for example, escallonia and berberis, which are evergreen and forsythia, which is deciduous. Lavender, hebe and box can be grown as low, dividing formal hedges rather than garden boundaries.

Formal hedges require regular clipping to keep them in shape and to prevent them becoming bare at the base and straggly. The time to trim is in June after nesting birds have reared their young, and again in July and August as necessary. Try not to cut hedges any later in the season, especially in areas prone to frost, where the cold can penetrate into the less-hardened wood in the centre of the hedge and kill the plants.

Always shape evergreen hedges to taper in at the top: a fall of snow can have enough weight to push a hedge wide open at the top and destroy the shape. Cut both sides before the top and use a line along the face of the top to ensure that it is cut level.

A level, uniformly dark green, weed-free lawn is a thing of beauty.

thinking about grass

The lawn is a sort of love it, hate it aspect of gardening and, as I've said elsewhere, I love to hate it. Let me tell you the bad news first and then I will tell you the really bad news. The maintenance of a good-quality lawn takes time, money and a lot of hard work. Now, by good quality I mean a lawn that is level, without obvious humps, lumps, bumps, hollows, dips or mole hills. It will be uniformly green, not go yellow in summer and stop short of being sodden wet in winter. Added to this it will be reasonably free of weeds, especially dandelions, daisies, buttercup, speedwell and moss. Here I must declare an interest: I have a grass area and it doesn't fit this description so I do not call it a lawn. I used to have three grass areas but I grew up and got a bit of sense.

Lots of people have good lawns and some have excellent specimens but even a lawnaholic will have to admit that it takes time. The operations go something like this: edge the grass, spray for weeds, apply lawn sand, spike, feed, scarify, grit the surface, autumn dress and spray for diseases. Did I forget to mention cutting the grass? Well, no matter, you only have to do it about 26 times from spring until autumn and then a few times in the winter when the weather is suitable. I have seen summers when we have hardly had 26 dry days in total!

Now, it is not my intention to put you off but I don't want you to opt for a lawn and then be disappointed: a lawn is for life, not just the summer holidays.

Creating a lawn from scratch Start by preparing the site. Remove any debris, builders' rubble and large stones that are on the surface and apply weedkiller such as glyphosate to the foliage of weeds. You need to allow at least four weeks for the chemical to work and if any perennial weeds reappear during this time, dig them out making sure to get up every root. Annual weeds need to be hoed off before they set seed.

Dig or rotovate the soil and level any humps and depressions. If there are large humps you may need to strip off the topsoil and level the subsoil, before replacing the topsoil and discarding the surplus subsoil.

Finally, rake the surface to level it, checking at regular intervals with a long wooden straight edge and a spirit level. Remove any remaining debris. Apply a general purpose fertilizer at 30 g (1 oz) per sq m and tread the surface to firm the soil. Give one final raking to remove the foot prints and leave the surface of the soil fine and firm, with no soft areas.

Growing a lawn from seed

Choose a mixture of seed that will produce the type of lawn you need. A mixture for a fine-quality lawn will contain seed of fescue and bent grass. if a hard-wearing lawn is required for a play area, some of the rye grasses will do better. There are special mixtures for dry sites and for light shade under trees

The condition of the soil and the season have to be considered. It takes very little rain to make the soil surface sticky and seed should not be sown until the surface dries out. Autumn sowing is best if your summers are hot and dry, allowing seed to become established before there is a dry period. A late spring sowing will grow away quickly and be well established by the late summer.

Tips

• Old grass is usually infested in spring with leather jackets, the grubs of the crane fly or daddy long legs, which eat the grass roots. Water the lawn and then cover it overnight with a black plastic sheet. In the morning remove the cover and all the leatherjackets will have come to the surface in time to make a good breakfast for the birds, especially the starlings.

• When cutting the grass try to vary the direction of cut each time to catch unawares the flat-growing, weed-type grass that lies down in front of the blades. This will also prevent the mower wheels constantly running over the same strip of lawn.

The seed should be broadcast over the area at a rate of 30 g (1 oz) per sq m. If there is a light wind scatter the seed by hand, with the wind and not against it. If you don't feel confident of sowing at the correct rate, mark the area into metre wide strips with cord, to help you check. Lightly rake the grass seed into the soil surface and if it hasn't rained after two days, water using a sprinkler. Warm moist weather will speed up the germination and the seedling grasses can appear inside two weeks. If the soil is dry or there is a cold period, it can take as long as four weeks before greenness appears. Try to stay off the grass until it is 5 cm (2 in) long. You can then give it its first cut using a rotary cutter set high to just top the grass. Cylinder mowers can't be used at this stage as they tend to pull the new grass and disturb the roots.

Laying turf Although turf is expensive, the effect is practically instant. The ideal time to lay turf is early autumn to late spring, providing the soil conditions are workable and the surface isn't wet or muddy and there is no frost on the ground or expected until the turf is laid.

Prepare the site in the same way as for sowing grass, with the surface fine, level and firm. Choose a grade of turf to suit the level of work and play the grass will have to tolerate. As with grass seeds there are different qualities of turf available, including top-quality fine grasses fit for a bowling green and hard-wearing mixtures for family use. The turf will be delivered rolled up and it is essential that it is laid as soon as possible to prevent it drying out. If it has to be kept overnight, store the rolls under cover in an airy place protected from rain.

Overleaf: The lawn sets off the plants and plants highlight the lawn.

When laying turf, it is essential to work from the grass that has already been laid and not on the bare earth. Stand on a plank to distribute your weight and avoid damaging the turf. Roll the grass out in a straight line and butt the second turf tightly to the first. Turf is supplied with only a thin layer of soil and is easily damaged if it is not carried carefully. The second row of turf is laid like a second layer of bricks in a wall, so that the joints are not in line with the joints in the first row. Firm the row of turf with the back of a metal rake, move the plank over and repeat until the area is covered. After the turf is laid, water regularly if there is no rain. After four weeks the roots will have anchored the turf to the soil. You can start to cut the new lawn as soon as the grass is long enough. Cracks may appear if the turf was not laid tightly, but these can be filled with a peat/soil mixture brushed into the grass.

Initial lawn care Water as necessary in periods of hot dry weather and cut the grass on a regular basis, gradually lowering the height of the mower blades to cut the grass shorter. But don't scalp the grass, as close-cut lawns are more prone to being colonized by moss. Weeds will appear, especially in lawns grown from seed, but don't apply weedkillers for at least six months – this will allow the grass time to become established. Avoid using high-nitrogen fertilizers for the same length of time, as it is more important for the grass plants to build up strong root systems than to produce a lot of leaf (which nitrogen would encourage).

Cutting the grass Deciding which way to cut the grass is the first hurdle. You have a range of options from small push mowers that are hard work, through to

An uneven application of fertilizer will result in the overdosed areas being scorched or killed.

pedestrian-operated rotary and cylinder cutters, where you walk behind a machine that is power driven by petrol, battery or mains electricity. Then there are hover cutters that float on a cushion of air rather than on wheels.

Rotary mowers do not leave as fine a cut as cylinder cutters. With rotaries, the blades rotate parallel with the grass surface, whereas cylinder blades spin down towards the grass and are close together, resulting in a finer cut with the grass finely chopped up. Mulching mowers literally chop up the grass to a fine mulch that can stay on the lawn and will disappear into the surface.

There are several schools of thought on the subject of grass cuttings, but the most popular advice is to leave the cuttings on the lawn after the first cut and again after the last cut of the season. In between they can either be collected in the grass box and removed or left on the lawn. If the clippings are being removed, you will need a dumping area out of sight. If they are being used in the compost heap, only thin layers of about 10 cm (4 in) can be added at any one time or they won't rot down properly.

Try to choose a machine whose height of cut can be adjusted. It is advisable not to cut too low at the start of the season or during very dry weather. The recommended height will depend on the type of grass, as some varieties can tolerate closer cutting than others, but as a rough guide 1.5 cm (½ in) to 2.5 cm (1 in) is fine in summer.

A roller at the rear of the grass cutter produces the light and dark green stripes beloved by all and reminiscent of the Wembley pitch. As you walk up and down, the roller flattens the grass in opposite directions and the light shines on the flat blades. If the grass was all rolled in the same direction, there would be no shading.

Rejuvenating an old lawn
It is amazing what you can do with an old overgrown, weedy grass area that used to be a lawn. If the site is level, half your battle is won. In spring, summer or early autumn, rough cut with a rotary mower or use a strimmer to remove most of the long grass, raking it off and cutting again until you get it to about

Plantain and daisies will soon smother the finer grasses if you don't keep them under control.

8–10 cm (3–4 in) high. Allow the grass to recover and start growing again and then apply a selective lawn weedkiller to kill a broad range of grass weeds, following the manufacturer's instructions. After a few days, cut the grass again and give it an application of lawn fertilizer to encourage growth. If you require a first-class, Wembley look-alike lawn, you have just wasted your time but if you will settle for a level, green, reasonably weed-free grass area that looks good you have probably just achieved it.

Weeding and feeding
Whenever the subject of lawns crops up you will hear the words 'weed and feed' used together. The grass is treated for weeds and at the same time it is fed with a high-nitrogen fertilizer. Weeds growing strongly from the application of fertilizer are softer and so are more easily killed with the selective weedkiller that attacks weeds without damaging the grass. The grass benefits from the fertilizer and quickly fills the space left by the dead weeds.

planning a patio

A patio is like a room outdoors and when the weather is suitable it can be used for relaxation, entertaining and eating. Essentially, it is an area of level hard surface in the garden where you can sit in sun or shade with table and chairs and, hopefully, enjoy the surroundings. The surface may be gravel, crazy paving (broken paving slabs), concrete slabs, pre-formed tiles, bricks, setts, natural slate, York or Cotswold stone. The total area may be enclosed by planted beds or the patio can be raised above the surrounding garden, reached by steps up from a lawn or path.

Having the patio as an extension to the house is ideal for enjoying a cup of coffee and a quick look at the paper before work. The main factor when choosing the site is sun. A sunless site is to be avoided at all cost: it will be cold, and the patio surface will turn green through lack of light, which encourages algae to grow.

There is no good reason for having just one patio and, if you have space, a second area away from the house at the end of a path, through lawn or shrubbery, will give you a choice of places to sit. While the patio should be in a sunny position, it is useful to have a section shaded for use when the sun gets too hot or where the drinks can be kept cool. A wooden pergola covering part of the patio and draped in climbers will provide the shade required. The sound and sight of running water add to the idyllic image and why not finish off with two birch trees 3 m (10 ft) apart to cast some shade and to swing a hammock from!

Laying the foundations

• It is essential that the patio is laid on a firm foundation and that surface water can run off. Start by excavating to a depth of 20 cm (8 in) below the finished level – keep the topsoil for use elsewhere. This is the chance to drain areas that are damp (using the method on page 23), but don't try to make a patio on very wet ground.

• Form a layer of clean 5 cm (2 in) stone 10 cm (4 in) deep and consolidate it using a vibrating hammer (which you can hire from garden centres or DIY hire shops).

• Lay a layer of landscape fabric on top to prevent weeds growing up and surface with a 5 cm (2 in) layer of vibrated sand.

• Create a very slight slope, so that water will run off the surface. A gradient of 25 mm in 1.8 m (1 in in 6 ft) sloping away from the house walls is sufficient. Using a straight edge and a spirit level to ensure accuracy, drive in wooden pegs 1.8 m (6 ft) apart, with each peg 25 mm (1 in) lower than the one before. Ensure that there are no depressions in the vibrated sand between the pegs, so that you have an evenly sloping surface. Then remove the pegs and lay your chosen surface on the sand. Bricks, tiles and setts should be laid tight together and fine dry sand brushed into the gaps and vibrated. Slabs and crazy paving need grouting with a very wet mix of four parts cement and one part sand, brushed into the joints. Brush off excess mortar the following day. When old stone is being laid, there is usually a difference in the thickness of the pieces and it may be necessary to bed each piece individually on a fairly weak, dry mortar mix of four parts sand to one part cement.

Roses drape a rustic arch leading into the patio.

Points to watch out for

• Over time the surface of sandstone slabs will flake off in layers and will be made worse by frost action.

• If the patio is next to a wall, leave holes in the surface at the base of the wall for climbing plants.

• Iron containers will rust and stain the patio surface.

• Make the patio big enough to accommodate furniture and guests.

• Make any steps from the patio to the garden from the same material to give continuity.

Wisteria drapes a timber pergola. Wisteria needs to be pruned after flowering and again in late winter. The effort is rewarded by a glorious display of flowers and beautiful fragrance, followed in late summer and autumn by velvety pods.

pergola

A pergola is an open timber structure tall enough to stand under and ideal for supporting climbing plants. It is often built in the form of an arch or as an open roof over a patio. For a large pergola the timber can be rustic peeled bark poles or cut timber as bulky as possible, with cross beams of equal size. Smaller structures can be made of lighter materials, such as wrought iron or wooden lattice work, but remember that some materials will require more maintenance than others. Timber needs staining or preserving; metal should be treated for rust.

Where a pergola is used to shade a patio, uprights must not obstruct the main area of the patio. You will need substantial timbers, so ensure that they are well concreted into the ground and that the cross beams are at least 2.5 m (8 ft) above ground level, to allow plants to grow over the bars without trailing down at head height. Choose climbers that look interesting for a good part of the year with leaf,

flower and fruit. Vines perform well and provide edible grapes in mild climates and wisteria, if pruned and trained, will be a mass of flowers during late spring and early summer.

Points to watch out for

• Form recessed joints where the vertical posts meet the cross bars and use galvanized nails that won't rust.

• Use well-seasoned wood to avoid the timber warping and splitting.

• When concreting the posts into the ground, leave space for planting climbers and provide galvanized or plastic mesh support to get the plants growing up and over the top.

• When making an arch over a path, position the uprights at least 60 cm (24 in) back from the sides of the path, to allow room for plants to grow up without blocking the way through.

play area

If you are creating a separate area for children to play in, site it close to the house where it can be clearly seen. A see-through fence, such as split chestnut stakes spaced apart and wired together, will allow anyone supervising to at least blink without the children disappearing.

Grass is an ideal play surface in summer but in winter it will become churned up into mud very quickly. An area of 13 mm (½ in) diameter round gravel may be hard on bare feet but at least it is dry and mud free underfoot. Bark mulch spread 10 cm (4 in) deep will cushion falls and is ideal where there are no dogs or cats to use it as a toilet area.

Play equipment needs to be well spaced out with nothing immediately behind or in front of a swing, for obvious reasons. Where uprights of swings, climbing frames, etc. are concreted into the ground, the concrete should be 15 cm (6 in) below the soil surface and be covered with soil or mulch. Outdoor sand pits are always popular. They need to be free draining, with a base that can be brushed clean when changing the sand. A lightweight cover will keep animals out when the pit is not in use. Any shrubs planted in the area must be able to withstand a bit of abuse and be free of thorns and spines. Plants such as buddleia, the butterfly bush, can tolerate a lot of damage. Broken branches will serve as a form of crude pruning, which is just what this shrub needs every year.

A Wendy house in the play area can be used to shelter in if a shower of rain comes on and is a useful place to store the toys that can't stay outside permanently.

If the garden is too small to subdivide, allow the children free range. Encourage them to help with the whole garden and to remove their toys to make way for the lawn mower.

Lawns are an ideal site for climbing frames, but placing matting or coarse bark round the base will ensure soft landings anywhere.

garden ornaments

Garden seat Larger gardens can accommodate more than one seat. Position some in sun and some in shade, to take in views of special parts of the garden. They come in all shapes and materials, including stone, hardwood, rustic timber and plastic, but have at least one that is comfortable to the point that you can doze off on it without going numb. In winter you may want to bring one or two under cover.

Bird bath A bird bath is another permanent fixture and every garden should have one. It doesn't have to be elaborate and providing it is shallow, the birds will use it. Position it where it can be seen from the house and you will get hours of enjoyment as birds bathe and drink, but don't forget to keep it topped up with water!

Garden furniture can be both practical and ornamental and, whether you choose to sit in the sun or the shade, position your seating so that you can delight in the scent of nearby shrubs.

A bird bath makes a focal point. Site it so that you can see it from the house and enjoy the activity of the birds.

Sun dial A sun dial usually stays out all year and the only rule to be observed is that it should be in full sun all day long. You'll probably never use it but there is always one visitor who wants to tell the time and thinks he knows how to set the dial.

Points to watch out for

• More and more garden ornaments are being stolen each year: secure with a bolt and chain attached to a permanent stake all those that are left outside.

• Full sun will bleach hardwood seats over a period of time. Give them a little protection and oil them lightly each spring with linseed oil.

• It is hard to mow grass around the base of ornaments. Set them on a hard surface that is flush with the grass.

• Plastic summer furniture will blow all over the place if left out in windy weather and is sure to damage your prize plants. Fix it to the ground or store it under cover when not in use.

water features

No garden should be without one of these. The sound and sight of moving water is all things to all people. It is relaxing, interesting, fascinating and above all rewarding if you have done the work yourself. Features can range from little trickles to a crashing crescendo tumbling over rocks like white water and down a waterfall into a pool of flowering plants and darting fish.

Large or small, if the water feature can be seen and heard from parts of the garden in summer and from the house in winter it more than earns its space in the garden. Birds will bathe in shallow pools and frogs breed in the pond and knowing that both reduce the slug and snail population is more than a bonus.

Small water features can be purchased in kit form complete with a submersible pump and ready to install. A wall-mounted lion's head spouting water into a bowl below or a miniature fountain depositing water onto round cobbles or trickling over a circular mill stone will sit neatly on the smallest patio and make you feel cooler on a hot day.

Constructing a water feature is a serious undertaking. Unlike many other garden projects, where there is a bit of latitude and a few mistakes can be made without having much effect, a water feature has to be 100 per cent perfect. Water is very unforgiving and if levels are not exactly right, or the flow is too fierce or, worst of all, if there is a leak, then the whole job may have to be redone from scratch.

Plants round a pond don't only create interest and soften the edges; by shading the water they also reduce the risk of algae.

Building a pond Ponds are easier to construct if the soil and subsoil are not too difficult to dig. It's a good idea to check with a few test holes that you won't hit rock just below the surface. It is also an advantage to have a level site. On a sloping site the low side has to be built up to keep the top of the pond at the same level. But if you have a flat site at the base of a slope, you have a ready-made location for a waterfall. All you need is a small upper pond or an outlet between rocks for the water to be pumped up to, then it can flow down to the bottom pond. Where there is no suitable slope or high ground, the soil dug out to make the pond can be earthed up to provide height close by.

Lining the pond It is important to decide early on what material you are going to use to form the pond. You have several options.

• In some areas, the local clay is suitable for coating the sides and the base. If the pond is kept full of water so that the clay doesn't dry out, it will act as a seal.

• Concrete can be used to line the pool if there is no settlement of the ground, which would cause it to crack. Coat the dry concrete with a waterproofing sealant, painting it on before the pond is filled with water.

• Moulded pre-formed rigid liners of fibre glass are strong and virtually indestructible. They are made in different shapes and sizes and you can add on sections to form waterfalls and cascades with moulded edges to give the appearance of rocks.

• Liners are available in different qualities, from cheap plastic that may last for a few years to heavy duty pvc and butyl, guaranteed to last anything from 20 years to a lifetime. The advantage of using a liner is that you can decide the shape and size, including depth, of the pond.

• When a liner is being used, the base and sides of the hole must be firm and able to withstand the weight of the water, which will be considerable. Bed the liner on a 5 cm (2 in) layer of fine sand or underfelt to prevent any small sharp stones puncturing it. When working in the pond on a flexible liner, remove your boots or at least clean them, in case there are stones embedded in the soles.

The ideal depth A pond may be shallow or deep, but a deep pond is more difficult to clean out: 75–90 cm (30–36 in) is a good depth for fish and plants, combined with a couple of shallow shelves at the sides at a depth of 20–45 cm (8–18 in) to allow for plants that like shallow water, such as the white bog arum *Calla palustris* and two striking irises, *Iris laevigata*, which has blue flowers, and *I. versicolor*, whose violet flowers have purple veins and a hint of gold.

The sides can slope gently, but not too much or the liner becomes obvious. While the pond is filling, keep the liner taut to avoid wrinkles. If the sides are curved, fold the liner into tidy pleats which the water will hold in place.

Don't be tempted to trim off the surplus liner at the edges until the pond is full and leave an overlap of 30 cm (12 in) all around the top. A pond may be surrounded with grass or planted up to the edge with plants such as primula, hosta and iris which will be reflected in the water. If you plan to lay a surround for walking on, it will have to be firm, secure and smooth, to prevent any risk of falling in. Lay paving slabs, tiles, slate or flat stones on top of the liner on a bed of wet mortar. Arrange them so that they overhang the edge of the pond by 5 cm (2 in) to hide the liner above water level.

Streams and waterfalls Miniature streams and waterfalls linked to a pond can be made using a liner in exactly the same way as the pond. The sides need only be deep enough to hold the flow of water. The breadth of the

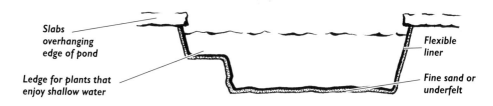

Construct a pond carefully using good-quality materials and it will last a lifetime.

Slabs overhanging edge of pond

Ledge for plants that enjoy shallow water

Flexible liner

Fine sand or underfelt

stream determines the speed the water flows: narrow gorge-like streams flow fast, while the water in broad, unimpeded areas moves smoothly.

Where separate liners meet, for example, where a stream joins a pond, the two liners need to have a generous overlap. The liner carrying the water down has to overhang the pond liner, to allow the water to flow into the pond. If the stream liner is under the pond liner, the water will run below the liner and ultimately drain the pond.

Installing a pump The most popular type of pump is the submersible version, placed in the bottom of the pond. To create a waterfall, the water is pumped up through a flexible hose buried in the soil nearby. The hose should have as large a diameter as possible. The outlet can be disguised among rocks or it can feed into a top pond which then overflows down towards the source and the water is circulated back up. A fountain may be incorporated into the feature but take care that during windy weather the spray doesn't blow out of the pond and cause the level to drop.

There is always the worry of young children falling into the pond, so if this is a possibility cover the surface of the pond with wire mesh. A shallow pond can be filled to the brim with cobble stones that change colour when wet. A fountain can operate through the stones and looks intriguing – where is the water coming from and going to?

Water and well-worn rock make a great combination. In this Australian garden, the half-hardy purple agapanthus is happy outside.

Points to watch out for

• Water and electricity don't mix. Always employ a qualified electrician to connect the pump and use armoured cable to run the power from the house. Bury the cable 60 cm (24 in) deep in a trench, with yellow plastic tape over the cable warning of live electricity.

• If you are installing outside lights at the same time as a pump, they will have to be wired separately, as the pump will be used during the day when the lights aren't needed.

• Remember where hoses are buried so that you don't stick the garden fork through them.

• Algae and green water will form if there is no movement of water or if the pond is in full sun. A fountain or waterfall will keep the water moving and if part of the pond is shaded by plants, the problem won't be as bad.

• Site a pond away from deciduous trees as the leaves tend to blow into the pond in autumn. If you don't clear the leaves out, they produce a gas as they rot down which is harmful to fish, plus they clog up pump filters.

• Where water flows into a pond from a stream, direct it over a flat rock that overhangs the pond. The falling water will cause more of a splash.

• Allow a new pump to run for 24 hours, keeping a regular watch to make sure your feature is not losing water. Never allow the pump to run without water or it will overheat.

From the citrus tree trained across the roof to the white, trumpet-shaped calla lily (*Zantedeschia*) in the centre, a glasshouse enables you to grow a range of Mediterranean and tropical plants that in many areas are more commonly seen as houseplants.

gardening with a glasshouse

A glasshouse adds a whole new dimension to gardening. The horror of working outside in rotten weather dlminishes when you scamper into the micro climate of a house of glass and can look out and see the rain belting down. There is so much that you can grow under glass, including fruit and vegetables full of flavour. Home-grown tomatoes, cucumbers, peaches, grapes, peppers and aubergine are all possible.

Propagation of plants becomes easier too and young plants will grow away more quickly. Collections of glasshouse plants such as alpines and cacti can become a real hobby.

Types of glasshouse Purchasing a glasshouse is going to dig a deep hole in the total gardening budget and you must resist the temptation to go for the cheapest. I can assure you that you get what you pay for and a cheap house made of inferior materials will cause unnecessary trouble in years to come. The first decision is whether to choose a timber or alloy model and while a cedar wood or hardwood house is a thing of beauty and easy to maintain, the initial cost may well be prohibitive. A softwood timber glasshouse will be more reasonable but will require regular painting – a slow tedious job involving scaffolding to get at the roof.

Good-quality alloy glasshouses are reasonably priced and are maintenance free, requiring no painting. They let in more daylight but are not as warm as a timber house. Timber glazing bars allow you to drive in nails and screws and to fix shelves. With a metal house, if too much weight is suspended from the glazing bars, they can bend, causing the roof glass to crack.

Deciding on size Cost is again a factor when deciding on the size of the glasshouse, but I recommend that you purchase a house at least one size up from the smallest, the additional cost being more than justified in the extra space. A 2.4 m × 1.8 m (8 ft × 6 ft) house is about the smallest you should contemplate. Smaller sizes really don't allow you much room to work. 2.4 m × 3 m (8 ft × 10 ft) is a lovely size, allowing you to grow a range of plants and justifying the inclusion of a small bench for propagating and potting.

Ventilation Ventilation of the glasshouse is very important and is the best defence against plant diseases. Ideally there should be a movement of air through the house and that is possible if there are side and roof ventilators. Cold air is drawn in through the bottom vents and as the air warms up, it rises and escapes through the roof openings.

A power supply is of great benefit for heat and additional light and to allow you to add on all the extras that are so useful: automatic ventilators, timing switches and soil-warming cables to speed up propagation. The electricity supply must be installed by a qualified electrician using armoured cable. All connections and plugs must be waterproof and operate via a contact breaker to prevent accidents.

A water tap close to the glasshouse is an advantage. It is

also a good idea to collect the rainwater off the glasshouse roof and store it in a water butt for watering.

The floor of the glasshouse can be solid concrete, laid with paving slabs or simply soil with a path down the centre. Growing directly in the soil has enormous advantages for ease of watering and feeding, but once soil becomes tired or diseased it will have to be dug out to a depth of 45 cm (18 in), and replaced with fresh virgin loam.

Where to site a glasshouse For convenience sake, the glasshouse should be reasonably close to the house with a path connecting the two – leaving you with no good reason not to visit even when the weather is bad. It will also be less expensive to run a power supply out to it from the house. Choose a level site out in the open. Don't choose a spot under trees or in a shady area: in winter, plants need all the daylight they can get. Unless your glasshouse is very long it won't matter if it is running north-south or east-west but if at all possible don't position it with the door facing into the coldest winds. Arrange to have the glasshouse erected by the supplier: self assembly can be more difficult than it looks.

Heating a glasshouse economically Heating a glasshouse is a serious business and can result in enormous fuel bills, whether you use electricity, gas or oil. Initally, you should aim to provide heat sufficient to keep the glasshouse frost free. Use a thermostat and timer to control the temperature and, if possible, in late autumn line the inside with clear polythene to act in the same way as double glazing and conserve heat. The polythene can be taken straight across at the eaves to form a false flat roof, leaving less air to be heated. Take it down in spring, of course. If you have only a few plants that require frost protection, another fuel-saving tip is to move them all away from the entrance behind a curtain or partition of polythene and heat only that portion of the house. Paraffin heaters can be used to keep the temperature above freezing but remember that for every litre of oil burnt, one litre of water is released into

Points to watch out for

• In summer the sunny side of the roof may need to be shaded as very strong sun will scorch foliage. Spray the glass with special glasshouse white paint that is easily washed off in autumn.

• Dirt and algae will collect where panes of glass overlap. You will need to slide them out and clean them each spring.

• Make the inside path as narrow as possible and stop it short of the end of the glasshouse to leave more space for growing.

• When growing grapes, net the windows with muslin in late summer to stop wasps entering and destroying the ripe fruit before you have a chance to pick it.

the atmosphere at a time when you are trying to keep humidity levels low. Fan heaters that can be reversed to blow cold air will be of use in summer when temperatures tend to be too high.

Putting a glasshouse to good use

I have referred earlier to growing edible crops under glass and while it is not easy to grow different crops in the same area, it can be successful if care and attention is given to hygiene. Some plants will require higher temperatures and others will need more water and humidity at a time when you are trying to keep the foliage of others dry. But if plants are widely spaced, it can still work. You will need to use as much ventilation as possible to get air moving through the house and on sunny days, the door can be left open. Plants that do better in the glasshouse soil may be planted on one side, while those in pots and growbags can be positioned on the opposite side. Keep a close watch out for pests as they will spread rapidly in an enclosed environment.

Whitefly are particularly hard to control. Diseases may attack the roots, stems, leaves and the fruit: if in doubt, dump any sick or suspect plants rather than risk losing all of your crops.

What to grow

Having decided on the type of glasshouse, the site and equipment, you must now decide what to grow. The controlled environment of a glasshouse allows you to succeed with plants that would not survive outside. You can also consider a range of plants that do well when grown without protection but that do even better under cover and, in the case of fruit such as strawberries, crop earlier at a time when they are expensive to buy. In cooler climates, permanent glasshouse plants include edible crops such as peaches, grapes and figs, planted directly into the soil and grown up the wall and over the roof. Annual crops include tomato, cucumber, corn on the cob, peppers and aubergine – all of which can be raised from seed or purchased as small plants.

A colourful display, including begonias, fuchsias and geraniums, flourishes under glass.

What to grow in a greenhouse

Home-grown tomatoes

The flavour of your own tomatoes is a thing to be marvelled at. Compared to commercially grown fruit purchased in a store the taste is so much better. They are an easy crop to grow and while mistakes can be made, and in a poor season pests and diseases may claim some plants, there are usually more than enough tomatoes to feed you, your friends and the neighbours.

Tomatoes can be raised from seed but it is easier to buy them as young plants from garden centres, all ready for planting out. Because of their popularity, there is a good selection of varieties available.

In a frost-free glasshouse, plants may be started off as early as mid March and you can be picking tomatoes in late May.

How to grow

• If the glasshouse soil is new and has never cropped tomatoes or potatoes (potatoes are in the same family as tomatoes and suffer from similar diseases) then I would grow the tomatoes in the soil. Incorporate lots of compost or old farmyard manure before planting and a base dressing of 60 g (2 oz) of a balanced general purpose fertilizer per sq m. Water the soil before planting and try not to give much more water until the first fruit are starting to swell.

• Where crops have been grown before or where the floor of the house is flagged over they can be planted in pots or in growbags – bags of soilless compost with added nutrients. Lay the bag flat and cut holes in the polythene and put the plants into the compost.

Most bags are marked for three planting holes but if you have enough space in the glasshouse, two plants to a bag will give better results.

• Tomato plants need to be supported as they grow. Attach a length of soft string to a wire running along the inside of the roof. Tie the other end loosely to the base of the plant and twist the string around the stem as the plant grows. Trusses of yellow flowers will appear, shortly after they will be replaced by the young green fruit.

Watering and feeding on a regular basis is essential. By the time the third truss of fruit has appeared they will be using up to 4 litres (8 pt) of water every other day. Each plant will provide 3–5 kg (6–11 lb) of fruit.

Varieties to grow

Varieties come and go with dozens of new 'improved' ones each year. If you are growing for flavour then these varieties are worth trying.

Gardeners' Delight Small cherry-sized tomatoes with a tangy taste.
Alicante Produces early crops of well-flavoured medium sized fruit.
Sungold The orange fruit is bite sized and produced over a long period into late autumn.
Moneymaker An old variety that is still popular and easy to grow, with reasonable flavour and medium-sized fruit.

Cool cucumbers

This is another easy-to-grow crop and the results justify taking that extra little bit of trouble. Like tomatoes, cucumbers can be grown from seed or purchased as young plants. Choose an all female variety that won't produce male flowers: fertilized cucumbers are bitter.

• Grow the plants in growbags (two per bag) or in large pots, at least 30 cm (12 in) plus diameter, in a rich, free-draining compost. Keep the compost moist at all times but don't allow it to become waterlogged.

• Train the plants in a similar way to tomatoes using string to support them. Check them every day as cucumbers grow very quickly. The fruit is produced at the leaf axils, so remove all the side shoots and any fruit that form on the bottom 60 cm (24 in) of the plant.

• Provide lots of ventilation and wet the path or floor on warm sunny days to encourage a moist atmosphere.

• Once the first fruit have started to swell feed with a high potash tomato feed every week. Pick the fruit as they ripen. An average plant will produce between six and 10 good sized fruit.

Varieties to grow

Aidas An all-female variety with smooth-skinned fruit, suitable for growing in an unheated glasshouse.
Petita Lots of small fruit with a good flavour.
Kyoto A Japanese type that is really easy to grow.

Warning

Even the all-female varieties can produce an occasional male flower, especially if the plant is under stress. Female flowers are easily recognised as they have a miniature cucumber behind the yellow flower; the male flowers merely have a thin stalk.

Corn on the cob (sweet corn)

Sweet corn is one of those crops that is best eaten immediately after picking. The sugar content very quickly converts to starch and even one hour will make a difference to the flavour.

• Grow them from seed or buy plants. They will grow in a cold glasshouse either in large pots or in the border soil, but don't like being disturbed, so plant them out before they become pot bound. Plant 45 cm (18 in) apart and don't allow the roots to dry out at any stage.

• The silky brown tassel at the top of the plant is the male flower and this should be gently shaken daily to assist pollination. On average each plant will produce one or two good cobs.

Varieties to grow

Royal Sweet Golden yellow kernels and very sweet, this variety will tolerate cooler conditions and produces 18 cm (7 in) cobs.

Honey Bantam Bicolour This variety has a mixture of yellow and creamy white kernels and is very sweet. It matures early with 18 cm (7 in) cobs.

Tip

It is important that the cobs are picked as soon as they are ripe. When the silks (the tuft of threads at the end of the cob) have turned brown, peel back part of the sheath that surrounds the kernel. Squeeze a couple of the grains: if the liquid is watery the cob is not ripe. If the liquid is creamy the cob is ready to pick, but if the grain exudes a thick doughy mass, it is past its best. Don't cut the cob but twist it off the stem.

Melons

There is no reason why you can't grow melons that have a flavour every bit as good as imported fruit.

• Grow melons in exactly the same way as cucumbers, either raised from seed or as bought plants. Plant two per growbag and don't firm the plants in. Plant them at the same depth as they were in the pots or slightly raised above the compost. Water the plants to settle them in, but avoid watering the leaves or stems.

• Melons grown along the ground will be more vulnerable to slug and snail attacks. Support the fruit off the ground using a handful of straw or pieces of slate. Ideally, grow them up and along wires, fixed 30 cm (12 in) apart. Train main stems along these wires and remove the growing tip after five leaves. Fruit develops on the side shoots.

• Unlike cucumbers, melons have to be pollinated so don't remove the male flowers. Once a small fruit has formed, stop the side shoot two leaves beyond it. Thin the fruit out to leave a maximum of five per plant, to ensure they swell to a reasonable size. Net the individual melons using an old pair of tights or a hair net to support them.

Varieties to grow

Charmel This form of Charentais melon is fast growing and has a deep orange, sweet flesh with a wonderful aroma.

Sweetheart An early cropper, ideal for growing in an unheated glasshouse.

Tip

It can be difficult to know when melons are ripe. One way is to smell them and if they have that unmistakable melon aroma, they are ready to eat. If you press gently at the tip it should be slightly soft.

Aubergine (egg plant)

Aubergines are a talking point in the glasshouse as well as on the table, especially when you point out that they are home grown. Aubergines are as easy to grow as tomatoes and take up less space. They can be purchased as young plants or grown from seed, but the seed needs to be sown in late February in a propagator at a temperature of 20°C (70°F). Set out two plants per growbag and stake with a cane. When the plant is 30 cm (12 in) high, nip out the growing tip to encourage the plant to become bushy. Feed weekly with a tomato fertilizer once the fruit start to form. Aubergines should be picked while the skin is still shiny. Under good conditions, a plant will be capable of growing five aubergines. Once they have started to swell, the remainder of the flowers should be removed.

Varieties to grow

Black Prince Crops early and produces large fruit.
Moneymaker Early fruiting. Crops well with good flavour.

Capsicum (peppers)

There are two types of peppers: sweet and hot – and some of the hot can be very hot. They are easy to grow; just follow the method for aubergines. Frequent spraying with water will help pollination and reduce the spread of red spider mite, which is a serious pest of peppers. Depending on variety, one plant can produce up to 40 fruit.

Varieties to grow

Big Bertha One of the largest sweet peppers, it will produce fruit 25 cm (10 in) long and crops early.

Thai Dragon This variety should carry a warning. The carrot-shaped shiny red fruit are 10 cm (4 in) long and just one plant will produce enough hot peppers for all your needs.

Strawberries

It is not that you can't grow perfect strawberries outside in the garden, but when they are grown in a glasshouse they ripen much earlier in the season. It is advisable to buy certified stock of strawberry runners that are guaranteed to be free of disease: look for well-rooted plants as early in the autumn as possible. Pot the plants into a soil-based compost and leave them outside in a sheltered position until January. Bring them into the glasshouse and keep them watered without any feeding until they flower. Pollinate the flowers with a soft brush, moving it gently from one flower to another to transfer pollen and to help fruit production. Give as much ventilation as possible to reduce the risk of grey mould. The plants will start to crop in mid spring, two months before those grown outside. If the light is good, one plant will yield 240 g (8 oz) fruit.

Varieties to grow

Royal Sovereign Certified stock of this old variety is sometimes hard to come by, but it has superb flavour.
Elvira The large, conical fruit crop well with a very good flavour.

Aubergines, tomatoes, sweet corn, peppers and strawberries, all fresh from the garden. Even those fruit and vegetables which grow perfectly well out of doors have an extended season thanks to the protected environment of the glasshouse.

The right plants for the right place: this geometric foliage is the perfect foil for the stark shapes and strong colours of the house behind it. Notice the mulch round the plants, which allows each specimen to stand on its own without the spaces in between being smothered in weeds.

plants for special places

There are fussy plants and others that will put up with whatever conditions they have to face, but even the unfussy have preferences and will show their unhappiness through stunted growth, discoloured foliage and a lack of flowers and fruit. If your soil and climate are average, with no extremes, you are very fortunate and will be able to grow a wide variety of plants with only the very particular refusing to thrive. When you become familiar with your garden, you choose the most suitable plants for the conditions you are able to provide. The plants I have suggested for each location are everyday varieties that are tried and tested. I have also slipped in one that is a 'bit more exotic' to give you the edge over the Joneses, especially if they profess to be expert gardeners who know their onions.

Plants for full sun

Many of the plants we grow in full sun are plants that enjoy Mediterranean conditions where the sun and the heat are complemented by light, sandy or stony free-draining soil. Choose the warmest, most sheltered site and if necessary, provide the plants with protection from frost and cold winds.

top ten

Anthemis tinctoria 'E. C. Buxton'
  Perennial
Cerastium tomentosum (snow in
  summer) Perennial
Cistus × *cyprius* Evergreen shrub
Diascia rigescens Perennial
Geranium endressii. Perennial
Gleditsia triacanthos 'Sunburst'
  Deciduous tree
Helianthemum 'Raspberry Ripple'
  Evergreen shrub
Juniperus chinensis 'Kuriwao Gold'
  Conifer
Phlomis fruticosa (Jerusalem sage)

five more to try

Campanula persicifolia Herbaceous
  perennial
Carpenteria californica Evergreen shrub
Euphorbia characias subsp. *wulfenii*
  Evergreen shrub
Fremontodendron californicum
  Evergreen shrub
Gypsophila paniculata Herbaceous
  perennial

a bit more exotic

Campsis × *tagliabuana* 'Mme Galen'
  Vigorous climber

Full details of all these plants can be found in the directory on pages 178–189

Plants for shade

It is easy to appreciate a bit of shade when you see the scorch damage that full sun is capable of. But there are some types of shade with accompanying soil that plants are less happy in. Dense shade caused by evergreen trees, combined with large drips of rain from the leaves, an impoverished soil and a mat of tree roots is, at best. tolerated by some plants. The cold shade on the sunless side of a tall building is often made worse by a chilly draught tunnelled around the corners of the walls. Wet shaded sites also restrict the choice of plants. The following species will succeed where others give up.

top ten

Crinodendron hookerianum (lantern
  tree) Evergreen shrub
Daphne laureola (spurge laurel)
  Evergreen shrub
Euonymus fortunei 'Emerald Gaiety'
  Evergreen shrub
Hedera colchica 'Dentata Variegata'
  (Persian ivy) Evergreen climber
Hosta 'Big Daddy' Herbaceous
  perennial
Lamium maculatum Evergreen
  perennial
Pachysandra terminalis Evergreen
  perennial
Skimmia japonica 'Wakehurst White'
  Evergreen shrub
Tolmiea menziesii (pick-a-back plant)
  Herbaceous perennial.
Vinca major 'Variegata' (periwinkle)
  Evergreen shrub.

five more to try

Aucuba japonica Evergreen shrub
Dicentra formosa Herbaceous
  perennial
Fatsia japonica Evergreen shrub
Sarcococca confusa Evergreen shrub
Viola labradorica Evergreen perennial

a bit more exotic

Rhodotypos scandens Deciduous shrub

A shady border overhung by a mature beech tree.

Plants for sandy soil

Sandy soils are quick to warm up and free draining, but in a season with low rainfall they will need irrigating. Mulching using compost, bark or a deep layer of gravel will help conserve moisture in the soil. Suitable plants adapt to the desert-like conditions by sending their roots far and wide and deep in search of water. Feeding them with a liquid foliar drench is quick acting and reduces the risk of the nutrients leaching away. Loose sandy or gritty soil is easily blown around by the wind and can cut off seedlings and young plants at soil level or abrade their stems.

—————————●—————————

top ten

Agapanthus 'Blue Moon' Herbaceous
    perennial
Ballota acetabulosa Evergreen
    subshrub
Brachyglottis monroi Evergreen shrub
Callistemon citrinus (crimson bottlebrush)
    Evergreen shrub
Cistus × *purpureus* Evergreen shrub
Eryngium bourgatii Herbaceous perennial
Lespedeza thunbergii Deciduous sub-shrub
Limonium platyphyllum 'Violetta' (sea
    lavender) Herbaceous perennial
Romneya coulteri (tree poppy)
    Deciduous subshrub
Santolina chamaecyparissus (cotton
    lavender) Evergreen shrub

five more to try

Acanthus hirsutus Herbaceous perennial
Agastache foeniculum Perennial
Artemisia 'Powis Castle' Evergreen
    perennial
Indigofera amblyantha Deciduous shrub
Linum narbonense Herbaceous perennial

a bit more exotic

Grevillea 'Canberra Gem' Evergreen shrub

Berberis darwinii is evergreen and spiny, with dark orange flowers in spring. These berries are the autumn display.

Plants for clay soil

A heavy clay soil is every gardener's nightmare – sticky when wet and hard and cracked when dry. Improving the drainage and opening the soil by incorporating lots of grit and organic matter will help, as will avoiding cultivating the soil when it is wet. If deep mulches are applied annually, the surface rooting area will be improved. In its favour, a clay soil is well supplied with nutrients, including trace elements. There is a whole range of plants that can be successfully grown in heavy clay. When planting, fork up the bottom of the planting hole so that the roots of the plant can penetrate the clay subsoil more easily and water can also drain away quickly. If you don't do this, the hole becomes a sump and the plant roots get waterlogged.

—————————●—————————

top ten

Aster novae-angliae 'Harrington's Pink'
    Deciduous perennial
Berberis darwinii Evergreen shrub
Chaenomeles × *superba* 'Crimson and Gold'
    (Japanese quince) Deciduous shrub
Choisya ternata (Mexican orange
    blossom) Evergreen shrub
Cotoneaster frigidus 'Cornubia' Semi-
    evergreen shrub
Monarda 'Cambridge Scarlet' (bergamot)
    Herbaceous perennial
Potentilla fruticosa 'Elizabeth' Deciduous
    shrub
Pulmonaria saccharata (lungwort,
    Jerusalem sage) Evergreen perennial
Sambucus nigra 'Guincho Purple' (black
    elder or bour tree) Deciduous shrub
Spiraea japonica 'Goldflame' Deciduous
    shrub

five more to try

Cytisus 'Lena' Deciduous shrub
Helenium 'Moerheim Beauty' Herbaceous
    perennial
Kirengeshoma palmata Herbaceous perennial
Magnolia × *soulangeana* Deciduous tree
Philadelphus 'Virginal' Deciduous shrub

a bit more exotic

Neillia thibetica Deciduous shrub

Plants for acid soil

A comparatively small number of plants enjoy a lime-free soil, but those that do will just not succeed in an alkaline soil – most will die in such conditions. They include some of our best-loved plants such as rhododendrons, azaleas, pieris and most of the heathers. One way to grow lime haters in a garden that is not ideal is to form raised beds by building low walls or using railway sleepers and filling them to a depth of 60 cm (24 in) with a lime-free compost – usually sold as ericaceous compost.

_____●_____

top ten
Calluna vulgaris 'H. E. Beale' Evergreen
    shrub
Camellia × *williamsii* 'Anticipation'
    Evergreen shrub
Celmisia spectabilis (New Zealand
    daisy) Evergreen perennial
Desfontainia spinosa Evergreen shrub
Enkianthus cernuus rubens Deciduous
    shrub
Kalmia latifolia (calico bush) Evergreen
    shrub
Lithodora diffusa 'Heavenly Blue'
    Evergreen shrub
Meconopsis grandis (Himalayan blue
    poppy) Herbaceous perennial
Pieris 'Forest Flame' Evergreen shrub
Rhododendron 'Moerheim' Dwarf
    evergreen shrub

five more to try
Erica cinerea Evergreen shrub
Eucryphia × *nymansensis* Evergreen tree
Gentiana × *macaulayi* Semi-evergreen
    perennial
Leptospermum scoparium Evergreen shrub
Phlox stolonifera Evergreen perennial

a bit more exotic
Clethra delavayi (sweet pepper bush)
    Deciduous shrub

Summer- flowering *Verbascum chaixii* 'Album'.

Plants for alkaline (limy) soils

Alkaline soils are ideal for a wide range of plants, whose roots seem to enjoy the free-draining, light, warm conditions. The addition of organic matter in the form of compost, rotted manures and mulches will make the soil more water retentive, and irrigation during dry periods will help the plants to get established quickly. An excess of lime can cause a defficiency of other trace elements, locking them up in the soil and showing as a discoloration on the leaf. Iron and magnesium both show as yellowing of the leaf or chlorosis, caused by too limy a soil.

_____●_____

top ten
Campanula glomerata 'Superba' (clustered
    bell flower) Herbaceous perennial
Deutzia hookeriana 'Mont Rose'
    Deciduous shrub
Dianthus gratianopolitanus (cheddar pink)
    Evergreen perennial
Kolkwitzia amabilis 'Pink Cloud' (beauty
    bush) Deciduous shrub
Malus floribunda (Japanese crab apple)
    Deciduous tree
Philadelphus 'Belle Etoile' (mock orange)
    Deciduous shrub
Pulsatilla vulgaris (pasque flower)
    Herbaceous perennial
Sorbus aria 'Lutescens' (whitebeam)
    Deciduous tree
Syringa meyeri 'Palibin' (lilac) Deciduous
    shrub
Verbascum chaixii 'Album' (nettle-leaved
    mullein) Semi-evergreen perennial

five more to try
Buddlea davidii Deciduous shrub
Euphorbia myrsinites Evergreen perennial
Osmanthus delavayi Evergreen shrub
Santolina rosmarinifolia Evergreen shrub
Sarcococca hookeriana Evergreen shrub

a bit more exotic
Cercis siliquastrum (Judas tree)
    Deciduous tree

Plants for exposed sites

Cold biting wind can dry out the foliage of newly planted shrubs and trees before they are able to take up moisture and so kill the plant. It can also loosen plants in the ground. Tall young herbaceous plants need to be staked to prevent them being blown over before they flower. Check staked plants in autumn and spring to ensure that stakes have not come loose and straps are not too tight. A temporary screen of hessian or netting will protect new plants until they get established. For a more permanent form of shelter, plants themselves provide the best wind break. They allow the wind to filter through the branches, whereas solid fences or walls force the wind to blow over the top and cause heavy turbulence on the side that is supposed to be sheltered.

top ten

Achillea filipendulina Evergreen perennial
Arbutus unedo (strawberry tree) Evergreen tree
Betula pendula (silver birch) Deciduous tree
Bupleurum fruticosum (shrubby hare's ear) Evergreen shrub
Crataegus monogyna (common hawthorn, may, quick) Deciduous tree
Laburnum × *watereri* 'Vossii' (golden rain) Deciduous tree
Nepeta × *faassenii* (catmint) Herbaceous perennial
Sorbus aucuparia (rowan, mountain ash) Deciduous tree
Spiraea 'Arguta' (bridal wreath) Deciduous shrub
Ulex europaeus 'Flore Pleno' (gorse, whin, furze) Evergreen shrub

five more to try

Acer pseudoplatanus Deciduous tree
Euonymus europaeus 'Red Cascade' Deciduous shrub
Gaultheria shallon Evergreen shrub
Prunus spinosa (blackthorn, sloe) Deciduous tree
Rosa rugosa Deciduous shrub

a bit more exotic

Ledum groenlandicum (Labrador tea) Evergreen shrub

Spiraea **'Arguta' forms a dense bush.**

Plants with aromatic foliage

A great number of aromatic plants are natives of the Mediterranean, where they enjoy light, free-draining, stony soils that are low in nutrients and moisture, plus lots of sun. The addition of sharp sand and coarse grit will help to lighten heavy soils, while choosing a site in full sun but sheltered from cold winds, frost and heavy rain, will reduce the risk of the plants dying in their first winter.

top ten

Caryopteris × *clandonensis* 'Kew Blue' Deciduous shrub
Lavandula angustifolia (English lavender) Evergreen shrub
Myrtus communis (common myrtle) Evergreen shrub
Perovskia 'Blue Spire' Deciduous sub-shrub
Prostranthera cuneata (alpine mint bush) Evergreen shrub
Rosmarinus officinalis (rosemary) Evergreen shrub
Ruta graveolens 'Jackman's Blue' (rue) Evergreen sub-shrub
Santolina chamaecyparissus Evergreen shrub
Skimmia × *confusa* 'Kew Green' Evergreen shrub
Thuja occidentalis (white cedar) Evergreen conifer

five more to try

Aloysia triphylla (lemon verbena) Evergreen shrub
Eucalyptus gunnii Evergreen tree
Illicium anisatum (Chinese arise) Evergreen shrub
Lavandula stoechas (French lavender) Evergreen shrub
Populus balsamifera Deciduous tree

a bit more exotic

Umbellularia californica (headache tree) Evergreen tree

Plants for seaside sites

There is no shortage of plants that can be grown in coastal areas but as well as tolerating severe winds, they must be able to put up with salt deposits on their foliage. Many perennials will thrive at the seaside, though they may be susceptible to bad weather in spring when the new shoots are emerging. Shrubs may be cut back by severe spring weather, especially if they put on a late flush of soft growth the previous autumn. But it usually acts as a form of natural clipping and the plants soon recover and grow away quite happily. Evergreens are prone to leaf scorch on the seaward side of the plant, when salt-laden winds burn the foliage and conifers are particularly vulnerable.

———————•———————

top ten

Anthemis punctata subsp. *cupaniana*
   Herbaceous perennial
Artemisia arborescens (wormwood)
   Evergreen shrub
Centranthus ruber (red valerian).
   Herbaceous perennial

Escallonia rubra var. *macrantha* Evergreen
   shrub
Fascicularia bicolor subsp. *bicolor* Terrestrial
   bromeliad
Fuchsia magellanica Deciduous shrub
Hippophae rhamnoides (sea buckthorn)
   Deciduous tree
Olearia macrodonta Evergreen shrub
Othonna cheirifolia Evergreen shrub
Tamarix ramosissima (tamarisk)
   Deciduous shrub

five more to try

Elaeagnus pungens 'Maculata' Evergreen
   shrub
Hebe × *franciscana* 'Variegata' Evergreen
   shrub
Lupinus arboreus (tree lupin) Evergreen
   shrub
Populus alba (poplar) Deciduous tree
Spartium junceum (Spanish broom)
   Deciduous shrub

a bit more exotic

Escallonia 'Iveyi' Evergreen shrub

Red-flowered *Centranthus ruber* enjoys a maritime site and spreads over a wide area.

Plants for cut flowers

Not all species last well in water. The plants listed here make ideal cut flowers. If you want lots of flowers, plant a cutting bed of annuals and perennials, leaving those in the main beds for colour in the garden. Make the cutting bed in a sheltered site and support plants to prevent wind damage. The soil should be moisture retentive but not too rich: excessive nitrogenous fertilizer will encourages leaf growth instead of flowers.

———————•———————

top ten

Achillea 'Coronation Gold' (yarrow)
   Evergreen perennial
Astilbe × *arendsii* 'Fanal' Deciduous
   perennial
Callistephus chinensis 'Ostrich Plume'
   (China aster) Annual
Camellia × *williamsii* 'Anticipation'
   Evergreen shrub
Chrysanthemum Herbaceous perennial
Delphinium 'Butterball' Herbaceous
   perennial
Forsythia × *intermedia* 'Karl Sax'
   Deciduous shrub
Geum 'Mrs J. Bradshaw' Herbaceous
   perennial
Paeonia lactiflora 'Bowl of Beauty'
   Herbaceous perennial
Rosa Deciduous shrub
Zantedeschia aethiopica (arum lily)
   Herbaceous perennial

five more to try

Freesia Perennial grown from corms
Kniphofia 'Wrexham Buttercup'
   Herbaceous perennial
Rhododendron decorum Evergreen shrub
Rudbeckia fulgida Herbaceous perennial
Tulipa 'Fringed Elegance' Bulb

a bit more exotic

Yucca gloriosa Evergreen shrub

A sheltered garden allows tender protea (on the left) to grow, and prevents the flower heads of the white agapanthus being damaged by the wind.

Plants for sheltered gardens

I haven't met a gardener who hasn't wished for a part of his garden to be different to whatever nature has provided and I am as bad as the rest. Like most northern hemisphere gardeners, I would love to be able to grow outside all those tender plants that exist only in heated conservatories in my part of the world. Wishful thinking, I know, but there is a range of plants that, given the most favoured spot in the garden, will survive and even thrive. Then, if you wish, you really can be one up on your gardening friends. But don't brag too much: sooner or later a freak frost or prolonged period of wet or dry weather will kill your treasures.

Walls facing the afternoon sun and sheltered from cold winds will suit a lot of delicate plants. Lightening the soil by the addition of grit and using a mulch of white gravel to reflect the light will all help. Providing overhead shelter from the worst of the winter rain will do much to prevent tender plants from becoming waterlogged. Small plants may be protected by covering them with a sheet of glass raised on bricks. Cover larger plants with clear plastic or polythene stretched over a framework of batons or canes, like a wigwam.

---

top ten

Echium wildpretii Herbaceous perennial
Fremontodendron mexicanum Evergreen shrub
Hedychium densiflorum (ginger lily) Herbaceous perennial
Lapageria rosea (Chilean bell flower) Evergreen climber
Myosotidium hortensia (Chatham Island forget-me-not) Evergreen perennial
Paeonia cambessedesii Herbaceous perennial
Paulownia tomentosa (foxglove tree) Deciduous tree
Pittosporum tobira (Japanese mock orange) Evergreen tree
Protea cynaroides (king protea) Evergreen shrub
Trachelospermum jasminoides (star jasmine) Evergreen climber

five more to try

Acacia dealbata Evergreen shrub
Agapanthus africanus Evergreen perennial
Agave americana 'Marginata' Succulent
Correa backhouseana Evergreen shrub
Disanthus cercidifolius Deciduous shrub

a bit more exotic

Pseudopanax ferox Evergreen tree

Actinidia kolmikta produces fragrant white flowers in summer, but is grown primarily for its stunning foliage.

Plants for walls

One of the biggest problems with growing plants up a wall is that the soil conditions at the base of the wall can be totally unsuitable. The area is usually contaminated with builders' rubble and if the wall is part of the house, the rain doesn't wet the soil because of the roof overhang. Any available moisture is absorbed by the porous wall and concrete foundation before plants can take it up, and it will be necessary to water regularly and enrich the soil with compost. Some plants may be positioned with their roots 30 cm (12 in) away from the wall and then trained towards it.

From an aesthetic point of view, consider the colour of the wall. White or cream flowers will be lost against a white-plastered surface, as will red-flowering climbers on red brick. In the northern hemisphere, east-facing walls are not suitable for spring-flowering plants, as the morning sun after a frost can scorch buds. South-facing walls can be very hot and are good for growing and training a

fruiting peach tree on. West-facing walls get the evening sun and are ideal for most plants, especially those that need pampering. North-facing walls are sunless and cold but there are still plenty of plants that will succeed and flower there. In the southern hemisphere, north-facing is sunny and south-facing likely to be cheerless.

The automatic choice of plant for a wall is a climber, but there are many excellent free-standing shrubs that, without support, will hug a wall.

top ten
Camellia sasanqua 'Narumigata' Evergreen shrub, sunny wall
Ceanothus 'Puget Blue' Evergreen shrub, sunny wall
Chaenomeles speciosa 'Moerloosei' (flowering quince) Deciduous shrub, sunny wall
Cytisus battandieri (pineapple broom) Semi-evergreen shrub, sunny wall
Euonymus fortunei 'Silver Queen' Evergreen shrub, sunny or shaded wall

Exochorda x *macrantha* 'The Bride' (pearl bush) Deciduous shrub, sunny or shaded wall
Hedera canariensis 'Gloire de Marengo' (Canary Island ivy) Evergreen climber, sunny or shaded wall
Hydrangea anomala subsp. *petiolaris* (climbing hydrangea) Deciduous climber, shaded wall
Lonicera sempervirens (trumpet honeysuckle) Evergreen shrub, shaded wall
Parthenocissus henryana (Virginia creeper) Deciduous climber, sunny or shaded wall.

five more to try
Actinidia kolomikta Deciduous climber, sunny wall
Akebia quinata Evergreen climber, sunny wall
Clematis armandii Evergreen climber, sunny wall
Clianthus puniceus 'Albus' Evergreen climber, sunny wall
Jasminum officinale f. *affine* Deciduous climber, sunny wall

a bit more exotic
Mandevilla laxa (Chilean jasmine) Deciduous climber, sunny wall

Plants for barrier planting

The first line of defence for most gardens is the boundary. It is so much nicer and more natural in most locations to use living plants for the perimeter to form a hedge or boundary planting. The screen may be necessary for privacy or shelter or even security, and deciduous or evergreen plants or a mixture of both can be used. Plants allow the wind to filter through rather than blowing over the top and causing turbulence on the garden side. At the same time, the leaves and branches filter out traffic noise. Hedges can be formal or informal depending on how they are clipped (see page 92 for more information).

For a long-term planting such as a hedge, the site should be well prepared with lots of compost and old farmyard manure added to the bottom of the planting pit. Incorporate some slow-acting fertilizer, such as bone meal, into the soil as you fill it back in. Choose a site that is weed free, especially of perennial weeds. If they are allowed to become established among hedging plants they will be difficult to remove and use the hedge as a secure base camp from which to spread at will. A clipping or pruning when plants are young will thicken up the hedge at the base, with less risk of gaps occuring low down in the hedge.

————————●————————

top ten

Alnus cordata (Italian alder) Deciduous tree
Berberis x *stenophylla* Evergreen shrub
Cotoneaster lacteus Evergreen shrub
x *Cupressocyparis leylandii* 'Castlewellan' (Golden leyland) Evergreen conifer
Elaeagnus x *ebbingei* 'Limelight' Evergreen shrub
Griselinia littoralis Evergreen shrub
Ilex aquifolium (common holly) Evergreen shrub or tree
Prunus laurocerasus (laurel, cherry laurel) Evergreen shrub
Taxus baccata (yew) Evergreen conifer
Thuja plicata (western red cedar) Evergreen conifer

five more to try

Chamaecyparis lawsoniana Evergreen conifer
Escallonia 'Pride of Donard' Evergreen shrub
Fagus sylvatica Deciduous tree
Pittosporum tenuifolium Evergreen tree
Viburnum tinus Evergreen shrub

a bit more exotic

Drimys lanceolata (mountain pepper) Evergreen shrub.

Viburnum tinus is evergreen and flowers in winter, bringing welcome cheer to the garden. A deciduous viburnum, *V.* x *carlcephalum*, is worth growing for its red autumn foliage.

Plants for autumn leaf colour

There are few sights more spectacular than autumn sunlight on a mature Japanese maple, its rich canopy a blaze of red. Yet it needs only one gale or night's frost to bring the display to an end with the leaves scattered to the four corners. If you are planting for autumn colour, choose a sheltered site where the wind can't remove the leaves prematurely. Avoid extremes of dry and wet ground, and areas in deep shade. A feed in early summer will encourage the plant to make new shoots and even more leaves that will change colour. It's not only deciduous trees that change colour in autumn: some garden conifers do too, such as *Thuja orientalis* 'Rosedalis', which has bright yellow foliage in spring, grey-green in summer and plum-purple in late autumn.

---

top ten

Acer palmatum 'Chitoseyama' (Japanese maple) Deciduous tree

Amelanchier lamarckii (snowy mespilus) Deciduous shrub or tree

Cercidiphyllum japonicum (Katsura tree) Deciduous tree

Cotinus 'Grace' (smoke bush) Deciduous shrub

Euonymus alatus (winged spindle) Deciduous shrub

Fothergilla major Deciduous shrub

Liquidambar styraciflua (sweet gum) Deciduous tree

Parrotia persica (Persian ironwood) Deciduous tree

Prunus sargentii Deciduous tree

Rhus typhina 'Dissecta' (stag's horn sumach) Deciduous shrub

five more to try

Carya ovata (hickory) Deciduous tree

Malus tschonoskii (crab apple) Deciduous tree

Nandina domestica 'Fire Power' (heavenly bamboo) Deciduous shrub

Quercus rubra (red oak) Deciduous tree

Sorbus sargentiana (rowan) Deciduous tree

a bit more exotic

Nyssa sinensis (Chinese tupelo) Deciduous tree

Rowan (*Sorbus*) and cherry (*Prunus*) in brilliant shades of autumn colour contrast with the variegated holly (*Ilex*).

Poppies will self-seed to reappear next year.

Plants for the wild garden

Like any other part of the garden, the wild garden has to be managed. If not, it ceases to be wild, becoming instead an overgrown, weed-infested piece of ground. It is worth remembering that many wild flowers are, in fact, fully qualified weeds and while buttercup, ragweed, bindweed and willow herb all have pretty flowers, they are awful weeds to let loose in the garden. They are quick to spread and very difficult to control. Luckily, there are lots of wild plants that are harmless in the garden and add greatly to the overall display while requiring minimum attention. They are happy to grow in impoverished soil in woodland or open ground, providing they are not smothered by more aggressive plants.

top ten

Aquilegia vulgaris (Granny's bonnet) Herbaceous perennial

Centaurea cyanus (cornflower) Annual

Corylus avellana (hazel) Deciduous shrub

Digitalis purpurea (foxglove) Biennial or short-lived perennial

Geranium pratense (meadow cranesbill) Herbaceous perennial

Hyacinthoides non-scripta (English bluebell) Bulbous perennial

Leucanthemum vulgare (ox-eye daisy) Herbaceous perennial

Papaver rhoeas (corn poppy, Flanders poppy) Annual

Primula vulgaris (primrose) Evergreen perennial

Rosa rubignosa (sweet briar) Deciduous shrub

five more to try

Alchemilla alpina (alpine lady's mantle) Herbaceous perennial

Arum maculatum (lords and ladies) Tuberous perennial

Gentiana verna (spring gentian) Evergreen perennial

Iris pseudacorus (yellow flag) Evergreen rhizomatous perennial

Pulsatilla vulgaris (pasque flower) Herbaceous perennial

a bit more exotic

Dactylorhiza fuchsii (common spotted orchid) Deciduous perennial

Snake's head fritillary (*Fritillaria meleagris*) naturalized in the meadow at Magdalen College, Oxford. Fritillaries are ideal scattered through an area of grass that can be left uncut, but will not survive in a lawn that is mowed regularly.

take any two plants

Cheese and wine, peaches and cream – they just seem to go together and so it is with some groups of plants. Allowing for height, climate and soil type, the plants almost seem to grow better together and bring out the best in their companions, fitting into the garden plan as an area of planting that will be noticed and copied.

plant combinations

If there is more than one plant in your garden, you have a combination of plants. Putting plants together is an aspect of gardening that is totally personal and your opinions and ideas will constantly change.

Colour of flower, leaf, berry and bark all have to be considered. Many gardeners are clinical in their approach to a mixture of colours. I have no hang ups and have seldom seen a mixed planting where the colour scheme upset me. On the other hand, I really do like a blue and yellow combination and nowhere is this more striking than with conifers such as *Chamaecyparis pisifera* 'Filifera Aurea', which is golden, and steel blue *C. pisifera* 'Boulevard'.

Thought has to be given to the time of flowering. It can be difficult – not to say frustrating – to achieve the colour combination of your dreams when one or two plants flower earlier or later than they are supposed to. One way to overcome this critical timing is to combine flower colour with leaf colour instead. Still on a blue and yellow theme, the evergreen *Ceanothus* 'Puget Blue', which has deep blue flowers in late spring and early summer can be planted in front of *Sambucus racemosa*. 'Plumosa Aurea', the golden cut-leaved elder, for example.

Shape and texture play an important role in combining plants. It can be a relief to introduce a complete contrast in plant shape: for example, a spiky-leaved plant such as *Yucca gloriosa* planted as a dot plant among clipped and shaped *Buxus sempervirens* can look the part and raise interest. In the same way, the sword-like leaves of *Phormium tenax* seem to complement the enormous leaves of *Gunnera manicata* and will remain on guard all winter when the impressive gunnera has died down.

Slow-growing conifers are good enough to fill a garden with every colour, shape and texture from upright, pencil-thin junipers and dumpy, dense thuja, to mat-forming junipers, with spiky, ferny or soft foliage in every shade of green, yellow, blue and grey.

Plant height can be crucial. Bigger plants can overpower their smaller neighbours and the larger plant in a duo will hide the smaller one if they are badly positioned.

You can also make combinations of spring and autumn species, where the plants enjoy each other's company but come into their own at different times rather than creating a complementary display. For example in spring, bulbs such as crocus will create interest in an otherwise dull bed of summer and autumn-flowering heathers.

Any two plants can be choreographed to make a good combination. Here, clematis tumbling down the wall forms a superb backdrop for the herbs arranged in tiers on the steps.

heathers and conifers

This is a favourite combination and one that has stood the test of time. Heathers are mainly low growing, forming carpets of colour, though there are exceptions in the form of tree heathers that will grow to 7 m (23 ft). Even these can be accommodated in the planting scheme. Conifers come in all sizes but the types I would encourage you to try are slow-growing species such as *Chamaecyparis pisifera* 'Boulevard', which looks compact and well behaved but will eventually grow to 9 m (30 ft); and dwarf conifers such as *Juniperus communis* 'Compressa', which grows to only 90 cm (36 in).

The site for the mixed bed needs to be in an open situation in full sun with well-drained soil that is retentive of moisture and acidic, with a pH of less than 7. If you have alkaline soil you can restrict yourself to lime-tolerant heathers such as *Erica carnea* and *E. vagans* which have lots of varieties; while for conifers, some of the junipers and dwarf pines will be fine. Alternatively, you can raise the beds by adding acidic soil on top and keeping the roots of the plants above the original limy soil. Or you can simply grow the plants in containers of ericaceous compost.

Space the heathers at 45 cm (18 in), in bold, irregular drifts to provide splashes of colour throughout the year. Don't forget to include some of the coloured foliage varieties. Flat-growing conifers may be mixed through the heathers to provide winter foliage colour and the more upright species can then be dotted through the planting to add shape and texture.

Good varieties

Heathers

Calluna vulgaris varieties
Erica carnea varieties
Erica cinerea 'Fiddler's Gold'
Erica vagans 'Mrs D F Maxwell'

Conifers

Juniperus procumbens
Picea glauca var. *albertiana* 'Conica'
Thuja occidentalis 'Rheingold'

Maintenance of the planting is minimal as the dense ground cover will reduce weeds, and both heathers and conifers have long lives. Little pruning is necessary, although the dead

Do's and don'ts

• Don't add peat to the soil to make it more acidic unless you mix it thoroughly through the topsoil. If peat dries out it is very difficult to re-wet it and the plants will suffer.

• Don't allow the heathers to grow into the conifers, as the foliage of both will turn brown.

• Don't plant the conifers too close together.

• Do mulch the heathers with old compost in autumn and wash it into the soil surface.

• Do clip the heathers after flowering

• Do keep on top of the weeds during the first year.

flowers should be clipped off the heathers after flowering to keep the plants compact. Pests and diseases are few but if you have planted one of the low-growing blue spruces (*Picea pungens* 'Glauca prostrata', for example), watch out for a red spider mite attack in summer. These insects will defoliate the plant if given a chance, so spray at four weekly intervals with a systemic pesticide to control them.

Heathers and dwarf conifers are unequalled as a combination, providing complementary textures and a terrific palette of colours.

roses and dwarf bulbs

Roses are one of our all-time favourites. Bush roses are colourful, repeat flowering, many are fragrant and they are available in a broad range of colours. The trouble is that they make a display only from early summer to mid autumn. The rest of the year they are frankly dead looking. Lots of plant combinations have been tried to cheer them up, including heathers and ground coverers such as ajuga and vinca, but none is really satisfactory because they all climb part way up the stems. The best method I have found is to use dwarf bulbs. By planting spring- and autumn-flowering crocus, dwarf tulips and snowdrops, the bed of roses will be in colour for most of the year. The foliage of dwarf bulbs dies away quickly or, if you prefer, the bulbs can be lifted after flowering and stored for replanting the following season.

Rosa **'Pot o' Gold' forms a neater bush than many roses, but it is still not very interesting in spring. An underplanting of bulbs will make the bed more cheerful.**

The site should be out in the open, not shaded and on a good loam or clay soil. Dig in lots of compost and farmyard manure and cultivate deeply to loosen the soil and give the roots a good start.

Bush roses are budded on to a rootstock and the union between the two must not be buried too deeply, as this encourages suckers from the rootstock to grow. If these are not removed quickly and as close to the stem or root as possible, they will grow faster than the variety and eventually take over.

Do's and don'ts

• Don't mix colours and varieties of roses in a small bed; one mass of colour will look better.

• Don't plant new roses in a bed where roses have already been grown: they will suffer from rose sickness.

• Don't allow suckers (shoots) to grow from the rose rootstock.

• Do choose scented rose varieties, such as 'Fragrant Cloud' or 'Irish Eyes'.

• Do feed regularly in summer with a rose fertilizer.

• Don't plant the bulbs too close to the roses.

• Do plant a good quantity of each variety of bulb – groups of 30-50 are ideal.

Dig a planting hole larger than the grafted spread of the roots and add a handful of bone meal to the hole around the roots of each rose. Bush roses should be planted 60 cm (24 in) apart. After firming the soil around the roots, shorten the shoots to 10–15 cm (4–6 in) and remove any weak or damaged stems.

Roses require routine maintenance: remove the dead flowers and feed them throughout the summer. Cut the plants back in early winter, removing about half of the shoots. Do the main pruning in early spring, cutting back shoots to 20-30 cm (8-12 in) from the ground and removing any weak and diseased stems.

In order that they remain good friends it is essential that the bulbs don't compete with the roses. Plant dwarf varieties of bulbs that flower when the roses are dormant. These don't have an excess of foliage and are quick to die down, leaving the roses centre stage for the summer. Bulbs of crocus, snowdrop, tulip, scilla, anemone, aconite and miniature iris will all add colour to the bed and for the autumn, plant hardy cyclamen.

shrubs and herbaceous plants

Herbaceous borders are back in fashion, but they still suffer from the problem that made them unpopular years ago – the fact that they can look dead and uninteresting in winter. Most perennials die down in late autumn, leaving a few evergreens that flower in winter such as hellebores to keep the border looking alive. Bulbs can help to fill the gap but since herbaceous plants have to be lifted and divided every few years there is a risk of disturbing the bulbs.

Mixing some shrubs into the border is the best way to add colour and plant and leaf shape to brighten the winter show. Choose evergreen shrubs, especially those that have variegated foliage to boost the off-season display. Try to design in shrubs which won't get too large, otherwise they tend to swamp the bed and hide the main summer display of perennials. A few winter-flowering deciduous shrubs can be included, such as *Daphne mezereum* – its compact shape and superb perfume more than compensate for the lack of leaves.

The herbaceous border is prone to weeds and if they invade a clump of plants, it is usually best to dump the clump rather than trying to remove the weeds. It is essential that you start with a bed free of perennial weeds and that you are careful not to import weeds with clumps of free plants given to you by 'friends'.

Do's and don'ts

• Don't plant all the shrubs at one end of the border: mix them through the bed.

• Don't plant tall-growing shrubs that will swamp the other plants.

• Don't use summer-flowering shrubs: their effect will be lost when the herbaceous plants in the border are looking at their best.

• Do divide the herbaceous perennials every three years.

• Do keep a close eye out for slugs and snails as they love tender young shoots.

• Do plant shrubs to extend the flowering season to autumn and spring as well as winter.

• Do cut the herbaceous perennials back in autumn to tidy the bed.

Shades of green and gold provided by conifers, hostas and euonymus, with a splash of blue ceanothus.

A colourful display of bulbs naturalized in grass. The foliage of the narcissus will last a lot longer
than that of the *Anemone blanda*, so mowing will have to be delayed until it has died down.

lawns and bulbs

With a bit of thought this can be the best garden
combination of all. Lawns can be boringly green (or yellow)
and require a lot of maintenance to keep them in a
presentable state. I once heard a lawn described as a
collective term for a lot of weeds. It can become strikingly
beautiful if dwarf bulbs are naturalized through it and
allowed to multiply each year, forming drifts of colour. The
level of maintenance is not increased as the dying foliage is
removed with the grass. The trick is to avoid tall-growing
bulbs with large leaves, such as daffodils, and those that
flower in late spring, long after grass cutting has started.

A new lawn sown or laid as turf in the autumn is ideal,
as this is the best time to plant bulbs. Plant them just before
the seed is sown or the turf laid and they will grow
through the grass. A dense planting will look more
impressive and be more memorable than a scattering of
flowers dotted all over the lawn.

Established lawns require a bit more work. The turf
needs to be lifted, the bulbs spread on the soil, and the turf
replaced. Or individual holes can be made in the grass, a
bulb placed in each hole and infilled with fine soil.

Do's and don'ts

• Don't apply weedkillers to the lawn until all bulb foliage
has died down and the bulbs are dormant.

• Don't cut the grass until the bulb foliage has died away
– usually about six weeks after flowering.

• Do give the grass a cut in late autumn before the bulbs
start to grow, to keep it short at flowering time.

• Don't use summer-flowering bulbs in the lawn, for
obvious reasons.

• Do feed the bulbs immediately after flowering and
before the foliage dies down.

• Do plant the bulbs at a depth of two to three times the
height of the bulb.

Dwarf narcissus, crocus and snowdrops make a
wonderful show in the spring. Where an area of grass can
be allowed to remain uncut for a longer period, then
bluebells, fritillaries and wild orchids may be encouraged. In
autumn, *Cyclamen hederifolium* followed by *Cyclamen coum*
will make a brave show in short grass.

trees and ground cover

Deciduous trees add height and shape to a garden and provide interest all year round – as even in winter the bare, twiggy tracery of branches adds to the overall picture. There are trees to suit even the very smallest of gardens but they can be difficult to underplant. All trees cast a shadow and if the garden is well endowed with different trees, the amount of shade can be considerable. Tree roots spread far and wide in search of water and nutrients and, as a result, the ground directly under the canopy of the tree is dry, riddled with roots, impoverished and in shade. Any rain that does penetrate in summer when the tree is in leaf falls as large drops that have collected on the leaves and these can damage small plants or wash away soil.

Do's and don'ts

• Don't try to cultivate the soil under the trees as you will damage the roots, instead form planting holes between the roots and carefully insert small container-grown plants.

• Don't use long stakes to support the newly planted trees. Short stakes allow the tree to build up a better root system (see also Staking, Training and Tying, page 40).

• Don't try to establish ground-cover plants in soil that has a perennial weed problem. Deal with it first.

• Don't allow the plants to go short of water during the first season until the roots are established.

• Do plant the trees at the right spacing, to prevent them growing into their neighbours.

• Do remove the bulk of the leaves that fall in autumn, as they will smother the smaller ground coverers.

• Do use plants that will spread to cover all the bare ground such as bugle (*Ajuga*), pachysandra and periwinkle (*Vinca*).

• Do plant some evergreen shrubs as a contrast to deciduous trees – *Sarcococca*, the sweetly scented Christmas box, is ideal.

Unless your garden is 1000 sq m in size, avoid planting large forest trees such as oak, beech and ash. Instead, go for the garden forms of the mountain ash (*Sorbus*), flowering cherry (*Prunus*), false acacia (*Robinia*) and the crab apples (*Malus*). It is usual to buy garden trees as standards, grown on a clear stem or trunk with no side branches below 2 m (6 ft 6 in), or as half standards, with a bare trunk 1 m (3 ft) high. To make best use of the space and to cover the soil, underplant the trees with plants that can survive in shady, dry, root-infested ground .

As their name suggests, ground-cover plants are plants that cover the soil. While many of them are low growing, others are of reasonable height with dense foliage that prevents weeds growing below them. Species that can tolerate the conditions under the trees include *Geranium macrorrhizum*, *Lamium maculatum* and the fern *Polypodium vulgare*. They form a lower level of interest while covering the soil and reducing weeding. With a little planning, it is possible to have year round colour by incorporating some bulbs such as winter aconites, hardy cyclamen and *Anemone blanda*, which will naturalize, spreading through the other plants.

The white-barked birch (*Betula utilis* var. *jacquemontii*) underplanted with the bugle plant (*Ajuga reptans*) and foxgloves (*Digitalis*).

The bog garden comes right to the door of the
summer house, allowing you to sit in the dry while
enjoying the lush atmosphere all around you.

garden styles

In the good old days, when gardens were the size of a small farm, there was space for herbaceous borders, walled-in fruit and vegetable plots, topiary and any other style that happened to be in fashion. Today's gardens tend to be smaller, but it is still desirable to subdivide them, to form gardens within the garden. This chapter offers suggestions to suit most needs and tastes, and if you put seating in each area you will be able to relax in whichever surrounding takes your fancy.

herbaceous garden

A good herbaceous border is something you walk right up to, look straight at and soak up the variety of colour, shape and texture. In season, it can be the most spectacular feature in the garden.

Positioning the borders

Rest assured that there are perennials for every garden. To make the right choice, get to know your soil conditions. Most perennials enjoy soil that retains moisture but doesn't become waterlogged, and they prefer an open site that gets some sun. But this is only a general rule and you will find exceptions listed in Plants for Special Places (page 115).

The bed, usually called a border, can be any shape and size, positioned in the lawn as an island bed or as a double border either side of a path with matching plants in each bed. It can be narrow or broad, and the edge can be straight or curved. If the bed is in front of a hedge or fence, keep tall plants to the back, stepping down in height to the low-growing species at the front. Where paths or lawn bound both sides of the border, it can be designed with the tallest plants in the centre and graded down to both sides.

Hedges send their roots out far and wide in search of water and nutrients, so plant perennials at least 90 cm (36 in) away from the base of a hedge. This will also make it easier to get to the hedge to trim it and collect the clippings.

Cultivation

Bare earth borders should be dug over to a full spade depth removing all the weeds. Use a garden fork if perennial weeds are present, to reduce the risk of chopping up the roots. Break up the lumps of soil and incorporate a 10 cm (4 in) layer of compost and bonemeal fertilizer at 60 g (2 oz) per sq m to give the soil a bit of body. A heavy soil can be opened up and lightened by the addition of grit. Bear in mind that this is your last chance to work the soil thoroughly for a few years. An all-out effort will be rewarded by an unparalleled display of foliage and flower.

Choosing the plants

There is seldom any difficulty in obtaining perennial plants. Most garden centres have a wide selection, complete with coloured picture label and cultural instructions. Always try to purchase plants that are growing strongly. Avoid the period from late summer through to early spring when plants are not at their best or are resting, which makes it hard to judge if they are good quality.

Be selective when offered free 'bits' by neighbours and friends. Try to find out the plant's proper name and check it out before introducing it to the garden. If the plant is surplus to another gardener's requirements, there is a fair chance that it is invasive and little better than a weed. On the other hand, the offering may well be a little treasure worth planting, but make sure all the roots are its own and you are not introducing someone else's weeds alongside it.

As well as height and spread and season of flowering, bear in mind that the foliage of many perennials can be interesting – the ornamental rhubarb (*Rheum palmatum*) for example – and the shape and texture of some plants give a border maximum interest.

Plan the planting scheme to allow for a range of heights, while making sure that dwarf plants are not screened by taller varieties and that each plant's overall spread is catered for. If in doubt, allow about 90 cm (36 in) between

The summer border opposite shows what can be achieved with a successful mixture of colours, heights and textures.

1. *Achillea* (yarrow) is a good flower for cutting and drying, but if you don't pick it, it has attractive winter foliage.
2. *Helianthus* stand tall at the back of a border without the need for support.
3. *Sedum spectabile* (ice plant) flowers in late summer and is loved by butterflies and bees.
4. Silver- and grey-leaved plants such as *Senecio cineraria* (shown here), *Santolina chamaecyparissus*, *Stachys byzantina* and lavender enjoy a free-draining soil in full sun.
5. *Monarda* (bergamot) is worth growing for its profusion of flowers and scented leaves. Choose mildew-resistant varieties such as 'Croftway Pink'.

plants and if they don't utilize all the space, you can easily interplant them with dwarf bulbs to fill the gaps and extend the season of colour.

Herbaceous borders are usually thought of as height-of-summer displays. There is undoubtedly an enormous range of summer-flowering plants but, with careful selection, it is possible to have perennials to provide colour during all four seasons. As herbaceous perennials re-emerge in spring, the new young growths appear as bronze, purple, pink and every shade of green, many unfurling into strikingly shaped

10 easy perennials

Alchemilla mollis (lady's mantle) A great plant for the front of a border

Astilbe x arendsii 'Fanal' Guaranteed to flower

Bergenia **'Ballawley'** (elephant's ears)

Digitalis purpurea Excelsior Group (foxglove) Just right for that cottage-garden look

Geranium **'Ann Folkard'** Will spread quickly in most soils

Kniphofia **'Bees Sunset'** (red hot poker) Flowers best if it is not disturbed

Lupinus **'Chandelier'** (lupin) Easy to grow, with the disadvantage that slugs love them

Papaver orientale **'Allegro'** (poppy) Probably the best known of the perennial poppies

Rudbeckia fulgida var. sullivantii **'Goldsturm'** Flowers from mid summer until late autumn

Stachys byzantina (lamb's ears) Woolly grey ground cover

A herbaceous border must have

- Moisture-retentive soil
- No perennial weeds
- Shelter from wind
- Site in sun with some shade
- Slug and snail control

foliage. The autumn asters, popularly known as Michaelmas daisies, *Tricyrtis formosana* (toad lilies), *Anemone hupehensis* (Japanese anemones) and *Strobilanthes atropurpureus* all continue the late summer display well into autunm. Even on the darkest winter day a border can present splashes of colour from hellebores in flower and decorative seed heads, not forgetting all the dwarf winter-flowering bulbs such as crocus, snowdrops, cyclamen and winter aconite.

Apart from weeds, the only serious drawback to a herbaceous border is the damage caused by slugs and snails. It is a mistake not to do everything possible to limit their numbers and to create barriers to separate them from what they consider to be breakfast, lunch and dinner with hostas for afters (see control methods on page 64.)

A well-planted herbaceous border will provide long periods of interest and colour and smother all but the strongest weeds. The perennial variegated grass (*Arundo*) in the foreground and the purple-leaved cannas are unusual and eye-catching choices.

Timber edging and gravel paths separate beds of salad from herbs, brassicas and root crops. Lavender makes a colourful, aromatic background.

kitchen garden

The kitchen garden is so called because it supplies the kitchen with fruit and vegetables. If it can be sited close to the house and connected to the kitchen door by an access path so much the better. Some form of screening can be an advantage at certain times of the year when the area is untidy with debris and half-cleared crops.

The area doesn't need to be large: close cropping with quick-maturing vegetables such as spring onions, radish and lettuce between rows of fruit will utilize the space. It is amazing how much food can be grown in a plot 4 m x 5 m (13 ft by 16ft).

When growing vegetables you will need to rotate the crops each year, so that the same types of vegetable are not continually grown in the same piece of ground. This will reduce the risk of diseases building up in the soil and allow fertilizer and lime to be applied to those crops that need them.

If rabbits are a problem in your garden, enclose the area with a fence to keep them out. To stop them burrowing under the fence, bury some netting below it and net across the gate as well.

Growing vegetables from seed

There is something very satisfying about sowing vegetables, watching them grow, looking after them and then harvesting them and enjoying that home-grown flavour.

Except in very small gardens where space is at a premium, the majority of vegetables should be sown in a seed bed and remain there until they are harvested or transplanted. In either case, it is important that the bed is well prepared and there is no point in starting to cultivate until the soil is workable. In winter, the area should be covered with a 15 cm (6 in) layer of rotted farmyard manure, then dug over and left rough for the frost to break down. By spring the lumps are easily worked with a rake or a fork, to leave a fairly fine tilth with no lumps or large stones. Don't cultivate too deeply; the seed bed needs to be firm but not packed down. Scatter a general purpose fertilizer at 60 g (2 oz) per sq m and rake it into the top 8 cm (3 in). A final rake over to level the site and remove any debris and you are ready for sowing.

Tips

• Birds cause enormous damage to fruit crops and pigeons are fond of green vegetables, removing the leaves faster than they can grow. Fine mesh plastic nets on a timber or metal structure 2 metres (6ft 6 in) high and covering 20 sq m (12ft x 15ft) should protect sufficient crops, providing the nets don't become damaged and allow birds to enter.

• On light, sandy, soils growing a hedge of lavender around the kitchen garden will look attractive and the aromatic foliage will disguise the smell of carrot leaves and foil the deadly carrot fly, which is attracted by their scent. It lays its eggs beside the young carrot and the resulting grub tunnels into the root and destroys it. Another method is to make a 30 cm (12 in) high screen of horticultural fleece around the bed of carrots to keep the low-flying insects out.

Soft and bush fruit

Fruit is very much a part of the kitchen garden and picking summer fruit can be memorable. Strawberries and raspberries often disappear from the basket before they get to the kitchen door. Black, red and white currants all make traditional desserts, as do gooseberries, blackberries and loganberries.

Aim to buy certified stock of fruit that has been declared free from a whole range of diseases that cause a reduction in yield and stunt the plants. Most soft fruits like a sunny site sheltered from cold winds and a soil that has been enriched with lots of compost and old farmyard manure. Space rows well apart so that the bushes are not shading each other. Raspberry canes can grow to 2 m (6 ft 6 in) high: keep them to the north side of the plot to avoid casting shade. If there is more than one line of canes, the rows should be 2 m (6 ft 6 in) apart for the same reason.

Growing raspberries

Raspberries are supported on wires running the length of the row. You need two wires attached to timber posts and fixed at 60 cm (24 in) and 150 cm (60 in) above the ground respectively. The fruiting stems of the raspberry must be tied to the wires 10 cm (4 in) apart. When pruning, any tall shoots should be cut back to 1.8 m (6 ft) and surplus stems removed at ground level. This makes it easier to pick the fruit. After fruiting those stems are cut off as close to the ground as possible and are replaced by that year's new shoots.

Growing strawberries

Strawberries should be grown in weed free soil and can be planted on level ground. But if the earth is wet, the plants can be set on ridges of soil 1 m (3 ft 3in) apart. Space the plants 45 cm (18 in) apart in the rows. The strawberry plants should be planted at the same depth as they were when potted up. The earlier they can be planted in the autumn, when the soil is still warm, the larger the crop will be the following summer.

It is amazing how much produce can be grown in a small area and still leave space for sweet peas.

mediterranean garden

It may not be possible to have a Mediterranean-style area in your garden – you need a site in full sun and if the ground slopes, it should face the sun. To me, a Mediterranean garden conjures up images of hot gravel and stones, heavy dry heat, the sound of insects, terracotta-painted walls, shady seats, figs, vines and plumbago growing up the walls, plus a mixture of aromatic smells.

The chosen spot has to be the most favoured in the garden, sheltered from the wind and cold frosts in the spring. Most Mediterranean plants hate to have wet feet, so the soil will need to be free draining, with lots of added grit to keep it loose, open and easily warmed by the sun. Surface the beds with a layer of gravel, which will warm up quickly, hold the heat and act as a mulch to reduce weeding. On heavy clay soils it just won't work – the soil dries out and forms surface cracks during hot periods, causing roots to suffer and water to drain away below the root zone. Instead, create a planting area by building walls of timber sleepers or ornamental bricks and filling the raised bed with imported sandy soil to keep the plant roots well above the clay.

Plants that are not totally hardy can be grown in terracotta pots and moved to a frost-proof glasshouse or conservatory before the winter sets in. If your budget will only run to plain plastic pots, plunge them them into the bed up to the rim and rake the gravel back over. They can be lifted and cleaned off ready for frost-free winter storage. Deciduous plants that start to grow early in the year and are prone to damage but not killed by frost, can be protected by covering the plant with chopped-up bracken, straw or coarse bark mulch. Remove it after all risk of frost is over in late spring.

Great plants for Mediterranean-style gardens

Amaryllis belladonna Not fully hardy bulb

Carpenteria californica Evergreen shrub

Fabiana imbricata f. violacea Evergreen shrub.

Hibiscus syriacus 'Oiseau Bleu' Deciduous shrub

Lavandula angustifolia (English lavender) Evergreen aromatic shrub

Lavandula stoechas (French lavender) Evergreen aromatic shrub

Yucca gloriosa **'Variegata'** (Spanish dagger) Evergreen perennial

Don't forget all the edibles for warm, sunny walls: figs, vines, cherries and peaches. Then there are the herbs that, if grown in a hot dry soil, will have a much enhanced flavour – sage and thyme, for example.

Tip

Soft shoots produced late in the season are more prone to damage from frost than shoots that are well hardened. In early autumn, give all the plants in the Mediterranean garden a liquid feed high in potash but with no nitrogen fertilizer. The potash will harden up the young growths and omitting nitrogen won't prompt the plant into fresh growth.

Left: **If you can grow oranges, you can have a Mediterranean-type garden. This is the real thing, in Mallorca, Spain. In more temperate climates the citrus trees (1) would need to be grown in containers and moved to shelter in winter. Cyclamen (2) will survive outside only in frost-free areas.**
Right: **Spiky-leaved architectural plants and tiled paths give a hot Mediterranean feel to this New Zealand garden.**

cottage garden

Original cottage gardens were the result of random planting of bits and pieces given by friends and cuttings taken from the 'big house'. There was seldom any overall design and if a plant proved through time to be too large it was simply moved to another position. Space was at a premium, most of the ground being used for growing essential food crops so the less useful but more decorative plants filled the gaps and covered walls and fences.

When I imagine a cottage garden, I think of brick or gravel surfaced paths edged with stones or bricks and plants tumbling over. A mass of bright and muted colours splashed over the ground and plants of every shape and size mixed at random. Above all, I can almost take hold of the jumble of scents that evoke childhood memories.

As an area within a larger plot, the cottage garden doesn't have to be particularly big. You can give it its own boundary by surrounding it with a low fence. Use rustic

peeled bark trellis or an old-fashioned picket fence and grow perennials such as hollyhocks (*Alcea rosea*) and delphiniums or scrambling climbers such as clematis, roses and honeysuckle (*Lonicera*) up and over the fence. The area can be in full sun or light shade where foxgloves (*Digitalis*), poppies (*Papaver*), monkshood (*Aconitum*), columbine (*Aquilegia*) and evening primrose (*Oenothera*) will soon spread by seed.

Preparing the ground

Take your time preparing the soil and eliminate as many weeds as possible before planting. Heavy wet soils may need to be drained or opened up by digging a 5 cm (2 in) layer of coarse washed grit into the top 25 cm (10 in) of soil. Cottage gardens were never short of old farmyard manure, it was the one thing that there was plenty of, and it took the place of compost and fertilizer. Today it is not so readily available and if you can't get hold of any, dig in as much compost as possible and apply 30 g (1 oz) of slow-release bone meal per sq m to the roots at planting time.

A small rustic alcove complete with wooden seat provides somewhere to sit in relaxing surroundings and enjoy afternoon tea among the scent of honeysuckle, lavender and pinks (*Dianthus*).

Tip
Any gaps in the planting scheme can be filled in summer by sowing seed of annuals such as nasturtium (*Tropaeolum*) and cornflower (*Centaurea cyanus*) directly into the spaces, thinning them out as necessary.

The mixture of perennials and lack of order combine to give a cottagey feel.

Great plants for cottage gardens
Alcea rosea **'Chater's Double'** (hollyhock) Biennial
Lathyrus latifolius (everlasting pea) Perennial
Lathyrus odoratus (sweet pea) Annual
Philadelphus **'Belle Etoile'** (bride's blossom) Shrub
Rosmarinus officinalis (rosemary) Shrub
Tropaeolum **Gleam Series** (nasturtium) Annual

bog garden

If you have an area in the garden which is permanently wet or waterlogged and it is either too expensive to drain or there is no suitable outlet to take the water away, then turn the problem to your advantage and convert the area into a bog garden. The first thing to find out is whether the soil remains wet all year round or if it is only a problem in winter or after prolonged rainfall. To succeed as a bog garden, the site needs to be constantly wet – plants that like those conditions won't survive if the soil dries out for a lengthy period. On the other hand, soil that is so waterlogged that it becomes stagnant and starts to smell won't support many plants and the area will attract mosquitoes. If there is too much surface water, one option is to raise the soil level, allowing the plant roots to be in the wet while the crown of the plant is above the water.

Stepping stones through the planted areas will keep your footwear clean and at the same time let you see the plants growing in their own habitat. The area can be in sun or shade as there are plants that thrive in either.

Faking it Even if there is no suitably wet part in your garden, you can still have a bog area. Construct one by digging out a hole about 30 cm (12 in) deep and lining it with plastic sheeting, with a few holes pierced in the sides and base. Mix the excavated soil with an equal amount of moisture-retaining compost and replace the soil. The plastic retains the water, keeping the soil in the pit wet, yet it will drain slowly to prevent the soil becoming saturated. Don't try to make a bog garden on sandy and gravelly types of soil. They do not retain moisture. Bog gardens are often constructed beside a garden pond and the overflow is directed into the bog, helping to keep the soil constantly wet. When it becomes necessary to feed the plants, usually in late spring, use a high potash feed and water it in. If your bog garden is close to the pond, don't let it drift into the open water.

Tip

When creating a bog garden from scratch, add a layer of wet rotted manure or leaf mould in the base of the hole, on top of the liner, to help retain moisture. Don't use peat – if it is allowed to dry out it is practically impossible to re-wet.

Candelabra primulas, astilbe and irises all enjoy having their feet in a moist soil.

Five great plants for wet areas

Astilbe Many varieties. Perennial
Clethra alnifolia (sweet pepper bush) Shrub
Hosta Many varieties. Perennial
Primula florindae (giant cowslip) Perennial
Rheum palmatum 'Atrosanguineum' (ornamental rhubarb) Perennial

woodland garden

A woodland garden cannot be arrived at overnight unless you have bought a wood, but if the planting is done carefully with the right species of plants, it is surprising how quickly it can come into being. The area of trees need not be massive – indeed, a woodland effect can be created in the corner of a medium-sized garden. A sheltered site will allow the young trees to grow away quickly to form cover, although in many instances the main reason for planting trees is so that they will provide the initial shelter for the rest of the plants in the garden; it is only later that their value as a copse or wood becomes apparent. Try to choose a site that will get the sun at some part of the day and then, when the trees grow up, rays of sunlight can be encouraged to shine through into little glades, lighting up a chosen specimen in the surrounding gloom.

Dappled shade is enjoyed by primulas, hostas, rodgersia, irises and rhododendrons.

Five great woodland trees

Betula pendula (silver birch) Deciduous
Fagus sylvatica (beech) Deciduous
Pinus nigra (Austrian pine) Evergreen conifer
Quercus rubra (red oak) Deciduous
Sorbus acuparia (rowan, mountain ash) Deciduous

Most soils will be satisfactory for woodland plants, providing there is sufficient depth for a good root run. Avoid thin soils overlying rock or chalk that is close to the surface, as the trees will become stunted and may die during a dry summer.

Pathways can be allowed to meander through the wood and cross over the existing tracks, giving the impression of a much larger area. They can be surfaced with chipped or peeled bark and edged with cut branches or logs.

A mixture of trees will produce a more interesting woodland, with lots of colours and leaf shapes. Mixing evergreens such as pine, holly and spruce with deciduous species such as beech, oak, rowan and ash will provide interest all year round and support a diverse range of wildlife.

If you are not in a hurry, plant young sapling trees called whips. Larger trees not only cost a lot more but are slower to become established and a percentage may die as a result of transplanting. Planting 2 m (6 ft 6in) apart will allow the trees to form cover quickly and encourage them to grow with straight trunks. If the wood becomes too dense, thin it by removing the worst shaped specimens and the least interesting varieties.

Tip

In the early years, fence the woodland area with rabbit-proof fencing to prevent these creatures from eating the young tree bark, which will stunt or kill the plant. Make very sure that you fence the rabbits out and that there are none hiding in the long grass inside the wood when the fence is erected or all your efforts will be wasted.

During the first few years, keep grass and weeds in the vicinity under control to prevent your plants getting choked. This is best achieved by applying weedkiller or placing a 60 cm (24 in) collar of old

Woodland shade is ideal for ferns, elephant's ears (*Bergenia*), hostas and Solomon's seal (*Polygonatum*). All form useful ground cover beneath the canopy of trees.

carpet around the base of each plant, making sure to water them regularly, as the collar will run the rain off.

As the trees grow they will form a canopy, cutting out light and preventing weeds from growing. Autumn leaf fall will ensure that after a few years a layer of leaf mould will build up and act as a mulch. Shade-loving ground-covering plants can be planted as an underskirt to provide you with one of the most interesting parts of the garden.

Five ground coverers

Cyclamen coum
Daphne laureola (spurge laurel)
Pachysandra terminalis (Japanese spurge)
Sarcococca humilis (Christmas box)
Vinca minor **'Azurea Flore Pleno'** (periwinkle)

3.

2.

wild flower garden

Wild gardens can be very beautiful, but contrary to their name, they can be slow to mature and are not easy to manage. But if your garden is large, a wild garden is a great way to use part of the space.

Wild gardens I like, but there is a thin line between what I like and what I thoroughly dislike. There are wild gardens and there are neglected, overgrown and weed-infested gardens.

In winter a wild garden can look unkempt, with long grass and little colour. For this reason, it should be tucked into a spot not too obvious from the house. It is the sort of area that you should come upon when out for a garden walk, or deliberately visit when it is in season and looking its best or stroll through on your way to another part of the garden. It can be in full sun or partial shade; a sloping site is acceptable, as the grass hasn't to be mown too frequently. Even a small corner will accommodate a lot of different plants and will soon become a haven for a range of interesting wild life.

Soil type Any soil type will do but if you can avoid the extremes of acidic and alkaline, you will be able to accommodate a larger range of plants. Most wild flowers prefer an impoverished soil. They dislike ground that has been enriched with fertilizer, which will encourage growth at the expense of flowers and, in many cases, even kill the plants or cause them to suffer from competition from other plants. Some gardeners are fortunate enough to have a deep loam soil: if you are one of the lucky ones, remove most of the soil from the wild garden area and reuse it where it will be appreciated, just leaving a thin layer over the subsoil. There are wild plant species for all types of soil, but heavy wet soils are more difficult to work with.

Keeping the garden going Germination of the seed of annual wild flowers can be hit or miss. Some types of plant have a greater chance of success than others and quite often by the start of the third season, some of the original species will have died out. Young seedlings can be suffocated by strongly growing grass and other weeds.

Rather than relying on nature, you can harvest about half of the seed by cutting off the seed heads and shaking them over a sheet of paper. Tip seed into paper bags and store it in a cool dry cupboard over winter. Sow some of it in the wild area in spring and the rest into seed trays, to give the young plants a head start.

Thin the seedlings out and plant strong young plants into the garden. Before planting out, any existing vegetation where the plants are to be set out can be spaded off, to allow the plants to grow away unhindered for the first few weeks until they become established and large enough to fend for themselves.

Wild flower bulbs Bulbs play an important part in the wild flower garden, providing colour year after year and multiplying speedily. *Fritillaria meleagris*, the snake's head fritillary, and dwarf narcissus will colonize meadow land. It is important that the grass isn't cut until after the bulbs' foliage has died down and the wild flowers have shed their seed.

Wild flower gardens should not be left to run riot. This is a carefully thought-out patch within a larger, well-maintained garden.
1. **Poppies will multiply rapidly.**
2. **Alliums can be left to self-seed.**
3. **Rudbeckia (just coming into flower here) will supply a golden late-summer display when the poppies and alliums fade.**

Five great wild flowers

Achillea millefolium (yarrow) Perennial

Centaurea cyanus (cornflower) Annual

Leucanthemum vulgare (ox-eye daisy) Perennial

Papaver rhoeas (field poppy) Annual

Primula veris (cowslip) Perennial

scented garden

Scented, aromatic or perfumed – call them whatever pleases you – these are the plants that bring memories flooding back from childhood, when the days were hot and it never rained in summer. One whiff of sweet pea, lilac, lavender or pinks and you are transported back to the very garden. They say that you can't buy memories, but for the price of a packet of seed or a few pounds for a plant, you can have not only memories but you can choose the ones you want.

Some scented plants are best known for their foliage, such as rosemary, sage and prostanthera (mint bush). Planted close to paths, they release their aroma as you brush against them. Others rely on their flowers for scent, such as lily and lilac, while yet more are endowed with both scented flowers and foliage, good examples being lavender and choisya. Some give of their best after a shower of rain in the evening, when a walk in the moonlight can bring you face to face with the heady perfume of wallflower or night-scented stock.

Paths edged with lavender and a tunnel of roses lead you along a scented trail into the herb garden.

Great scented plants

Choisya ternata (Mexican orange blossom) Shrub with scented flowers and leaves

Daphne mezereum Shrub with fragrant flowers

Lavendula stoechas (French lavender) Shrub with scented flowers and leaves

Perovskia atriplicifolia (Russian sage) Sub-shrub with aromatic leaves

Roses, especially the older varieties. Shrubs and climbers with scented flowers

Viburnum x carlcephalum Shrub with scented flowers

Lonicera fragrantissima (honeysuckle) Climber with scented flowers

Convallaria majalis (lily of the valley) Ground cover with scented flowers

Jasminum officinale (jasmine) Climber with fragrant flowers

Mediterranean plants Many aromatic plants are Mediterranean and appreciate full sun and can tolerate drought conditions. The leaves give off their scent when the oils in the foliage are released. This occurs when temperatures are high. Pruning every year will encourage new growth with young foliage that performs better. Mediterranean species enjoy a soil that is well drained and of an open gritty texture. If your soil is heavy and poorly drained, a bed can be made up with a lighter soil and raised to provide better drainage. Raising the planting area will also bring the plants with their flowers and foliage closer to the nose; raised beds are especially useful for gardeners in wheelchairs. Grow some of the scented plants in pots on the patio and in beds close to garden seats to enjoy the perfume.

It is possible to have scent in the garden every month of the year. A must for mid-winter is *Sarcococca confusa*, the Christmas box, with its tiny white flowers that drench the surrounding area with fragrance.

foliage garden

First-time gardeners may be excused for shying away from foliage gardens and opting instead for flower colour. Yet leaves can be dramatic and eye catching. Leaves come in every shape, colour and size, making bold architectural structures that the gardener can rely on and use to highlight and frame flowering plants. Deciduous foliage often changes colour with the seasons, giving of its best in autumn when it changes spectacularly from green to red, purple and gold.

When screening the garden for privacy or shelter evergreen foliage comes into its own, with escallonia, berberis and yew all in demand.

The song claims that there are 40 shades of green and if that is the case, you can have them all in the garden in a choice of matt or gloss. Ferns such as *Matteuccia struthiopteris*, the shuttlecock fern, unfurl pale green leaves in spring that quickly grow to 1.8 m (6 ft). Then there are ornamental grasses such as the miscanthus, some of which can grow to 3 m (10 ft) between spring and autumn. Leaves are available in every colour from green splashed with white – hostas are typical – to just about black as with the low-growing, grass-like *Ophiopogon planiscapis* 'Nigrescens'. Nature has allowed for those gardeners with limited space by providing species that change their leaf colour with the seasons.

Deciduous and evergreen plants may be used to complement one another; the bold, fingered, evergreen leaves of *Fatsia japonica* highlighting the bare tracery of twiggy stems of *Betula jacquemontii*, or the glossy evergreen of the holly mixed in a hedge of deciduous beech with its brown crinkly dead leaves and tightly wrapped, thin, pointed buds.

Rheum palmatum 'Atrosanguineum' has striking foliage which contrasts with the rounded leaves of *Ligularia dentata* 'Desdemona'.

Foliage comes into its own in winter when there is less flower colour to compete and the leaves are suddenly highlighted. Flower arrangers fill their gardens with plants with odd-shaped leaves as essential backdrops to the flowers.

Tip
Generally the best way to feed plants is to use a balanced fertilizer containing nitrogen, phosphate and potash to encourage growth and flowering. If the foliage is the plant's main claim to fame, then by feeding with a high nitrogen fertilizer, the leaves will be larger and there will be more of them.

Five great foliage plants

Acer japonicum 'Vitifolium' Deciduous tree for autumn colour

Hosta 'Wide Brim' Perennial with green and white leaves

Rodgersia pinnata 'Superba' Perennial with big divided leaves

Stachys byzantina Perennial with woolly leaves

Yucca gloriosa Perennial with sword-like leaves

Broad, level, well-surfaced paths and raised beds make gardening easier for those in wheelchairs. This Californian garden was designed from scratch with the disabled in mind, but the same principles can be applied to an established space on a smaller scale.

retired person's garden

A garden for retirement should be low maintenance and easy to manage. I know that it is after retirement that lots of gardeners get most joy out of their garden but, sooner or later, the body slows down and gardening tasks that were once easy take longer to complete. Heavy construction work and any major jobs should be done by a garden contractor. I have already said that the jobs that require most time are weeding, grass cutting, pruning, digging, watering and planting. With a little careful planning, it is possible to reduce the hours spent on each task.

Prevention is better than cure   Control of weeds is covered on pages 30–33, but it is far better if weeds are prevented from growing, rather than trying to get rid of them. Mulching is a good way to keep weeds at bay using shredded bark or gravel. Using a layer of landscape fabric as a membrane under the mulch will stop deep rooted weeds appearing, yet allow rain to percolate through to the soil. Of course you can carry on cultivating by digging and hoeing on a regular basis, but this is harder on the back and arms.

Cutting and pruning Keep the size of the lawn to a minimum and you'll need only a small mower to cut it. Lawns need constant work to keep them looking good and regular weeding, feeding, spiking and raking all take a lot more time if the lawn is large.

Pruning cannot be ignored, but with some thought and a careful choice of plants it can be kept to a minimum. There are lots of plants that require little or no pruning, including *Daphne mezereum*, azalea and hamamelis (witch hazel). Shrubs that need a lot of pruning include forsythia, philadelphus and weigela. If they go unpruned they will cease to flower and become untidy with lots of old straggly branches. So root them out and replant with low-maintenance shrubs.

Digging and watering

Cultivation of the soil is heavy work and often unnecessary. If a planting hole is well prepared, there is no need to cultivate the whole bed. Restricting the area that you dig lessens the risk of replenishing weeds by bringing more seeds to the surface every time the soil is turned over. Ground coverers such as *Ajuga* (bugle) and *Vinca* (periwinkle) planted into weed-free soil will reduce the area of bare soil for weeds to colonize.

The need to water the garden is reduced when mulches are used. After the first growing season, when the roots of the plants have travelled out in search of moisture, it really should not be necessary to water them except during very dry summers. The trouble with watering is that once you start, you have to carry on until it rains.

Planting If done properly the first time, planting should not cause much trouble for a few years, especially if shrubs are used in preference to shorter-lived perennials. Space the plants at the correct distance to avoid having to thin them later. Try to keep the number of annuals in the garden to a minimum. Planting them is time consuming and then they have to be removed and dumped or composted in the autumn. Avoid plants that sucker such as *Rhus typhina* (the stag's horn sumac) and those that have to be regularly trained on walls and fences to prevent them becoming a tangled mass of shoots.

As we get older it takes less of an excuse to keep us indoors and it is pleasant if the garden can be seen and appreciated from the warmth of the house. Be sure to landscape close up to the dwelling and grow scented plants under opening windows.

> **Five great low-maintenance shrubs**
>
> *Camellia x williamsii* 'Anticipation'
>
> *Cordyline australis*
>
> *Hamamelis mollis*
>
> *Magnolia stellata*
>
> *Pieris japonica*

The garden's design Raised beds are an advantage for those who find it difficult to bend over; and brick retaining walls can be sat on while weeding. Soil can be altered to give a choice of acid or alkaline, allowing you to grow a wider range of plants.

Make paths as wide as possible to allow two people to walk side by side and to accommodate a walking frame or a wheelchair. The surface should be firm. Where there is a change of levels, slope the path rather than constructing steps which are difficult to negotiate in later years.

Container growing is a useful method of gardening brought down to manageable proportions. There is an enormous range of small containers that can be moved about and planted up to give permanent or seasonal displays. Containers eliminate the need to weed or prune, although watering becomes a daily chore in a dry season. If you plant them up in a potting shed remember to place them in position before watering – the weight of the wet compost makes moving them much more difficult.

If hedges need to be planted, use informal flowering shrubs such as escallonia and roses, which require less clipping than more traditional formal hedges of laurel, privet and yew.

herb garden

'Herb' is a collective term for a whole range of useful plants that are useful to us. There are culinary herbs, medicinal, strewing and aromatic herbs, plus those used for herbal teas and for dyeing.

Unless you are feeding the five thousand a small patch of herbs in the kitchen garden should suffice. If you want to make a feature of the herb area you can create a knot garden, where small beds are kept separate by low hedges in a formal pattern. Dwarf box hedges are traditional but require regular clipping and are a great hiding place for snails. Lavender hedges are in keeping with the herbal theme and look attractive, but are short lived and need to be clipped every spring to encourage new growth from the base.

Herbs in containers Where only a few varieties are in demand herbs can be grown in a container on the patio or outside the kitchen door for convenience. Before you head off to the garden centre, give a bit of thought to which herbs you are likely to use, rather than buying a whole lot that you have heard of but will never get round to cooking with. Sage, rosemary and thyme are well worth growing, as are parsley, mint and bay. Mint is a bit of a thug and grown direct in a bed, it will spread all over the garden. It is best planted in an old bucket and plunged into the ground. Make sure the rim of the bucket is above soil level so that the mint can't escape. One bay tree will produce more than enough leaves for culinary use. Unless you are into alternative medicine, don't bother with the medicinal herbs, as they will only take up space and never be used.

Five decorative herbs
Allium schoenoprasum (chives)
Borago officinalis (borage)
Lavandula stoechas (French lavender)
Rosmarinus officinalis (rosemary)
Thymus x citriodorus **'Bertram Anderson'** (lemon thyme)

Plants grown in full sun in a well-drained, light gritty soil will reward you with the best flavour. When grown in containers ensure that there is good drainage by filling the bottom 10 cm (4 in) with large pieces of polystyrene. Cover them with horticultural fleece to stop the water washing the compost down into the base and blocking the drainage holes. Use an open, free-draining compost and don't fill the pot to the top, leaving room to water.

For best flavour
Young new growths and leaves have the best flavour, so encourage growth on plants such as sage and thyme each spring by pruning. A light clipping is all that is needed rather than cutting into the older wood, which may not reshoot.

A top dressing of equal parts grit and peat worked into the centre of woody species will encourage new roots to grow on the stem and rejuvenate the plant.

Avoid overfeeding herbs with nitrogen – and there is no need to enrich the soil with compost or manure at planting time. To ensure the soil is well drained, the herb garden can be planted in a raised bed in a sunny part of the garden and creeping herbs such as thyme can be planted along the edge and allowed to grow over the sides and trail down.

Tip
It is possible to have fresh mint and parsley all winter if they are given some protection from the elements. When small amounts are sufficient, grow them on the kitchen windowsill. In late autumn dig a few roots of parsley and pot up in compost in a container deep enough to hold the long root. Trim off older leaves and water well. New growth will soon appear. The roots of the mint are just below the soil surface and can be lifted, laid on a shallow container and covered with 2 cm (1 in) of compost and watered in. The new shoots will appear quickly and can be nipped off for use.

Clipped box hedges (1) contain the plants, leaving the gravel paths uncluttered. This showcase herb garden at the famous Ballymaloe Cookery School in Ireland contains, among many others, nasturtiums (2), sage (3), globe artichokes (4), fennel (5) and evening primrose (6).

tropical garden

Even in cooler climates it is possible to give that tropical, lush look and enclosed feeling to part of the garden. Lots of leafy plants, shade and moisture are essential for success and the site needs to be sheltered and warm. Plants such as coleus (*Solenostemon*) with their wonderfully coloured leaves are normally thought of as conservatory or house plants in my part of the world, but they can be moved outside in their containers for the summer. The holiday will do them good and they will enjoy the cooler conditions and provide that exotic look at the time when the garden is most in use.

Site A warm, sheltered part of the garden overhung with mature trees is ideal, but in a new garden it may be necessary to settle for a sunny corner protected from the wind and planted with large foliage plants to provide the future leaf canopy. Avoid low-lying areas, as they are often

frost pockets where the cold air drains down to the lowest part of the garden, damaging all but the hardiest of plants.

The soil needs to be free draining with no risk of water-logging, but needs to retain sufficient moisture to encourage mosses and ferns to cover the tropical floor and some of the best of the less aggressive clematis, such as *C.* 'Dr Ruppel', to scramble about higher up among the other plants.

Planting There is always the risk of ending up with a jungle, and even a tropical jungle is to be avoided. Correct spacing of the plants is important, as warm, moist growing conditions will encourage rampant growth, allowing the more aggressive species to take over, smothering smaller plants and generally becoming a nuisance. Mulching the soil with composted leaves will not only help to retain moisture and deter weeds, but will also add to the aesthetics, providing that humid feeling.

Feeding To encourage the plants to produce leafy growth, feed a high-nitrogen fertilizer at fortnightly intervals during the summer. In the autumn revert to high-potash fertilizer to harden the plants up for the winter.

The striking foliage of palm and banana raises the temperature in this back garden in Melbourne.

Five great 'tropical' plants
Echium pininana
Fatsia japonica
Ficus carica (common fig)
Gunnera manicata
Phormium tenax (New Zealand flax)

children's garden

There are two schools of thought; you can allow the children to have free run of the whole garden or a portion of the garden can be set aside for their exclusive use. I am very much in favour of giving them part of the garden, but I suppose consideration has to be given to their age and how well behaved the children in question are.

If none of the garden is out of bounds, then you must expect some damage to plants through youthful enthusiasm. It is not fair or enjoyable to be constantly shouting at them. And no matter how well behaved your own offspring are, their friends may well be little horrors with no respect for property or plants.

The big advantage in giving an area over to the children is that when they are young you can fence them in and keep an eye on them at the same time. Chose an area close to the house within sight of the kitchen window for peace of mind. All the toys can be kept inside the play area, which makes grass cutting a simple task without having to clear the lawn before you start the mower up.

Five easy plants for children
Tropaeolum majus (nasturtium)
Primula vulgaris (primrose)
Galanthus nivalis (snowdrop)
Fragaria x ananassa (strawberry)
Lathyrus odorata (sweet pea)

Gardening has to be interesting for children, with no early set backs. A sure way to success is to encourage them to grow something they like to eat. Quick-growing food crops include sugar snap peas, radishes, early finger carrots, lettuce and, best of all, strawberries. Plants that mature quickly are also satisying. Sunflowers from seeds are great fun: as well as the enormous 2.5 m (8 ft) high giants that need staking, there are dwarf sunflowers with large flowerheads.

Propagation has always interested children providing they can see results fast. Sowing seeds, planting and taking cuttings will all hold their attention if growing happens like magic. Seeds don't have to be sown in rows but can form letters or the child's name. Hebes, especially 'Purple Queen', and catmint will root like weeds. Cuttings will form small plants in about four weeks, grown outdoors in summer in a sandy soil, using a cut-down plastic drinks bottle as a miniature cloche.

Young gardeners Turning children into gardeners is every bit as pleasing as helping them to qualify in their chosen profession. Start them off with an area of ground that won't appear enormous yet is large enough to grow a variety of plants. A 2 m (6 ft 6 in) square plot is ideal. Make sure that it is free of any perennial weeds and cultivate the soil to leave it in a condition to be worked with small hand tools.

Tip

Pumpkins are great fun to grow from seed. If sown in May they will be ready for Halloween. The way to produce large fruit is to grow the plant on a raised bed that is free draining, with lots of added compost, and restrict the crop to one pumpkin per plant.

Safety first

• Don't allow children to handle sharp tools.

• Don't allow children anywhere near mechanical or electrical equipment.

• Don't use any chemicals in the children's garden.

• Don't allow pets into the children's garden in case they use it as a toilet area.

• Don't grow poisonous plants or plants that can cause a skin allergy.

• Do insist that children wash their hands after working in the garden.

• Make sure the soil is free of broken glass and nails, and remove any stones larger than 5 cm (2 in) across.

The tissue-paper-like flowers are the main reason for growing poppies, but the seed heads are also eye-catching in dried flower arrangements.

growing tips for favourite plants

You don't have to be a gardener to have a favourite flower, but when you decide to grow your own, you become a gardener.

I have so many favourites, and as the seasons change so does my loyalty. Some, such as roses, tend to be grown together in dedicated rose beds, while others, such as fuchsias, pop up here and there in mixed plantings. Clematis too may be dotted about, scrambling over fences, sheds and old trees.

Giving your favourite what it likes by way of feeding, pruning and soil type will undoubtedly make you its favourite, so take a tip from me…

clematis

There are small-flowered clematis and double-flowered clematis, spring-, summer-, autumn- and even winter-flowering varieties and while most of them are deciduous, there are some evergreen species, too. The majority of clematis are climbers, but there are some attractive herbaceous varieties that will stay at knee height. In other words, there are clematis to suit every taste and fill every niche in the garden.

Site and soil Most clematis dislike bitterly cold winds, preferring a more sheltered position. The exceptions are the small-flowered species such as *Clematis tangutica*, *C. alpina*, *C. montana* and *C. macropetala*, which are tough and able to withstand all but the worst of conditions. All clematis do best in a reasonably sunny site but can be grown in light shade; in fact, the pale-coloured, large-flowered varieties fade in strong sunlight. As climbers they love to scramble up and over fences, trellis, sheds and other trees and shrubs. Vigorous species such as *C. montana* are quite capable of climbing to the top of a 15 m (50 ft) tree.

Once they become established, clematis will grow successfully in most soils with the exception of extremes of wet or dry, but they

Group 1: *C. montana* 'Wilsonii'

Group 2: *C.* 'Vyvyan Pennell' and 'The President'

Group 3: *C. viticella* 'Abundance'

particularly enjoy a well-drained, moisture-retentive soil with lots of added farmyard manure, leaf mould or compost. They prefer a cool root run, with their roots in the shade and well covered with a moisture-retentive mulch (see page 46 for suggestions). This will not only help keep the roots cool and prevent the soil from drying out in summer, it will also encourage the lower part of the stem to root into the compost.

Planting Since they are always sold as container-grown plants, clematis can be planted at any time without causing a check in the plant's growth. If you are planting in summer, water well afterwards as the plants will be in full growth.

Follow the step-by-step planting instructions on page 37. It is particularly important to place the rootball in the hole at least 10 cm (4 in) deeper than it was in the pot. This encourages extra roots to form on the stem and offers some protection against clematis wilt disease (see under Pests and Diseases, below). Protect the new young shoots from slugs and snails by using pellets or trapping them in containers of beer.

Pruning Newly planted clematis should be pruned in early spring just above the first pair of shoots. Nip out the tips of the resulting shoots to encourage them to form more sideshoots and branch out into a multi-stemmed plant. Clematis fall into three types and, after the first year, the pruning for each type is different.

Group 1 comprises *Clematis armandii, Clematis cirrhosa, Clematis alpina, Clematis macropetala* and *Clematis montana.* Pruning is not necessary for any of these species, although if they have become too large or are taking over their support, they can be pruned as soon as flowering is finished. If the growth is a nuisance, cut them back hard and they will grow away as if they had never been touched, though if the plant is very large and mature it may be advisable to spread this treatment over a period of two or even three years.

Group 2 includes all the semi-double and double varieties and the early large-flowering types that flower before midsummer. These produce their blooms on short growths and will often flower again in late summer and early autumn. Some of the best known of this group are *Clematis florida, C. lanuginosa , C. patens.*, and the varieties *C.* 'Nelly Moser', *C.* 'Lasurstern' and *C.* ' The President'.

Not a lot of pruning is needed for this group. At the end of winter, simply cut out all the dead bits and

Group 1
Overgrown plants can be cut back after flowering. Remove weak or damaged growths and cut to reduce size.

Group 2
Prune in late winter remove weak and damaged shoots leaving a framework of strong well spaced shoots.

Group 3
Prune all shoots hard in late winter to 30 cm (12 in) above ground level. Remove dead shoots at ground level.

any very thin, weak shoots, cutting just above a pair of nice plump buds. Don't prune too hard or you will stop the clematis from producing its first flush of blooms. If the plant is totally overgrown, it can be cut hard after the first flush of flowers and the resulting new growths trained in to replace the old wood.

Group 3 includes *Clematis orientalis, Clematis texensis, Clematis viticella* and all the late large-flowering hybrids

This is where you can lose your temper, because they require severe pruning every year. They flower on the current year's growth so should be pruned hard in late winter. Look for the lowest pair of good strong buds on each main stem and cut just above them, removing everything that is growing beyond that. The plant will look butchered but, believe me, you will have an abundance of flowers the same year.

Feeding All clematis appreciate regular feeding and after pruning a balanced feed is needed to encourage the plant to produce strong healthy shoots.

Pests and diseases Probably the worst pests are also the most common – slugs and snails play havoc with clematis in the spring, eating through the main young shoots. When you have cut hard back to the lowest buds and then lost them to slugs, it is a worry until new growth appears. During the season you can find snails 5m (16ft) up a wall or tree heading for the tops of your clematis.

Wilt disease of clematis is caused by the fungus *Ascochyta clematidina*. It attacks the tips of the plant first, then the leaf stalks turn black where they join the leaf and the young growths wither. Little research has been done on this problem, and there is no sure-fire method of prevention or cure. A deeper-than-average planting hole may help, and if the disease does strike, cutting the plant right back to ground level is the best remedy. Sometimes the plant will recover from lower down, producing shoots at soil level. If you have lost a clematis to wilt disease, don't plant another in the same spot.

Waterlogged soil and slug damage can also cause ordinary wilting, without these symptoms.

Other pests such as greenfly and caterpillars can be a nuisance, but no more so than on other plants.

Growing in containers It is possible to grow clematis in a container but it will need to be as large as possible, with extra drainage holes and a good moisture-retentive, soil-based compost. A large wooden barrel is ideal or any container that is at least 60 cm (24 in) deep and 45 cm (18 in) wide. The pot plus compost will be heavy, so position it out of direct strong sun before filling and planting. Leave the top 10 cm (4 in) of the container free of compost to allow for watering and applying a mulch each spring.

Clematis suitable for growing in containers include varieties of *C. alpina* and *C. macropetala* and *C.* 'Doctor Ruppel', 'Vyvyan Pennell' (a double-flowered variety), 'Miss Bateman' and 'H F Young'.

***Clematis armandii* is evergreen and flowers in late winter with the exquisite scent of almonds.**

roses

Roses have been with us for a very long time and have, over the centuries, adapted and changed with the times almost as well as the human race. Today, breeders and people dedicated to rose growing strive to bring us new, better and more adaptable varieties to suit every situation in the garden. There are species roses, shrub roses, climbers, ramblers, cluster-flowered (floribunda), large-flowered bush (hybrid tea), patio, ground cover and miniature roses. It really is not necessary to know or to grow all the different types and the best advice I can give is to go out and buy the type of rose that is best suited to where you are going to plant it.

If a rose is to grow up a wall, trellis or arch, choose a climber, rambler or a vigorous shrub rose. Roses to be mass planted in a formal bed can be cluster or large flowered. Patio roses and miniature types do well in containers for the patio and if there is a steep bank to be covered then some of the recently introduced ground-cover roses are ideal. Ultimate height and spread need to be considered: there are vigorous roses and there are rampant ones such as *Rosa filipes* 'Kiftsgate', which will grow up and along for 12 m (40 ft).

Some roses are almost evergreen, such as the Flower Carpet series with white, pink, red and yellow in the range. When planting an island bed in the lawn, choose just one variety of rose rather than a mixture of varieties in different colours that are bound to flower at different times. The perfume of a well-scented bloom is a heady aroma that never fails to bring back memories and it is worth visiting some of the rose trial grounds in summer to check for yourself the fragrance of a particular rose. Some modern varieties have little or no scent and breeders seem more interested in colour, habit or disease resistance than in what our noses want. Perhaps that is why many of the older perfumed roses are still available while some of the more recent introductions have dropped out of the catalogues.

The highly scented gallica rose 'Charles de Mills', with its fully double flowers, makes a fragrant summer shrub and can also be trained over a support.

How to buy roses

There are two ways to buy roses; either as container-grown plants, which will not suffer a check in growth if planted carefully; then there are bare-root plants bought in the late autumn, winter or early spring. Bare-root plants can be purchased in garden centres, stores, direct from the nursery or by mail order. They will have no leaves or flowers but you will be able to see if the main roots are strong and healthy, and if there are lots of the small white fibrous roots which are essential for good growth. Immediately they arrive, take them out of any packaging and plant them. If the weather or the soil is not suitable for planting, the roses should be heeled into the ground as a temporary measure, so that their roots are in close contact with damp soil and covered to prevent them drying out. Choose a soil that is easily dug and firm the soil around the rose roots. When time and weather allow, put them in their permanent position, before the winter is over.

Pruning roses

Roses flower best on the young wood made that year: in other words, they flower on current growth. The principal of pruning roses is to remove the old wood and encourage new shoots. At pruning time you can also take the opportunity to remove dead, diseased, weak and crossing stems, thereby keeping the plant healthy and less cluttered.

Rosa 'Arthur Bell', cluster-flowered, double, yellow and with a beautiful scent.

Good varieties
'Alex's Red' Fragrant, double red flowers, 90 cm (36 in) high.

'Fragrant Cloud' Dark green leaves, very fragrant, large scarlet flowers, 75 cm (30 in) high

'Pot o' Gold' Very fragrant, double, golden-yellow flowers in clusters, 75 cm (30 in) high.

'Arthur Bell' Bright green leaves, fragrant, double, buttercup-yellow flowers, 90 cm (36 in) high.

'Evelyn Fison' Glossy, dark green foliage, double bright red flowers 70 cm (28 in) high.

'Playboy' Glossy, dark green foliage, semi-double, orange-yellow flowers, 75 cm (30 in) high.

Rosa complicata is a vigorous gallica rose which makes a sturdy and thorny hedge. It can reach a height and spread of 2.5 m (8 ft).

Pruning large-flowered and cluster-flowered roses
When The most reliable time is in the spring, when the buds are swelling and can be clearly seen. In areas where there is less risk of frost, they can be pruned early; in colder climes it will have to be done later. As well as spring pruning, established rose bushes are usually cut back by half in early winter, to reduce the risk of wind damage, which rocks the plant in the ground and injures the roots.

Where Cut out all damaged, dead and diseased branches and any stems that are spindly. Cut with sharp secateurs and make a clean sloping cut about 7 mm (¼ in) above a bud.

How much Reduce all the main stems to about 20 cm (8 in) from the ground. For cluster-flowered roses where the size of individual blooms is not so important, the main shoots may be shortened to 25-30 cm (10-12 in). All prunings should be removed from the bed and burnt to prevent the spread of diseases such as black spot.

Pruning shrub roses
When Late winter is a good time to do the little pruning that is necessary to most of the shrub roses.

Where With the old-fashioned species roses, very little pruning is necessary. Simply cut out the very old wood, the dead branches

…nd any stems that are diseased. Modern shrub roses should be …hortened back and tidied up.

How much The main shoots can be shortened by about one third.

Good varieties

'Charles de Mills' A gallica rose with quartered, fragrant double magenta-pink flowers in summer, 1. 2 m (4 ft) tall.

'Complicata' A gallica rose, vigorous, with large, single, pink flowers with pale pink centres, 2. 5 m (8 ft) high.

'Gertrude Jekyll' A modern shrub rose with large, double, deep pink, fragrant flowers in summer and autumn, 1. 5 m (5 ft) high.

Rosa 'Dublin Bay' is a trouble-free climber that can also be pruned to grow as a shrub.

Pruning climbers

When In autumn when flowering is finished.

Where The old wood is cut out as close to the ground as possible without leaving a stump and any weak shoots removed. Thin out the main stems to form a framework that can be tied in, rather than let it become a tangle of branches. Cut the side shoots back in autumn.

How much The side shoots should be shortened by two thirds.

Good varieties

'Gloire de Dijon' A noisette rose with dark green foliage and quartered, double, fragrant, creamy-buff flowers in summer and autumn, 5 m (16 ft) high.

'Dublin Bay' Dark green leaves, double, bright crimson flowers in summer and autumn, 2. 5 m (8 ft) high.

'Handel' Erect habit, dark green leaves, clusters of double, fragrant, cream flowers with deep pink edging, 3 m (10 ft) high.

Rosa 'Félicité Perpétue' is a joy to grow – vigorous, hardy, disease-free and almost evergreen in mild gardens, it is still in flower later in the season than many ramblers.

Pruning ramblers

When After flowering in late summer.

Where All the shoots that flowered should be cut out.

How much Only the new strong shoots that haven't flowered should remain, the old flowering shoots are cut out at ground level.

Good varieties

'Félicité Perpétue' Rosette-shaped, double pale pink to white flowers in summer, 5 m (16 ft) high.

'Wedding Day' Rampant grower, single, fragrant, creamy-white flowers that age to pale pink in summer, 10 m (33 ft) high.

Planting Do the planting properly. The rose is going to be in the same piece of ground for the rest of its life and that could be for the next 10 or 15 years. The conditions you provide now will affect its performance for all that time. Make the planting hole generous; at least twice the width of the container the rose was bought in or the spread of the bare roots. The depth of the planting hole needs to be 35-45 cm (14-18 in) with the base of the hole forked up to loosen the subsoil. Add a forkful of well-rotted farmyard manure to the base and then a layer of topsoil mixed with 60 g (2 oz) of bone meal. Check that the compost around the roots of container-grown roses is moist before planting – if it is dry, plunge the pot plus the rose in a bucket of water and leave for 20 minutes. Before planting, check for damage. If there are any broken stems, cut them back to a healthy bud below the damage. If there are any very long, thick roots, shorten them to half their length. Handle the rose carefully to avoid weakening the plant at the join or union where it was budded onto the rootstock, just above ground level. The rose should be planted with the union about 2 cm (1 in) below soil level. With bare-root roses, spread the roots out in the planting hole – don't allow them to tangle up and all spread in the same direction. Firm the soil around the roots to exclude any air pockets and water well to settle the soil.

Planting distance depends upon the type of rose and the ultimate size of the plant. As an average 45–60 cm (18–24 in) is adequate for most bedding roses; shrub roses will, on average, require 2 m (6 ft 6in) each way. Climbing varieties will need to be spaced 3 m (10 ft) apart and some of the vigorous ramblers can spread 10 m (33 ft).

Training roses With climbers and rambler roses, the main stems need to be trained into some order, otherwise they will scramble all over the place and the flowers won't be well displayed. Use a soft tying cord to bind the stems loosely to the support without damaging them. With bush-type roses, try to keep the centre of the plant free of crossing branches for ease of working. Shoots can be directed by pruning to a bud pointing in the direction that you want the new shoot to grow.

Feeding Proprietary rose fertilizers contain a mixture of nutrients, including small amounts of vital trace elements. A handful scattered per square metre, after pruning and again in mid summer, should keep the plant happy. Don't be tempted to apply a late feed: this can lead to soft growth which will be damaged by frost. A mulch of rotted farmyard manure in late winter or early spring will help retain moisture and keep down weeds while providing humus and nutrients.

Pests and diseases There is a race on to breed disease-resistant roses and some of the recent ground cover types, such as the Flower Carpet varieties, are resistant to the main problems. Black spot is probably the worst disease and a regular spray programme with a fungicide will help. Good hygiene is important too: removing diseased leaves and infected prunings will help to prevent the spores of the disease overwintering. Mildew and rust can also cause a lot of trouble in some seasons. The only insect that is a constant pest is greenfly: these appear in dense clusters on buds, young shoots and on the undersides of the leaves. Regular spraying with a systemic insecticide will help, but eventually they will build up a resistance to any one particular pesticide. Ladybirds eat an enormous number of greenfly.

Growing in containers Miniature and patio roses can be grown in containers and make a good show in the summer. The more compact varieties of bush roses will also be happy but the taller varieties and the climbers and rambler roses really need to be in a good loamy soil in a bed. Potting compost for container growing should be soil based with good drainage in the base of the container and lots of old farmyard manure added to the mixture. Don't allow the roses to dry out at any time and feed with rose fertilizer in spring and late summer. Use containers that can be moved: roses look dead in winter and need to be moved out of the public eye until the following early summer.

sweet peas

I have never met anyone who disliked sweet pea flowers. Their long slim stems carry graceful, butterfly-like flowers in a breathtaking range of colours. With the older varieties their incredible perfume seeps into every part of the garden. Most of the modern varieties have been bred with showy flowers in clear colours but little or no perfume.

There are two main types of sweet pea. Perennials grow strongly and flower in their second season, reappearing every spring and quickly scrambling up and over any support available. They produce flowers on short stems with minimal perfume. Then there is the annual sweet pea that we all know and love, *Lathyrus odoratus*.

Annual sweet peas not only supply colour and perfume but, given support, in a matter of weeks the young plants will grow to provide a tall screen offering privacy and shelter, and quite capable of screening unsightly parts of the garden.

There is no shortage of small plants in stores and garden centres during spring. Once they are hardened off, to accustom them to outside temperatures, they can be planted out in rows where they are to flower.

Annual sweet peas are easily grown from seed sown in autumn or in early spring in containers, but they have a large root system and like to be in a deep pot or tube that allows the roots to grow down without becoming tangled. The small round seeds have a tough outer skin that can slow up germination. A tip is to nick the seed coat with a knife or a nail file opposite the 'eye' of the seed – that will hasten germination, allowing the shoot to emerge more easily. Seed sown in the autumn must be overwintered in a frost-free glasshouse. Once the seedlings have two pairs of leaves, the growing tip of the shoot should be nipped out to encourage side shoots and form a bushy plant.

Sweet peas will flower all summer if they are dead-headed to prevent seed forming.

Planting Harden the plants off and plant out in the ground in late spring, when the soil has had a chance to warm up. The ground should be well prepared: for best results, dig a deep trench in winter, in full sun, and incorporate lots of old farmyard manure and compost to help retain the moisture. The roots of the sweet pea love a moist soil and should never be allowed to dry out. Layers of wet newspaper placed in the base of the trench will help to conserve moisture and prevent it draining down below the level of the roots.

Space the plants 25 cm (10 in) apart in a staggered double row on top of the backfilled trench, taking care not to damage the roots. Firm the soil around the roots without packing it too tightly. They will need some form of support for the tendrils to cling to – wire netting or canes can be used. The need to water regularly cannot be over-emphasized: a shortage will result in stunted plants and a scarcity of flowers.

Lathyrus **'Wiltshire Ripple', one of the many colour variations now available.**

Training When the plants start to flower, keep picking the blooms and remove any that are not perfect, to prevent them setting seed. Once this happens, the plant stops flowering and diverts its efforts into seed production.

If you are trying for top-quality blooms fit for exhibition, then the plants should be grown as cordons on a single stem with all the tendrils and side shoots removed and the stem tied in to a sturdy bamboo cane with soft string. The resulting flowers appear on long stems with many more flowers per stalk.

Feeding Sweet pea plants are greedy and require regular feeding for good growth and flower colour. The nitrogen percentage can be low as the plants are capable of manufacturing their own nitrogenous fertilizer but the levels of phosphate should be high, with the potash at the same level as the nitrogen. Three parts phosphate to one part each of nitrogen and potash is about right. Liquid feeds work well and the plants respond quickly, but never use a foliar feed when the sun is shining as the leaves may be scorched.

Pests and diseases Sweet pea plants are prone to some soil-borne fungal diseases that can cause them to wither and die, so it is advisable to choose a different site for the crop each year. Slugs and snails cause havoc to young plants by eating the young stems at ground level, and protection or traps will be necessary. Greenfly can be a nuisance during warm summers and can be controlled with systemic pesticides, but take care to avoid wetting the flowers as some of the chemicals can mark them.

Growing in containers Some varieties of sweet pea will grow to 2 m (6 ft 6in) and other dwarf types will only reach 60 cm (24 in). Tall varieties need a large deep container if they are to succeed and a good rich compost that retains moisture. The dwarf types are happy in earthenware pots on the patio in a sunny position, leaving 10 cm (4 in) free of compost at the top of the pot to accommodate watering and feeding.

lilies

Lilies are in a class of their own and don't they know it. With names such as *regale*, 'Limelight', 'Lovely Girl' and 'Madonna', they can not be blamed for acting superior. Even the varieties with downward facing flowers mostly turn their petals back so that we can get a good view and are really only being coy. Some species grow to 2 m (6 ft 6in) in height; others suitable for balcony or patio display grow only to 30 cm (12 in), such as *Lilium cernuum* (nodding lily).

Planting Lilies can be planted in spring or autumn, when they will flower the following year. They like a site in sun or dappled shade and are ideal for mixing through a shrubbery or herbaceous border.

The soil needs to be well prepared by adding lots of rotted farmyard manure and compost, especially if the soil is alkaline. They require an open, well-drained soil: if the soil is heavy, plant them on top of a 2.5 cm (1 in) layer of clean grit or sharp sand to stop them rotting. The planting hole should be 15 cm (6 in) deep for stem-rooting varieties such as *Lilium longiflorum* and *L. regale,* and 10 cm (4 in) deep for *Lilium candidum,* which likes to be just below the soil surface. Larger bulbs will need to be well spaced; a hole of 60 cm (24 in) diameter will take a group of three bulbs. Mark the position with a cane to avoid planting anything else on top of them, but take care not to spear the bulbs with the cane. A layer of sharp sand on the surface around the emerging shoots will help to deter slugs and snails, but it will still be necessary to inspect them every day and remove slugs as you find them.

Some lilies can be naturalized in fine grass, where they will appear each summer and spread quite quickly. *Lilium martagon* is ideal with its pendant wine red Turk's cap flowers. It can tolerate an alkaline soil and is able to withstand the worst of weather. Where the lilies are growing in the border, they should be lifted and divided every three to four years taking care not to damage the bulbs.

The appropriately named *Lilium regale* – **one of the most majestic of flowers.**

Pests and diseases Apart from slugs, snails and aphis, the worst pest is the lily beetle, whose grubs destroy the foliage and the flowers by chewing. The beetles are easily recognisable as they are bright red and the best control method is to pick them off and destroy them. Wash off the grubs with a paintbrush into a jar of water and dispose of them. Diseases include different rots that attack the bulb. Lily disease attacks foliage, forming brown spots and causing the leaves to wither. Affected plants should be lifted and burnt.

Growing in containers Dwarf lily varieties thrive in large pots and barrels, and for summer display coupled with perfume they are hard to beat. Provide extra drainage using old pieces of broken clay pots over the drainage hole and fill the pot with a loam-based compost. Position the bulbs 15 cm (6 in) apart and 15 cm (6 in) deep. Water regularly throughout the growing season but don't allow them to become waterlogged. Taller varieties will need staking and sheltering from the worst of the wind.

Acer palmatum in full autumn glory.

Japanese maples

Perfect in shape and spectacular in leaf, the Japanese acers, especially *Acer palmatum* and its many varieties, are top of the plant shopping list for most first-time gardeners. The only thing that stops them selling in millions is that they are more expensive than a lot of other plants..

All acers are deciduous, but some have highly coloured foliage from the moment they unfurl in the spring through until the first frosts. The leaves of *A. palmatum* 'Bloodgood' are dark red-purple all through the summer, turning bright red in autumn and grows to 5 m (16 ft). *A. p.* 'Shishio' has red leaves in spring that turn bright green in summer and return to red in autumn; it grows to 2.5 m (8 ft) high. Even small plants have that mature-tree look, spreading their branches almost horizontally, with layers of deeply cut hand-like leaves which move in the slightest breeze.

Don't be tempted to buy acers as bare-root plants – they will suffer a check in growth after they are planted and more than likely die. Plants sold in a ball of soil wrapped in hessian fare little better. The best chance of success is with container grown plants with a good rootball.

Choose a site in full sun or partial shade. All the *palmatum* varieties dislike a cold windy situation and spring frosts can burn the young emerging leaves and cause dieback on the new shoots.

The soil needs to be well cultivated, deep and enriched with compost. Acers prefer to grow in an acid, well-drained soil and since they may well outlive you, give them a good base dressing of bone meal at planting time.

Plant at the same depth as they were in the pot and water them in to settle the soil around the root ball. There is seldom a need to prune unless the plant has grown too big for the allotted space and even then cut back as little as possible, trying not to spoil the natural shape of the plant. A mulch of leaf mould is the only treat they need and they will give a generation of pleasure with the minimum of attention. Planted with hostas and ferns, the leaf colours are highlighted, while an underplanting of dwarf spring bulbs shows off the bare twiggy branches.

Growing in containers All Japanese maples love growing in containers, providing the containers are large enough and the compost is not allowed to dry out in summer. The big advantage is that the plants can be moved to a sheltered location in early spring when the emerging leaves are vulnerable. Leave room at the top of the pot for watering and a top up of fresh compost each spring. Eventually some varieties will have to be planted out in the garden, where they will continue to provide colour and shape.

poppies

There are all sorts of poppies, but the one thing that they have in common and makes you want to grow them is their tissue-paper flowers that present themselves on a daily basis for a long period. They come in a mixture of pastel 'hand-painted' shades and scorching reds which would do justice to a flamenco dancer. The field poppies in Monet's painting are also referred to as the Flanders poppy (*Papaver rhoeas*). *P. nudicaule* is another favourite and more commonly known as the Iceland poppy, in a selection of pastel shades. Another perennial with large flowers is, *P. orientale*, the oriental poppy; the variety 'Beauty of Livermere' has blowsy flowers stained with a black blotch at the base of each petal. As poppies flower in early summer, they can leave large gaps in the border for the rest of the season. For this reason they should be dotted through other later-flowering plants.

The seed heads are in great demand for dried flower arrangements and the seed can be saved and sown in odd corners of the garden.

Himalayan blue poppies and Welsh poppies belong to a different genus (*Meconopsis*) and prefer to grow in a moist, free-draining soil with lots of old compost added and in partial shade. Water regularly in summer and remove the flower heads as soon as they are finished, to encourage more flowers to form.

Planting   Annual poppies will do better in dry, free-draining soil that is low in nutrients. Grown from seed, they flower within weeks of sowing. *Papaver somniferum*, the opium poppy, has some wonderful varieties including the Paeony-Flowered Group which produce masses of fully double, frilly blooms in pink, purple, red and white. Sow in spring outside where they are to flower and cover the seed with fine soil. It is practically impossible to transplant annual poppies, so don't try to keep the thinnings.

Perennial poppies like a well-drained soil in a sunny position. They have deep fleshy roots, so cultivate the soil as deeply as possible before planting. Large clumps can be divided in spring or after flowering.

Removing the dead flowers before they set seed will encourage more flowers and extend the season.

Papaver rhoeas **'Mother of Pearl', a cultivar of the annual field or Flanders poppy.**

rhododendrons and azaleas

The only thing that stops me recommending that every garden should have one of these shrubs is their preference for an acid soil. Apart from that, there is something to suit every taste and every size of garden. Azaleas used to have their own genus, but are now classified as rhododendrons: the difference is that all rhododendrons are evergreen whereas most azaleas are deciduous (though I can recommend the evergreen Kurume hybrids).

Rhododendrons tend to have large leaves and large flowers, while azalea flowers are smaller and appear in clusters. There are varieties that flower in the northern hemisphere as early as January – *Rhododendron* 'Christmas Cheer' seldom flowers for the festive season, but generally follows hard on its heels. A selection of varieties will provide a succession of blooms until early summer.

Plants range in size from the lovely little scarlet-flowered *Rhododendron forrestii* at 20 cm (8 in) to the towering 15 m (50 ft) high *R. macabeanum* with its 30 cm (12 in) leaves and enormous trusses of deep yellow flowers, which have contrasting purple blotches on the inside.

Many rhododendron hybrids have the excellent *R. fortunei* as one of their parents. Any that you come across are worth growing. This one, *R.* 'Fred Wynniatt', grows to 4 m (13 ft) and can tolerate sun.

Soil and site Both rhododendrons and azaleas prefer a woodland situation in dappled shade, but will tolerate a more open site screened from the morning sun and shletered from cold winds. The soil must be well drained as the plants dislike waterlogged ground, enjoying moist conditions with added leaf mould and ericaceous compost. An acid soil with a pH of 4.5–5.5 is ideal. Rhododendrons are shallow rooted and you can do a lot of damage when hoeing weeds around their base. To avoid this problem, a mulch of compost or bark will help keep the surface of the soil moist, cool and weed free.

Planting Dig a planting hole larger than the pot or rootball of the plant and fork up the base of the hole to assist drainage. If the soil is dry, prepare the planting hole the previous day, fill it with a bucket of water and allow it to drain before planting. Add a handful of bonemeal to the soil as it is being replaced around the roots and plant the rhododendron at the same depth as in the pot. Firm the soil around the rootball and water well to settle the soil around the roots.

Pruning It is only necessary to remove branches in order to improve the shape of the plant or if they are crossing into the centre of the shrub or rubbing together. Old straggly plants may be cut hard and the branches will regrow from old wood. Dead-head after flowering to encourage growth rather than seed, taking care when removing the dead flowers not to damage the new shoots forming to either side.

Feeding An annual dressing of leaf mould in the spring is all that is needed. Take note of any foliage that turns pale yellow (chlorotic), as this is a symptom of a limy soil which does not give the plant sufficient iron or magnesium. In this case, apply these elements as a foliar feed.

Pest and diseases The only major pests are vine weevil larvae, which eat the roots, causing young plants to

R. 'Vuyk's Rosyred' is an evergreen dwarf azalea , ideal for a container. It flowers in mid-spring and reaches 75 cm (30 in).

wither and die; and the adult weevils disfigure the foliage by eating the edges of the leaves.

Growing in containers All rhododendrons and azaleas do well in containers, but their main season of display is spring and early summer. The larger-growing species and hardy hybrid varieties of rhododendron will eventually outgrow the biggest container and will have to be planted out in the open border, but until that time they will give years of display. Check that there are lots of drainage holes in the base of the pot and that the compost is acidic and free-draining. Leave space at the top of the pot for watering and top-dressing.

fuchsias

The fuchsia is a plant for everyone. Young or old, male or female, gardener or non-gardener, most people are charmed by their flowers and by their easy cultivation. They can be grown as a pot plant or an outdoor shrub, some varieties being totally hardy. They are available in the most wonderful range of colours with flowers shaped like ballet dancers.

Soil and site Outdoors, fuchsias should be planted in a well-drained, fertile soil that retains moisture. They need full sun or partial shade in an area protected from biting cold winds. For indoor pot plants a loam-based compost is best, although they will succeed in a soilless compost providing it is not allowed to dry out. Position the plants in a bright place, but not in strong, direct sunlight.

Fuchsia **'Marinka' has red stems and red midribs to the leaves and is excellent for a hanging basket.**

Planting Plant with the rootball 5 cm (2 in) deeper than when in the pot and mulch every autumn to protect the base from heavy frost. Apart from the hardy species such as *Fuchsia* 'Riccartonii' and *F.* 'Mrs Popple', most varieties die back to ground level in winter, reappearing in late spring when the young growths need protection from frost. I leave the dead woody stems as a marker, otherwise my size 10 boot does more damage than the frost.

Pruning Flowers are produced on young current season shoots, so prune hard in late spring to within a few buds of the older wood.

Feeding For outdoor shrubs, a general fertilizer such as Growmore may be applied in late spring at 30 g (1 oz) per sq m. Give the hardy species a high-potash feed in autumn to firm up the wood before winter.

During the growing season, feed indoor plants every three weeks with a balanced liquid fertilizer. In winter, keep the watering to a minimum, but don't allow the compost to dry out completely or the plant roots will shrivel and die.

Pests and diseases This is where fuchsias lose Brownie points. As pot plants they are susceptible to whitefly, greenfly, red spider mite, capsid bugs and vine weevil. They also suffer from grey mould fungus disease. Outdoors they are not so vulnerable, greenfly being the main problem.

Growing in containers Fuchsias are great plants for hanging baskets and as centre dot plants in larger containers. Varieties such as *F.* 'Cascade' (red and white), *F.* 'Hermiena' (purple and white) and *F.* 'Marinka' (red) are naturally trailing and, if they are fed every three weeks they will drape baskets, hiding them completely.

F. **'Cascade', a trailing variety with single flowers, can spread to cover a wall but needs to be protected from frost.**

Once you have identified some plants that appeal to you, you can have lots of fun combining them to create different effects. Mix flowers and foliage plants to provide variety and splashes of colour, or choose several plants of the same colour for a more subtle, harmonious look. Remember, your garden is a canvas on which you can paint any picture you like.

directory

This directory is a list of plants mentioned in How to Garden, with a description of the type of plant, its general appearance and ultimate height.

It is by no means an exhaustive list of plants I could recommend, but it will start you off. You will soon realize that the fun of choosing plants is exceeded only by the joy of watching them grow to maturity.

Find yourself a good garden centre with knowledgeable staff and pick their brains. They will welcome the chance to help you choose the right plant and will share in the pleasure of your success.

Acacia dealbata

Alcea rosea
'Chater's Double'

Allium schoenoprasum

Anthemis tinctoria
'E. C. Buxton'

Aquilegia vulgaris

Acacia dealbata (mimosa) Evergreen tree with hairy, fern-like, silvery green leaves and fragrant golden yellow flowers in winter and early spring. Grows best in a well-favoured site or on a sheltered south-facing (north-facing in the southern hemisphere) wall. Height 15 m (50 ft).

Acer (maple) Genus of mainly deciduous trees grown for autumn colour. ***A. japonicum*** 'Vitifolium' (Japanese maple) has broad, deeply lobed leaves colouring beautifully to brilliant red in autumn. Mature trees seed freely. Height 5 m (16 ft).
A. pseudoplatanus is the fast-growing common sycamore with dark green leaves and yellow flowers in spring, followed by green winged seed. Height 30 m (100 ft). For more information on the many varieties of ***Acer palmatum***, see page 172.

Achillea (yarrow) Genus of ornamental perennials.
A. 'Coronation Gold' is evergreen with silvery grey leaves and flat heads of small, golden yellow flowers in late summer and autumn. Height 80 cm (32 in). ***A. filipendulina***, another evergreen, has grey-green leaves and flat, plate-like, golden yellow flowerheads in summer and early autumn. Height 1.2 m (4 ft).
A. millefolium is a wild flower. It is mat-forming with pungent pale green leaves and flattened yellowish-white and pink flowerheads in midsummer. Height 60 cm (24 in).

Actinidia kolomikta Deciduous climber with dark green leaves that are tinged purple when young, developing white and pink variegations on the top half. Fragrant white flowers are borne in summer and female plants produce yellow-green fruit. Height 5 m (16 ft).

Agapanthus Genus of tall perennials with trumpet-shaped flowers and long strap-like leaves. ***A. africanus*** is clump-forming and evergreen, with large rounded umbels of blue flowers in late summer. Height 60 cm (24 in).
A. 'Blue Moon' is deciduous with pale blue flowers in late summer. Height 60 cm (24 in).

Agastache foeniculum Perennial with aniseed-smelling foliage, grey-green on the underside. Dense spikes of blue-violet flowers in summer and early autumn. Height 1 m (40 in).

Agave americana 'Marginata' Succulent with long, needle-sharp, fleshy grey-green leaves with pale yellow margins turning white with age. Spreading panicles of yellow-green flowers appear in summer. Height 2 m (6 ft 6 in).

Akebia quinata Semi-evergreen climber with dark green leaves, blue-green on the underside and tinged purple in the winter. Fragrant dark purple flowers appear in early spring, followed by 10 cm (4 in) long fruit. Height 10 m (33 ft).

Alcea rosea Chater's Double Group (hollyhock) Vigorous perennial with pale green leaves and tall spikes of double flowers in early summer, in a range of colours including white, yellow, pink, red and purple. Height 2 m (6 ft 6 in).

Alchemilla (lady's mantle) Genus of perennials with sprays of small green or yellow flowers. ***A. alpina*** is mat-forming with deep green leaves that are silver on the underside and small greenish-yellow flowers in summer. Height 10 cm (4 in). ***A. mollis*** is great for the front of a border or the edge of a path. Its pale green, wavy-edged leaves hold drops of water like beads of mercury. It spreads rapidly but is easily kept in place. Height 45 cm (18 in), spread 60 cm (24 in).

Allium schoenoprasum (chives) Bulbous perennial with thin, hollow, dark green leaves, used as a herb, plus purple or white flowers in summer. Height 30 cm (12 in).

Alnus cordata (Italian alder) Deciduous tree with glossy dark green leaves. Yellow-brown male catkins appear in late winter before the leaves. Height 25 m (80 ft).

Aloysia triphylla (lemon verbena) Bushy, deciduous shrub with lemon-scented, narrow, pale green leaves and pale lilac or white flowers in late summer. Height 3 m (10 ft).

Amaryllis belladonna Bulbous perennial with fleshy, strap-like leaves and pink, scented, funnel-shaped flowers on long stems in autumn. Height 60 cm (24 in).

Amelanchier (snowy mespilus) Deciduous shrubs or trees with brilliant spring and autumn leaf colour. ***A. canadensis*** has white flowers in spring, followed by small edible black fruit. The leaves of ***A. lamarckii*** turn from copper to green and then brilliant orange and red in autumn. Height 8 m (26 ft).

Anthemis Perennials with daisy-like flowers. ***A. punctata*** subsp. ***cupaniana*** has silvery green leaves turning grey-green in winter and white flowerheads in summer and early autumn. Height 30 cm (12 in). The flowers of ***A. tinctoria*** 'E. C. Buxton' are lemon yellow with deep yellow centres and are excellent for cutting. Height 60 cm (24 in).

Aquilegia vulgaris (granny's bonnet) Perennial with light green leaves, flowering in late spring and early summer in a range of cultivars and colours, from white through pink and blue to violet. Height 90 cm (36 in).

Arbutus unedo (strawberry tree) Evergreen tree with shiny mid green leaves and peeling, red-brown bark. The white flowers appear in autumn at the same time as the rough-skinned red fruit from the previous year's blossom. Height 8 m (26 ft).

Artemisia Evergreen shrubs with aromatic foliage. ***A. arborescens*** (wormwood) has ferny, silvery white foliage and small yellow flowers in summer and autumn. Height 90 cm (36 in). *A.* **'Powis Castle'** has silvery grey leaves and panicles of silver-yellow flowers in late summer. Height 60 cm (24 in).

Arum maculatum (lords and ladies, cuckoo-pint) Tuberous perennial with shiny green leaves. The flower is a greenish-yellow spathe or hood, with central purple-brown spadix in late spring, followed by spikes of red berries. Height 50 cm (20 in).

Aster novae-angliae **'Harrington's Pink'** (New England aster) Deciduous perennial with mid green leaves, flowering from midsummer until late autumn with sprays of light pink, daisy-like flowers with yellow centres. Height 1.2 m (4 ft).

Astilbe Genus of deciduous perennials for moist soil in shade. In really wet boggy conditions astilbes prefer some sun. Remove the flowers of white varieties as soon as they have finished flowering as the dead flower spike looks unkempt. *A.* **x** *arendsii* **'Fanal'** is one of my favourites, with dense panicles of deep red flowers in early summer. Height 60 cm (24 in), spread 90 cm (36 in).

Aubrieta Low-growing, evergreen perennials that are spring flowering in shades of pink, mauve and purple. Clip plants over after flowering to keep them compact. They enjoy a sunny site. Height 5 cm (2 in).

Aucuba japonica **'Crotonifolia'** (spotted laurel) Evergreen shrub with glossy mid green leaves speckled with bright yellow. It has small red-purple flowers in spring followed by red berries. Height 3 m (10 ft).

Aurinia saxatilis Spring-flowering evergreen with grey-green foliage and yellow flowers. Plants need to grow in full sun. Height 20 cm (8 in).

Ballota acetabulosa Bushy evergreen sub-shrub with grey-green leaves and white woolly shoots. Small purple-pink flowers are produced in late summer. Plants are not fully hardy. Height 60 cm (24 in).

Berberis Genus of berried shrubs. *B. darwinii* is evergreen with glossy, dark green spiny leaves. It flowers in late spring with a mass of pendant clusters of orange flowers, followed by blue-black fruit. Height 3 m (10 ft). *B.* **x** *stenophylla* has deep yellow flowers on arching branches in late spring, followed by blue-black fruit. It makes an impenetrable informal hedge. Height 3 m (10 ft).

Bergenia **'Ballawley'** (elephants' ears) Perennial with shining green leaves turning red-purple in winter. Bright crimson flowers on red stems appear in late winter and last until late spring. Plants tolerate shade and the leaf colour is even better if grown in poor soil. A good plant for winter; site it towards the front of the bed where it can be seen. Height and spread 60cm (24in).

Betula (birch) Deciduous trees with interesting bark. *B. pendula* (silver birch) has peeling, white-brown bark and mid green leaves, turning yellow in autumn. Pale brown male catkins are produced in spring. Height 25 m (80 ft). The leaves of *B. pendula* **'Youngii'** turn yellow in autumn; after they fall the twiggy, dome-shaped, 'weeping' tree seems to crouch in the garden waiting for spring.

Borago officinalis (borage) Annual with dull green, bristly foliage and star-shaped blue flowers in summer. Height 60 cm (24 in).

Brachyglottis monroi Evergreen shrub whose leathery, olive-green foilage is white on the underside. Yellow, daisy-like flowers are borne in summer. Height 90 cm (36 in).

Buddleja davidii (butterfly bush) Deciduous, fast-growing shrub with grey-green leaves and long panicles of purple or lilac flowers in summer and autumn. Height 3 m (10 ft).

Bupleurum fruticosum (shrubby hare's ear) Evergreen shrub with blue-green leaves and yellow, star-shaped flowers in summer and early autumn. Height 45 cm (18 in).

Callistemon citrinus (crimson bottlebrush) Evergreen shrub with dark green leaves. Spikes of crimson-red flowers are produced in late spring and early summer. Plants are not fully hardy and dislike cold winds. Height 2 m (6 ft 6 in).

Callistephus chinensis **'Ostrich Plume'** (China aster) Annual with mid-green leaves and long-stemmed, feathery double flowers in pink, red, crimson and mauve in summer and autumn. Height 60 cm (24 in).

Calluna (Scots heather or ling) Genus of evergreen perennials that range from small shrubs to ground cover. *C. vulgaris* **'H. E. Beale'** produces pale pink double flowers on long spikes during late summer and autumn. The flowers are excellent for cutting. Height 40 cm (16 in). *C. vulgaris* **'Kinlochruel'** has long clusters of double white flowers. Height 25 cm (10 in).

Camellia Genus of evergreen shrubs with glossy green leaves and peony-like flowers. *C.* **x** *williamsii* **'Donation'** has semi-double pink flowers in late winter and spring. Height 5 m (16 ft) high. The leaves of *C. sasanqua* **'Narumigata'** are paler on the underside; scented creamy white flowers flecked with pink appear in late autumn. Height 5 m (16 ft). *C.* **x** *williamsii* **'Anticipation'** has double, deep red flowers in late winter and early spring. During frosty weather, direct early morning sun can destroy the flowers. Height 4 m (13 ft).

Campanula Large genus of plants with bell-shaped flowers in summer. *C. glomerata* **'Superba'** is a deciduous perennial with dark green leaves and violet-blue flowers clustered at the ends of stiff stems. Height 60 cm

Aster novae angliae **'Harrington's Pink'**

Astilbe x arendsii **'Fanal'**

Berberis darwinii

Bergenia ciliata

Callistemon citrinus

Campsis x tagliabuana
'Madame Galen'

Carya ovata

Cerastium
tomentosam

Cercis siliquastrum
'Bodnantense'

Chaenomeles speciosa
'Moerloosei'

(24 in). **C. persicifolia** is an evergreen perennial that forms rosettes of bright green leaves and has white to mid blue, pendant flowers. Height 90 cm (36 in), spread 30 cm (12 in).

Campsis x tagliabuana 'Madame Galen' Vigorous deciduous climber that clings to its support by aerial roots. The orange-red flowers are trumpet shaped and carried in panicles during late summer and autumn. Height 10 m (33 ft).

Carpenteria californica Bushy evergreen shrub with glossy, dark green leaves and peeling orange-brown bark. Cup-shaped, fragrant white flowers with bright yellow stamens appear in midsummer. Height and spread 2 m (6 ft 6 in).

Carya ovata (hickory) Deciduous tree with peeling grey-brown bark and mid green leaves that turn brilliant yellow in autumn. It produces edible nuts. Height 20 m (65 ft).

Caryopteris x clandonensis 'Kew Blue' Deciduous shrub with aromatic grey-green leaves and dark blue flowers in late summer and autumn. Height 90 cm (36 in).

Ceanothus Genus of both evergreen and deciduous shrubs – one of the few plants to produce genuinely blue flowers. Most varieties like a sunny site. **C. 'Puget Blue'** is an evergreen with deeply veined dark green leaves and profuse deep blue flowers in late summer. Height 4 m (13 ft). **C. 'Italian Skies'**, also evergreen, has glossy, light green leaves and bright blue flowers in spring. Useful for ground cover, it spreads to 3 m (10 ft). Height 1.2 m (4 ft).

Celmisia spectabilis (New Zealand daisy) Evergreen perennial with leathery, silvery green leaves that are woolly on the underside. The large daisy flowerheads have white ray florets and bright yellow centres and are carried on long woolly white stems in early summer. Height 30 cm (12 in).

Centaurea cyanus (cornflower) Classic meadow wild flower. Cornflowers are annuals with mid green leaves. They produce dark blue flowers with violet inner petals in late spring and early summer. Height 60 cm (24 in).

Centranthus ruber (red valerian) Short-lived perennial with mid green leaves and fragrant funnel-shaped flowers in shades of white, pink or deep red. Blooms from late spring to late summer and likes a lime soil. Height 90cm (3ft).

Cerastium tomentosum (snow-in-summer) Rampant, mat forming perennial with grey woolly leaves. Plants are covered in star-shaped white flowers in late spring and summer. Height 8 cm (3 in).

Cercidiphyllum japonicum (Katsura tree) Deciduous tree. The mid green leaves are bronze when young and turn yellow, orange and finally red in autumn, when they smell of burnt sugar. The colour is best in an acid soil. Height 15 m (50 ft).

Cercis siliquastrum (Judas tree) Deciduous tree with heart-shaped blue-green leaves that are bronze when young, turning yellow in autumn. The deep purple-pink flowers appear in spring, before or with the young leaves. Height 8 m (26 ft).

Chaenomeles (flowering quince, japonica) Spring-flowering, deciduous shrubs with fragrant fruits. **C. speciosa 'Moerloosei'** has spiny branches, dark green leaves and white flowers flushed dark pink, followed by yellow fruit in autumn. Height 2 m (6 ft 6 in). **C. x superba 'Crimson and Gold'** has mid green leaves, spiny branches and dark red flowers with golden anthers. Height 90 cm (36 in).

Chamaecyparis (false cypress) Genus of evergreen conifers that vary in size. **C. lawsoniana** has a columnar shape and bright green leaves. Height 30 m (100 ft). **C. pisifera 'Boulevard'** has peeling red-brown bark and soft bluish foliage. Height 10 m (33 ft).

Choisya ternata (Mexican orange blossom) Evergreen shrub with aromatic, dark green foliage. Fragrant white flowers are produced in spring and again in early autumn. Height 2.5 m (8 ft).

Chrysanthemum (florists' chrysanthemum) Genus of perennials with flowers in a range of shapes. Either a spray or single heads of flowers are produced, depending on whether or not the plants were disbudded to leave only one bud to open. Available in a range of colours from late summer through until late autumn. Height 90–150 cm (3–5 ft).

Cistus (sun rose) Genus of evergreen, summer-flowering, bushy shrubs with sticky leaves and shoots. **C. x cyprius** has terminal clusters of three to six white flowers with crimson and yellow blotches on the base of the petals. Height 90 cm (36 in). **C. x purpureus** has deep pink flowers with maroon blotches. Height 90 cm (36 in).

Clematis see page 160.

Clethra Shrubs and small trees with spires of fragrant flowers. **C. alnifolia** (sweet pepper bush) is deciduous, with mid green leaves and white flowers tinged pink in late summer and autumn. Height 2.5 m (8 ft). **C. delavayi** has deep blue-green leaves and cup-shaped white flowers. Height 4 m (13 ft).

Clianthus puniceus 'Albus' (lobster claw) Evergreen shrub with dark green leaves that prefers a wall to scramble up. White flowers shaped like lobster claws appear in spring and early summer. Height 4 m (13 ft).

Convallaria majalis (lily of the valley) Perennial that spreads by rhizomes. Pairs of dark green leaves and sprays of bell-shaped, fragrant, waxy white flowers appear in late spring. Height 20 cm (8 in).

Cordyline australis (New Zealand cabbage palm) Evergreen tree with long, lance-shaped pale green leaves and large panicles of creamy white flowers in summer. As the tree matures the lower leaves fall off, leaving a bare trunk. Height 10 m (33 ft).

Cornus alba (dogwood) Deciduous shrub with red winter shoots and mid green leaves. Small white flowers in late spring are followed by white fruit with a touch of blue. Height 3 m (10 ft).

Correa backhouseana (Australian fuchsia) Evergreen shrub with dark green leaves that have hairy undersides. Tubular pink-red or cream flowers are produced from early winter until late spring. Height 2 m (6 ft 6 in).

Corylus avellana (hazel) Deciduous shrub with mid green leaves and yellow catkins in late winter and early spring. Height 4 m (13 ft).

Cotinus 'Grace' (smoke bush) Deciduous shrub with purple leaves turning bright, translucent red in autumn. Height 5 m (16 ft).

Cotoneaster Genus of shrubs valued for their bright red berries in late summer and autumn. **C. frigidus** 'Cornubia' is semi-evergreen with dark green leaves and white flowers. Height 6 m (20 ft). **C. lacteus** is evergreen and its dark green leaves are off-white on the underside. It makes an ideal informal hedge. Height 4 m (13 ft).

Crataegus (hawthorn) Deciduous trees with glossy dark green leaves and fragrant flowers, generally white with pink anthers, in spring, followed by dark red fruit. **C. monogyna** is commonly grown as a field hedge as its thorns deter animals. Height 10 m

(33 ft). For a change, try a red-flowering variety such as **C. laevigata** 'Paul's Scarlet'. Height 5 m (16 ft).

Crinodendron hookerianum (lantern tree) Evergreen shrub that prefers an acid soil. Lantern-shaped, deep pink or scarlet flowers appear from late spring through summer. As it is not totally hardy, the young growths are often damaged by late spring frosts. Height 6 m (20 ft).

x *Cupressocyparis leylandii* 'Castlewellan' (golden Leyland) Fast-growing evergreen conifer with bright yellow foliage, used for formal or informal hedging. Will quickly reach 25 m (80 ft) if you let it.

Cyclamen coum Tuberous perennial with leaves that are either plain deep green or have silver markings. Small white, pink or red flowers appear in winter, at the same time as the foliage. Height 5 cm (2 in).

Cytisus (broom) Genus of deciduous, semi-evergreen or evergreen shrubs that should be pruned immediately after flowering. Depending on the species, flowering may take place any time from early spring to autumn. **C. battandieri** (pineapple broom) is semi-evergreen with silver-grey leaves and pineapple-scented, clear yellow flowers in mid to late summer. Height 4 m (13 ft). **C. 'Lena'** is deciduous and its yellow flowers have bright red 'wings'. Height 1.8 m (6 ft).

Dactylorhiza fuchsii (common spotted orchid) Deciduous meadow or woodland orchid with purple-spotted leaves. White, pale pink or mauve flowers with deep red markings bloom in late spring and early summer. Height 45 cm (18 in).

Daphne Deservedly popular genus of sweet-scented flowering shrubs, a number of which bloom in winter

and very early spring, adding much needed cheer to the garden. **D. laureola** (spurge laurel) is an evergreen shrub with shiny, dark green, leathery leaves. Clusters of yellow-green flowers appear in late winter and spring, followed by black fruit. Height 90cm (36in). **D. mezereum** is a very fragrant deciduous species that flowers in mid to late winter before the leaves appear. Height 1.2 m (4 ft).

Delphinium 'Butterball' Herbaceous perennial with mid green leaves and semi-double off-white flowers with a deep yellow centre. Flowers are produced in early summer. Height 1.5 m (5 ft).

Desfontainia spinosa Evergreen shrub with glossy, dark green, spiny leaves. Tubular red flowers with yellow tips appear in summer and autumn. Height 2 m (6ft 6 in).

Deutzia x hybrida 'Mont Rose' Deciduous, summer-flowering shrub with dark green leaves and star-like deep pink flowers with yellow stamens. Height 1.2 m (4 ft).

Dianthus gratianopolitanus (cheddar pink) Evergreen perennial with grey-green leaves that produces single, deep pink, fragrant flowers in summer. Height 15 cm (6 in).

Diascia rigescens Herbaceous perennial with small, heart-shaped leaves. Tall spikes of deep pink flowers are produced in summer and will flower continuously if you remove dead flower heads. Diascias are not totally hardy in cold areas. Height 30 cm (12 in).

Dicentra formosa (wild bleeding heart) Deciduous perennial with mid green basal leaves and long arching stems of pink flowers in late spring and early summer. Height 45 cm (18 in).

Digitalis (foxglove) Genus of biennials or short-lived, summer-flowering perennials. **D. purpurea**

Choisya ternata

Cotoneaster frigidus 'Cornubia'

Crinodendron hookerianum

Delphinium 'Butterball'

Diascia rigescens

Digitalis purpurea

Elaeagnus pungens 'Maculata'

Eryngium giganteum

Escallonia 'Iveyi'

Fabiana imbricata f. violacea

has dark green leaves and tall one-sided spikes of white, pink or purple flowers speckled purple on the inside. Height 1-1.8 m (3-6 ft) **D. purpurea Excelsior Group** make a great show with their mid green leaves and tall spikes of yellow, white, pink or purple flowers arranged all round each stem. Deadhead after flowering, removing the whole stem to prevent the plant seeding all over the place. Height 2 m (6 ft 6 in), spread 60 cm (24 in).

Disanthus cercidifolius Deciduous shrub with blue-green leaves which turn purple, red, orange and yellow in late autumn. Fragrant red flowers appear in autumn. Height 3 m (10 ft).

Drimys lanceolata (mountain pepper) Evergreen shrub with aromatic, glossy, dark green leaves, with red shoots and white flowers in late spring. Makes a good informal barrier hedge. Height 4 m (13 ft).

Echium Genus that includes perennials with enormous spikes of flowers in late spring and summer. **E. pininana** is short-lived with large rough, hairy, silver-green leaves. Its stems of tiny powder-blue flowers can tower up to 5 m (16 ft). **E. wildpretii** has a rosette of light green leaves and a tall column of funnel-shaped red flowers. Height 2 m (6 ft 6 in).

Elaeagnus Genus including autumn-flowering evergreen shrubs, some with variegated foliage. They are good plants for maritime sites. **E. x ebbengii 'Limelight'** has silvery young leaves which turn golden yellow. Its flowers are pale green and creamy white and it makes a good informal hedge. Height 3 m (10 ft). **E. pungens 'Maculata'** has shiny dark green leaves marked with yellow in the centres, plus small white flowers. Height 4 m (13 ft).

Enkianthus cernuus f. rubens Deciduous shrub with bright green leaves turning purple-red in the autumn. Red bell-shaped flowers hang in clusters in late spring and early summer. Height 3 m (10 ft).

Erica (heather) Genus of evergreens from low-growing ground cover to large shrubs, with attractive foliage and bell-shaped flowers. **E. carnea 'Vivellii'** has deep magenta flowers and bronze foliage. **E. c. 'Springwood White'** trails over the ground with pure white flowers. Height 15 cm (6 in). **E. cinerea 'Fiddler's Gold'** flowers in late summer and autumn with golden-yellow foliage that deepens to red in winter. Height 25 cm (10 in). **E. vagans 'Mrs D. F. Maxwell'** has deep rose-pink flowers in autumn. Height 30 cm (12 in).

Eryngium bourgatii Herbaceous summer-flowering perennial with silver-veined, dark green basal leaves and blue stems. The blue flowers have silver-blue outer bracts. Height 45 cm (18 in).

Escallonia Genus of free-flowering, mainly evergreen shrubs with glossy, dark green leaves. **E. 'Iveyi'** has panicles of fragrant, pure white flowers in mid summer. Height 3 m (10 ft). **E. 'Pride of Donard'** has short sprays of bright red flowers in summer. Height 2 m (6 ft 6 in). **E. rubra var. macrantha** produces tubular bright red flowers in summer and early autumn. Height 3 m (10 ft).

Eucalyptus Genus of evergreen trees that quickly become large. They all have aromatic leaves and many varieties have glaucous blue foliage and patchwork bark. **E. gunnii** (cider gum) Fast-growing tree that sheds its pale green bark. The juvenile leaves are blue-green and rounded, the mature foliage elliptical or lance shaped and grey-green. Has small white flowers in summer. Height 25 m (80 ft).

Eucryphia x nymansensis 'Nymansay' Columnar evergreen tree with toothed leaves and cup-shaped white flowers in late summer and autumn. Height 15 m (50 ft).

Euonymus (spindle trees) Genus of both deciduous and evergreen shrubs. Deciduous species are grown for autumn colour; evergreens for year-round interest. **E. alatus** (winged spindle) is a deciduous shrub with dark green leaves that turn a brilliant red in autumn. The shoots have corky 'wings' and the fruits are purple. Height 2 m (6 ft 6 in). **E. europaeus 'Red Cascade'** is another deciduous shrub with red autumn foliage and fleshy red fruits that open to show the orange seeds. Height 3 m (10 ft). **E. fortunei 'Emerald Gaiety'** is a bushy evergreen with shiny bright green leaves and pure white margins that take on a pink tinge in winter. Height 90 cm (36 in). **E. f. 'Silver Queen'** is an evergreen with white-margined, dark green leaves, the white turning pink in winter, and small white fruit. Height 5 m (16 ft) as a climber.

Euphorbia Vast genus including evergreen shrubs and perennials with curious 'flowers' that are really cup-shaped bracts or leaves. **E. characias subsp. wulfenii** is a shrub with grey-green leaves and large clusters of yellow-green flowers in late spring and summer. Height 1 m (40 in). **E. myrsinites** is a perennial with succulent blue-green leaves and bright greenish-yellow flowers in spring. Height 10 cm (4 in).

Exochorda x macrantha 'The Bride' (pearl bush) Deciduous shrub with mid green leaves and white flowers in late spring and early summer. Height 2 m (6 ft 6 in).

Fabiana imbricata f. violacea Evergreen shrub with small, dark green, needle-like leaves and lavender-mauve flowers in early summer. Height 1 m (40 in).

Fagus sylvatica (beech) Large deciduous tree, which when kept clipped as a hedge holds its dead leaves throughout the winter. Tree height 30 m (100 ft).

Fascicularia bicolor subsp. *bicolor* Bromeliad with mid green leaves edged with spines. In temperate climates it is best grown in a conservatory. In summer the inner rosette of leaves turns brilliant red, forming a ring around the blue flowers. Height 80 cm (32 in).

Fatsia japonica Spreading evergreen shrub with large, deeply lobed, leathery, shiny green leaves. The umbels of creamy white flowers are produced in the autumn, followed by small black fruit. The cultivar *F. j.* 'Marginata' has creamy white edges to the leaves. Height 3 m (10 ft).

Ficus carica (common fig) Deciduous shrub with large, rounded and deeply lobed leaves. The green fruits ripen to dark green or brown and are the edible figs. Grows to a rounded plant 3 m (10 ft) high.

Forsythia Genus of deciduous shrubs with yellow flowers in spring. *F. x intermedia* 'Karl Sax' has mid green leaves that turn purple in autumn; it flowers in late winter and early spring. Height 2 m (6 ft 6 in). *F. x i.* 'Lynwood' has deep yellow flowers that appear in early spring before the foliage. Height 2.5 m (8 ft).

Fothergilla major Deciduous shrub with glossy dark green leaves that turn brilliant yellow, orange and red in autumn. It has fragrant white flowers in spring. Height 3 m (10 ft).

Freesia Perennial grown from a corm with long mid green leaves and yellow flowers in summer. Plants are generally not fully hardy. Height 45 cm (18 in).

Fremontodendron Genus of shrubs with saucer-shaped yellow flowers produced from late spring until autumn. *F. californicum* can be evergreen or semi-evergreen with dark green leaves. Height 8 m (25 ft). *F. mexicanum* is evergreen and its flowers are tinged red on the outside. It does best on a sunny, sheltered wall. Height 6 m (20 ft).

Fuchsia see page 176.

Galanthus nivalis (snowdrop) Bulbous winter-flowering perennial with narrow glaucous leaves and small white flowers with a green mark on each of the inner petals. The flowers smell of honey. Height 10 cm (4 in).

Gaultheria shallon Evergreen shrub with glossy dark green leaves. Urn-shaped small pink-white flowers in late spring and early summer are followed by purple fruit. The plant spreads by suckers. Height 1.2 m (4 ft).

Geranium Genus of useful hardy perennials for sun and shade. The young leaves of *G.* 'Ann Folkard' are pale green, ageing to a deep green. During summer and autumn large magenta flowers are borne in profusion, each bloom with a black centre and attractive deep purple veins. It will spread quickly in most soils but will not succeed in waterlogged ground. Height 60 cm (24 in), spread 90 cm (36 in). *G. endressii* has light green evergreen leaves that make a good backdrop to the icing-sugar pink flowers during summer and early autumn. The flowers deepen to dark pink as they age and should be removed after flowering. Height 45 cm (18 in). *G. macrorrhizum* is an evergreen with pink or white flowers in early summer. It will grow in shade. Height 45 cm (18 in). *G. pratense* (meadow cranesbill) has white, blue or purple flowers in early summer. Height 60 cm (24 in).

Geum 'Mrs. J. Bradshaw' Perennial with wrinkled mid green leaves and semi-double scarlet flowers in summer. Height 60 cm (24 in).

Gleditsia triacanthos 'Sunburst' Deciduous tree with golden spring foliage, becoming pale green in summer and deep yellow again in autumn. Young trees are subject to frost damage which burns the foliage. This variety doesn't produce seed pods. Height 11 m (36 ft).

Grevillea 'Canberra Gem' Evergreen shrub with spiky, pine-like green leaves and pink-red waxy flowers in early spring and again at later periods in the season. Plants are not fully hardy and require a sheltered site. Height 2 m (6 ft 6 in).

Griselinia littoralis Evergreen shrub with leathery, glossy, bright green leaves. Ideal for a formal or informal hedge in mild areas. Height 7 m (23 ft).

Gunnera manicata Perennial with enormous leaves – up to 2 m (6 ft 6 in) across. The leaves are deeply lobed and held on 2.5 m (8 ft) long prickly stems. Height 2m (6 ft 6 in).

Gypsophila paniculata (baby's breath) Deciduous perennial with narrow glaucous leaves and long-stemmed sprays of small white flowers in summer. Height 1 m (40 in).

Hamamelis mollis (Chinese witch hazel) Deciduous shrub with hairy mid green leaves that turn yellow in autumn. Fragrant golden yellow flowers appear before the foliage in mid and late winter. Height 4 m (13 ft).

Hebe Genus of evergreen shrubs of varying sizes, with characteristic spikes of flowers. *H. x franciscana* 'Variegata' has dull green leaves edged with creamy white and purple flowers in summer and autumn. Height 90 cm (36 in). *H.* 'Amy' (formerly known as *H.* 'Purple Queen') has dark green leaves that

Fascicularia bicolor subsp. *bicolor*

Ficus carica

Forsythia intermedia 'Karl Sax'

Fremontodendron californicum

Geranium pratense meadow cranesbill

Hedera canariensis
‘Gloire de Marengo’

Hibiscus syriacus
‘Oiseau Bleu’

Hippophae rhamnoides

Kalmia latifolia

Kniphofia
‘Bees Sunset’

are purple when young and bronze-purple in winter. Carries spikes of violet-purple flowers in late summer. Height 1.5 m (5 ft).

Hedera (ivy) Evergreen climbers with a range of different foliage. *H. canariensis* **‘Gloire de Marengo’** (Canary Island ivy) has light green leaves variegated white. Height 5 m (16 ft). *H. colchica* **‘Dentata Variegata’** (Persian ivy) has light green leaves with grey-green mottling and creamy white margins. It is useful for ground cover and grows well on a shady wall. Height 5 m (16 ft).

Hedychium densiflorum (ginger lily) Exotic perennial with glossy mid green leaves and fragrant yellow or orange flowers in late summer. Height 5 m (16 ft).

Helenium **‘Moerheim Beauty’** Deciduous perennial with mid green leaves and dark copper-red flowers with dark brown centres in summer. Height 90 cm (36 in).

Helianthemum (rock rose) Evergreen shrubs for sunny sites. *H. apenninum* (sun rose) is mat-forming and flowers from spring to mid summer in shades of white, pink, yellow and red. Clip over after flowering to keep the plant compact. Height 30 cm (12 in). *H.* **‘Raspberry Ripple’** has grey-green leaves. Its white flowers have deep pink centres, the colour spreading out to the edge of the petals. Height 20 cm (8 in).

Hibiscus syriacus **‘Oiseau Bleu’** Deciduous shrub with dark green leaves. Bright blue, trumpet-shaped flowers with red centres are produced in late summer and autumn. Height 3 m (10 ft).

Hippophae rhamnoides (sea buckthorn) Deciduous tree or large shrub with spiny shoots and grey green leaves. On female plants, the pale green spring flowers are followed by bright orange fruit. Height 7 m (23 ft).

Hosta Genus of summer-flowering herbaceous perennials for shady spots. Keep a close watch for snails and slugs which can destroy a plant in a couple of evenings. *H.* **‘Big Daddy’** has heart shaped, grey-blue, puckered leaves and white flowers in early summer. Height 60 cm (24 in). *H.* **‘Wide Brim’** is clump-forming with glaucous, dark green, puckered leaves and lavender-blue flowers. Height 45 cm (18 in).

Houttuynia cordata **Variegata Group** Perennial with red, green and yellow variegated leaves and white flowers. Plants will grow in full sun or light shade but like a moist soil. Height 30 cm (12 in).

Hyacinthoides non-scripta (English bluebell) Bulbous perennial with glossy dark green leaves and bell-shaped, scented, blue or white flowers in spring. Height 30 cm (12 in).

Hydrangea Genus of late-flowering shrubs and climbers. *H. macrophylla* is the species from which two cultivar groups were developed. Lacecaps have flattened heads of small fertile flowers surrounded by larger sterile flowers, while hortensia (mopheads) have spherical flowerheads of large sterile flowers. Height 2 m (6 ft 6 in). *H. anomala* **subsp. *petiolaris*** is a climber with dark green leaves that turn yellow in autumn. It produces white flowers in summer and in the northern hemisphere will grow well on a north-facing wall. Height 15 m (50 ft).

Iberis semperflorens (candytuft) Evergreen sub-shrub with dark green leaves and white flowers in late spring and early summer. For best results, grow in full sun and clip lightly after flowering to stop the plant becoming straggly. Height 30 cm (12 in).

Ilex aquifolium (common holly) Evergreen shrub or tree with glossy, dark green, spiny leaves and red berries in late autumn and winter.

Makes ideal formal or informal hedging. Height 25 m (80 ft).

Illicium anisatum Evergreen shrub or small tree with glossy leaves and fragrant, creamy white, star-shaped flowers in spring. Height 7 m (23 ft).

Indigofera amblyantha Deciduous shrub with bright green leaves and upright clusters of small pink flowers in summer and early autumn. Height 2 m (6 ft 6 in).

Iris pseudacorus (yellow flag) Vigorous perennial with long grey-green leaves and yellow flowers with brown or purple markings in late summer. Height 1 m (40 in).

Jasminum officinale f. *affine* (jasmine) Deciduous climber with mid green leaves and clusters of fragrant, pink-tinged white flowers in summer and early autumn. Height 10 m (33 ft).

Juniperus (juniper) Slow-growing conifers, including dwarf forms. *J. chinensis* **‘Kuriwao Gold’** enjoys a light sandy soil in full sun. It forms a rounded plant with bright yellow leaves. Height 2 m (6 ft 6 in). *J. communis* **‘Compressa’** is a dwarf form with small, sharp-pointed, deep green leaves. Height 90 cm (36 in). *J. procumbens* is mat forming with yellow-green needle-like leaves. Height 75 cm (30 in), spread 2 m (6 ft 6 in).

Kalmia latifolia (calico bush) Evergreen shrub with shiny, dark green leaves and white, pale pink or deep pink bowl-shaped flowers in late spring and early summer. The flower buds are crimped like icing-sugar decorations. Height 3 m (10 ft).

Kirengeshoma palmata Clump-forming perennial with purple stems and pale green leaves. Tubular pale yellow flowers appear in late summer and autumn. Height 1 m (40 in).

Kniphofia (red hot poker) Deciduous perennials with long, strap-like leaves and tall flower spikes. **K. 'Bees' Sunset'** has interesting orange-yellow flowers in summer. It flowers best if it is not disturbed and is grown in a rich, well-drained, sandy soil. Height 90 cm (36 in), spread 60 cm (24 in). **K. 'Wrexham Buttercup'** has bright yellow flowers in summer. Height 1. 2 m (4 ft).

Kolkwitzia amabilis 'Pink Cloud' (beauty bush) Deciduous shrub with dark green leaves. Bell-shaped pink flowers with a yellow throat appear in late spring and early summer. Height 3 m (10 ft).

Laburnum x watereri 'Vossii' (golden rain) Deciduous tree with dark green leaves and full hanging clusters of golden yellow flowers that are up to 60 cm (24 in) long. It flowers in late spring and early summer. Height 8 m (26 ft).

Lamium maculatum Evergreen perennial that spreads like wildfire and is. excellent for ground cover in deep shade. The heart-shaped leaves are often blotched with silver or pink and in summer the flowers can be purple, pink or sometimes white. Height 20 cm (8 in).

Lapageria rosea (Chilean bell flower) Evergreen climber with dark green leaves and bell-shaped, fleshy, deep pink flowers in summer and late autumn. In temperate climates, these plants prefer a cool conservatory. Height 5 m (16 ft).

Lathyrus latifolius (everlasting pea) Herbaceous perennial climber with blue-green foliage and sprays of pink or purple flowers in summer and autumn. Height 2 m (6 ft 6 in).

Lathyrus odoratus (sweet pea) See page 169.

Lavandula (lavender) Evergreen shrubs with aromatic leaves and fragrant flowers. **L. angustifolia** (English lavender) has grey-green leaves and spikes of deep purple flowers in late summer. Height 90 cm

(36 in). **L. a. 'Hidcote'** has silvery grey leaves and dark purple flowers in summer. Height 60 cm (24 in). **L. stoechas** (French lavender) has dark purple flowers with tufted paler bracts in late spring and summer. Height 60 cm (24 in).

Ledum groenlandicum (Labrador tea) Evergreen shrub with dark green leaves that are felted brown beneath and white flowers in late spring. Height 90 cm (36 in).

Leptospermum scoparium (New Zealand tea tree) Evergreen shrub with aromatic leaves and white or pink-tinged flowers in late spring and early summer. Height 3 m (10 ft).

Lespedeza thunbergii Deciduous sub-shrub with blue-green leaves on long arching shoots producing terminal clusters of purple-pink flowers in late autumn. Height 2 m (6 ft 6 in).

Leucanthemum vulgare (ox-eye daisy) Perennial with dark green leaves and white daisy-like flowers with yellow centres in late spring and early summer. Height 60 cm (24 in).

Ligustrum vulgare (privet) Semi-evergreen shrub with dark green leaves and panicles of scented white flowers in summer. Height 3 m (10 ft).

Limonium platyphyllum 'Violetta' (sea lavender) Deciduous perennial with dark green leaves up to 60 cm (24 in) long and spikes of deep violet flowers in late summer. Height 60 cm (24 in).

Linum narbonense Herbaceous perennial with mid green leaves and bright blue flowers with white centres in early and mid summer. The flowers are short-lived and fade on the day that they open. Height 45 cm (18 in).

Liquidambar styraciflua (sweet gum) Deciduous tree with light green leaves that turn orange and red in autumn. Height 20 m (65 ft).

Lithodora diffusa 'Heavenly Blue' Evergreen shrub with dark green leaves and deep blue flowers in late spring and early summer. Height 20 cm (8 in).

Lonicera sempervirens (trumpet honeysuckle) Evergreen climber with dark green leaves, blue-green on the underside. Tubular flowers are produced in summer and autumn: they are scarlet on the outside and yellow on the inside and are followed by red berries. Height 4 m (13 ft).

Lupinus (lupin) Herbaceous perennials and shrubs with upright flower spikes in summer. Lupins are easy to grow, but form large fleshy roots that don't like being moved. They suffer from attacks of greenfly, mildew and slugs. **L. arboreus** (tree lupin) is an evergreen or semi-evergreen shrub with grey-green leaves and fragrant yellow or occasionally pale blue flowers. Height 2 m (6 ft 6 in). **L. 'Chandelier'** has mid green palmate leaves that hold the raindrops and bright yellow flowers. Removing the old flower heads before seed pods form will encourage a second flush of flowers. Height and spread 90 cm (36 in).

Magnolia Genus of shrubs and trees. Those listed are deciduous and spring-flowering. **M. x soulangeana** can be a shrub or a small tree with dark green leaves and large goblet-shaped pink, purple or white flowers that appear both before and at the same time as the foliage. Height 6 m (20 ft). **M. x soulangeana 'Lennei'** gets away with being called a tree, though it grows more like a shrub. It is open branched with dark purple goblet-shaped flowers that are ivory white on the inside. Height 8 m (26 ft). **M. stellata** is a shrub with mid green leaves and silky flower buds that open to pure white or white tinged with pink. Height 3 m (10 ft).

Malus (crab apple) Small deciduous trees with spring blossom, autumn

Lapageria rosea

Lespedeza thunbergii

Liquidambar styraciflua

Magnolia x soulangeana

Malus 'Royalty'

Mandevilla laxa

Nyssa sinensis

Olearia macrodonta

Paeonia
cambessedesii

Phlox stolonifera
'Home Fires'

foliage and edible fruits. **M. 'Royalty'** is one of the best crabs. Its dark purple leaves turn red in autumn. In late spring it covers itself in deep crimson blossom, followed by small dark red fruit. Height 10 m (33 ft). **M. floribunda** (Japanese crab apple) has dark foliage and red buds that open to pale pink flowers in late spring, followed by small yellow fruit. Height 8 m (26 ft). **M. tschonoskii** has glossy mid green leaves that turn purple, red and orange. Its pink-flushed white flowers are followed by red fruit tinged with yellow and green. Height 8 m (26 ft).

Mandevilla laxa (Chilean jasmine) Deciduous climber with dark green leaves and tubular, very fragrant white flowers in summer and early autumn. Plants require a sheltered wall to survive. Height 3 m (10 ft).

Meconopsis grandis (Himalayan blue poppy) see page 173.

Monarda 'Cambridge Scarlet' (bergamot) Herbaceous perennial with purple-green leaves and scarlet flowers with deep red calyces in late summer and early autumn Height 90 cm (36 in).

Myosotidium hortensia (Chatham Island forget-me-not) Evergreen perennial with glossy, ribbed, bright green leaves and large clusters of mid blue flowers in early summer. Height 60 cm (24 in).

Myrtus communis (common myrtle) Evergreen shrub with dark green aromatic leaves. The white flowers with prominent white stamens are produced in late summer and early autumn. Height 3 m (10 ft).

Nandina domestica (heavenly bamboo) Evergreen shrub with bright green leaves that are reddish-purple when young and turn back to the same shade in winter. Panicles of white flowers with yellow anthers in mid summer are

followed by red fruit. Height 2 m (6 ft 6 in).

Neillia thibetica Deciduous shrub with bright green leaves and arching sprays of bell-shaped, bright pink flowers in early summer. Height 2 m (6 ft 6 in).

Nepeta x faassenii (catmint) Perennial with aromatic, silver-green, wrinkled leaves and spikes of mid blue flowers with purple spots in summer and early autumn. Height 45 cm (18 in).

Nyssa sinensis (Chinese tupelo) Deciduous tree with bronze leaves turning deep green and then orange, yellow and red in the autumn. Height 8 m (26 ft).

Olearia macrodonta Evergreen shrub with holly-like, glossy, dark green leaves that are white felted on the underside. Fragrant white daisy-like flowers with red-brown centres are borne in summer. Height 6 m (20 ft).

Osmanthus delavayi Evergreen shrub with leathery, dark green leaves and tubular, fragrant white flowers in spring. Height 4 m (13 ft).

Othonna cheirifolia Evergreen shrub with fleshy, pale green leaves and yellow daisy-like flowers in summer. Height 30 cm (12 in).

Pachysandra terminalis Evergreen perennial with shiny, dark green leaves and small white flowers in early summer. Height 20 cm (8 in).

Paeonia (peony) Genus of herbaceous perennials with large single or double flowers in early summer. Watch out for slugs eating the stems. **P. lactiflora 'Bowl of Beauty'** has mid green leaves and semi-double, pink-red flowers with creamy white centres. Height 90 cm (36 in). **P. cambessedesii** has dark green leaves with purple veins and purple under-sides. Its bowl-shaped flowers are deep pink with yellow stamens and red filaments. Height 45 cm (18 in).

Papaver orientale see page 173.

Parrotia persica (Persian ironwood) Brilliant tree for autumn colour, with glossy green leaves that flush yellow, orange and purple. The flowers are red, appearing in tiny clusters in late winter before the leaves. Height 7 m (23 ft).

Parthenocissus henryana (Virginia creeper) Deciduous climber with dark green leaves veined with white. The leaves turn red in autumn. Height 12 m (40 ft).

Paulownia tomentosa (foxglove tree) Deciduous tree with large bright green leaves and panicles of fragrant lilac flowers marked with purple and yellow on the inside. The fawn felt-like buds develop in the autumn and overwinter, opening in late spring. Height 10 m (33 ft).

Perovskia (Russian sage) Sub-shrubs with grey-white shoots and grey-green aromatic leaves. **P. atriplicifolia** has spires of small violet-blue flowers in summer and early autumn. Height 1.2 m (4 ft). **P. 'Blue Spire'** is deciduous and has violet-blue flowers in late summer and autumn. Height 1.2 m (4 ft).

Persicaria bistorta 'Superba' Evergreen perennial with dark green leaves turning red-bronze in autumn. Flowering from summer to autumn, the spikes of rose-red flowers fade to pink and finally become brown in winter. Height 25 cm (10 in).

Philadelphus (mock orange) Genus of deciduous shrubs with dark green leaves and very fragrant flowers. **P. 'Belle Etoile'** has single, cup-shaped white flowers with purple markings in the centre in late spring and early summer. Height 1.2 m (4 ft). **P. 'Virginal'** has double white flowers in midsummer. Height 3 m (10 ft).

Phlomis fruticosa (Jerusalem sage) Evergreen shrub with grey-green leaves and mustard-yellow flowers in early summer. Height 90 cm (36 in).

Phlox Genus of colourful perennial and annual flowering plants. The two listed are perennials. *P. stolonifera* (creeping phlox) has dark green leaves and pale to deep purple flowers in early summer. Height 10 cm (4 in). *P. subulata* is evergreen, flowering in late spring and early summer in shades of white, pink, purple and red. Height 15 cm (6 in).

Phormium tenax (New Zealand flax) Perennial with stiff upright leaves up to 3 m (10 ft) long, dark green on the upper surface and blue-green on the underside. Panicles of red-brown flowers are carried on 4 m (13 ft) stems in summer.

Picea glauca var. albertiana 'Conica' Slow-growing conifer, cone-shaped with pale green foliage. Eventual height 5 m (16 ft).

Pieris Genus of evergreen shrubs that flower in late winter and spring. **P. 'Forest Flame'** has shiny, dark green leaves that are brilliant red when young, turning pink and then green. Sprays of white flowers appear in spring. Height 2 m (6 ft 6 in). *P. japonica* has glossy mid green leaves and sprays of white flowers in late winter. Height 4 m (13 ft).

Pinus nigra (Austrian pine) Evergreen conifer with pairs of dark green leaves and 8 cm (3 in) long cones. Height 30 m (100 ft).

Pittosporum Evergreen shrubs and trees flowering in late spring and early summer, with scented flowers. **P. tenuifolium** forms a shrub or small tree with glossy, mid-green leaves with wavy margins. Small, honey-scented, dark red flowers are followed by black capsules. Height 10 m (33 ft). **P. tobira** (Japanese mock orange) has leathery, deep green leaves and creamy white, bell-shaped flowers, followed by brown capsules and red seed. Height 5 m (16 ft).

Polypodium vulgare (common polypody) Evergreen fern with leathery, dark green fronds. Height 30 cm (12 in).

Populus (poplar) Deciduous, fast-growing tall trees. **P. alba** (white poplar) has dark green leaves with white undersides, turning yellow in autumn. In spring the male catkins are red and the female catkins are green. Height 30 m (100 ft). **P. balsamifera** (balsam poplar) has balsam-scented buds and glossy dark green leaves that are pale green on the underside. The green catkins appear in early spring. Height 30 m (100 ft).

Potentilla fruticosa 'Elizabeth' Deciduous shrub with mid green leaves and bright yellow flowers in summer and early autumn. Height 90 cm (36 in).

Primula Perennial plants, spring and summer-flowering. Those listed are fragrant. *P. florindae* (giant cowslip) is deciduous with long mid green leaves and umbels of tubular, sulphur yellow flowers on long stems in summer. Height 90 cm (36 in). *P. veris* (cowslip) is deciduous with mid-green leaves and umbels of deep yellow flowers in spring. Height 30 cm (12 in). *P. vulgaris* (primrose) is evergreen with bright green leaves and pale yellow flowers in late winter and early spring. Height 20 cm (8 in)

Prostranthera cuneata. (alpine mint bush) Evergreen shrub with aromatic mid green leaves and white tubular flowers in spring. Height 60 cm (24 in).

Protea cynaroides (king protea) Evergreen shrub with grey-green leaves and deep red or pink bowl-shaped flowers. Height 1.5 m (5 ft).

Prunus (ornamental cherries and cherry laurels) Genus of trees that are covered with blossom in spring or summer. **P. 'Amanogawa'** has upright branches clothed in semi-double, fragrant, pale pink flowers in spring and good autumn leaf colour. The stiff branches resist wind damage, so that the blossom stays on the tree instead of becoming confetti just when the show is at its best. Height 4.5 m (15 ft). *P. laurocerasus* (laurel, cherry laurel) is an evergreen shrub with glossy, dark green leaves that are pale green on the underside. Fragrant white flowers in late spring are followed by red fruit that turns black. An ideal plant for formal or informal hedging. Height 8 m (25 ft). *P. sargentii* is deciduous. Its dark green leaves are red when young and turn bright red in early autumn. The flowers are pale pink and produced in spring. Height 15 m (50 ft). *P. spinosa* (blackthorn, sloe) forms a deciduous shrub or tree with spines and deep green leaves. White flowers appear before the leaves in early spring, followed by black, edible fruit. Height 5 m (16 ft). **P. x subhirtella 'Autumnalis'** will brighten your day in the dead of winter. It produces semi-double white flowers tinged with pink in mild weather from autumn through winter and on into spring. Height 8 m (26 ft).

Pseudopanax ferox Evergreen tree with long, thin, sharply pointed and toothed bronze-green leaves 45 cm (18 in) long. Panicles of green flowers are produced in late summer. Height 5 m (16 ft).

Pulmonaria saccharata (Jerusalem sage) Evergreen perennial with white-spotted, mid green leaves. It flowers in late winter and early spring with white, violet or red flowers with green calyces. Height 30 cm (12 in).

Pulsatilla vulgaris (pasque flower) Deciduous perennial with light green leaves and bell-shaped, silky, pale pink or purple flowers in spring. Height 20 cm (8 in).

Pyracantha Genus of evergreen shrubs with yellow, orange or red berries in autumn and winter and white flowers in spring. All species are thorny and grow well against a wall. Height up to 4.5 m (15 ft).

Pieris 'Forest Flame'

Potentilla fruticosa 'Elizabeth'

Primula veris

Protea cynaroides

Pyracantha 'Orange Glow'

Rodgersia pinnata
'Superba'

Romneya coulteri

Rudbekia fulgida

Sarcocca confusa

Skimmia confusa
'Kew Green'

Quercus rubra (red oak) Deciduous tree with dull dark green leaves that turn red, brown, yellow and orange in autumn. Height 30 m (100 ft).

Rheum palmatum **'Atrosanguineum'** (Chinese rhubarb) Perennial with thick leaf-stalks and large crimson leaves emerging from red buds and ageing to dark green. Large panicles of deep pink flowers appear in early summer. Height 2. 5 m (8 ft).

Rhododendron see page 174.

Rhodotypos scandens Deciduous shrub that dislikes heavy shade. It has deep green, heavily veined leaves and produces white, four-petalled flowers in spring and early summer. The flowers are followed by shiny black berries. Height 1. 5 m (5 ft).

Rhus typhina **'Dissecta'** (stag's horn sumach) Deciduous shrub with velvety red shoots and dark green leaves turning orange-red in autumn, when it also produces crimson fruit. Height 3 m (10 ft).

Rodgersia pinnata **'Superba'** Clump-forming perennial with heavily veined, dark green leaves, tinted bronze when young. It produces tall plumes of pink flowers in late summer. Height 1. 2 m (4 ft).

Romneya coulteri (tree poppy) Deciduous sub-shrub that dislikes cold winds. It has glaucous grey-green leaves and large pure white, tissue-paper-like flowers with prominent orange-yellow stamens, which are produced all summer. Height 2 m (6 ft 6 in).

Rosa see page 163.

Rosmarinus officinalis (rosemary) Evergreen shrub with aromatic, narrow, dark green leaves and deep blue to white flowers, which are produced in late spring and early summer and again in autumn. Height 1. 2 m (4 ft).

Rudbeckia Perennials and annuals with daisy-like flowers. **R. fulgida** (black-eyed Susan) is a perennial with mid green, hairy leaves and orange-yellow flowerheads with dark brown centres in late summer and autumn. Height 90 cm (36 in). The dark green foliage of **R.f. var. sullivantii 'Goldsturm'** is a contrast to the large golden yellow flowers, each with a dark brown button-like centre. This is a perennial, flowers from midsummer until late autumn and likes a well-drained soil. Height and spread 60 cm (24 in).

Ruta graveolens **'Jackman's Blue'** (rue) Evergreen sub-shrub with aromatic, glaucous, blue-green foliage and yellow flowers in summer. Height 90 cm (36 in).

Sambucus (elder) Deciduous shrubs or trees producing autumn berries. **S. nigra 'Aureomarginata'** has yellow-edged, dark green leaves and musk-scented white flowers in early summers. Height 5 m (16 ft). **S. n. 'Guincho Purple'** (black elder or bour tree) has dark green leaves turning purple in late summer. Scented, pink-tinged flowers on purple stalks are produced in early summer. Height 3 m (10 ft).

Santolina Small evergreen aromatic shrubs that flowers in summer. **S. chamaecyparissus** (cotton lavender) has grey-green leaves and bright yellow flowers on thin stems. Height 60 cm (24 in). **S. rosmarinifolia** has bright green foliage and yellow flowers. Height 60 cm (24 in).

Sarcococca (sweet box) Evergreen shrubs with fragrant white flowers in winter, followed by black fruit. All have glossy green leaves. **S. confusa** is the tallest growing, reaching 2 m (6 ft 6 in). **S. hookeriana** spreads by suckering. Height 1. 5 m (5 ft). **S. h. var. humilis** is a dwarf, suckering shrub with pink-tinged flowers. Height 60 cm (24 in).

Skimmia Evergreen shrubs flowering in late spring. **S. x confusa 'Kew Green'** has mid green leaves and creamy white fragrant male flowers. Height 2 m (6 ft 6 in).

S. japonica **'Fructu Albo'** has dark green leaves and green flower buds followed by white fruit. Height 60 cm (24 in).

Sorbus Deciduous trees with autumn foliage and colourful berries. **S. aucuparia** (rowan, mountain ash) has dark green leaves that turn red or yellow in autumn. White flowers in late spring are followed by orange-red berries. Height 15 m (50 ft). **S. aria 'Lutescens'** (whitebeam) has silvery grey young foliage later turning grey-green. White flowers in spring are followed by dark red berries. Height 10 m (33 ft). **S. sargentiana** has sticky mahogany-coloured buds in winter, followed by large deep green, pinnate leaves that turn the most spectacular red and orange in autumn. The fruit hangs in large deep red clusters. Grows slowly, but will eventually reach 10 m (33 ft). The arching branches of **S. vilmorinii** are weighed down with dark red berries that turn pink and finally pure white. The small pinnate leaves don't colour up in autumn, but form a good backdrop for the fruit. Height 4.5 m (15 ft).

Spartium junceum (Spanish broom) Deciduous shrub with dark green shoots and leaves that have silky hairs on the undersides. The flowers are golden yellow, fragrant, pea-like and appear from early summer until late autumn. Height 3 m (10 ft).

Spiraea Spring- and summer-flowering deciduous shrubs with starry flowers. **S. 'Arguta'** (bridal wreath) has bright green leaves and white flowers in spring. Height 2 m (6 ft 6 in). **S. japonica 'Gold Flame'** has bronze and red young leaves, becoming yellow and finally green, plus deep pink flowers in summer. Height 90 cm (36 in).

Stachys byzantina (formerly known as *S. lanata*; lambs' ears) Perennial with white woolly leaves and woolly pink-purple flowers from summer to early autumn. Likes a well-drained soil in full sun. Forms a useful ground-covering mat. Height 45 cm (18 in) high, spread 60 cm (24 in).

Syringa (lilac) Deciduous shrubs or small trees with fragrant flowers in late spring and early summer. *S. vulgaris* has mid-green leaves and conical clusters of mauve flowers. There are many named varieties producing single and double flowers in white, pink, blue, violet and mauve. Height 6 m (20 ft). *S. meyeri var. spontanea* **'Palibin'** forms a dense shrub with pale pink flowers. Height and spread 1.5 m (5 ft).

Tamarix ramosissima (tamarisk) Deciduous shrub with red stems and pale green leaves and sprays of pink flowers in late summer and early autumn. Height 4 m (13 ft).

Taxus baccata (yew) Evergreen conifer with dark green leaves and red fruit in autumn. Makes a good formal or informal hedge. Height 10 m (33 ft).

Thuja (cedar) Evergreen conifers. ***T. occidentalis*** (white cedar) has apple-scented pale green leaves and orange-brown bark. Height 15 m (50 ft). The cultivar **'Rheingold'** is slow-growing, eventually reaching 2 m (6 ft 6 in) with a conical shape and pale green foliage. ***T. plicata*** (western red cedar) has mid to dark green leaves that are pale green on the underside. It is useful for formal or informal hedging. Height 20–30 m (65–100 ft).

Thymus (thyme) Evergreen sub-shrubs and herbs with aromatic leaves that do best in full sun. ***T. x citriodorus* 'Bertram Anderson'** has lemon-scented, grey-green and yellow leaves and pale lavender-pink flowers in summer. Height 30 cm (12 in).

T. vulgaris has grey-green leaves and purple or white flowers in spring and early summer. Height 30 cm (12 in).

Tolmiea menziesii (pick-a-back plant) Herbaceous perennial with pale green leaves with prominent veins. Unusually, young plants are formed on the leaves, where the leaf and stalk meet. In late spring and early summer the plant produces scented flowers with green sepals and deep purple petals. Height 45 cm (18 in).

Trachelospermum jasminoides (star jasmine) Evergreen climber with shiny dark green leaves turning red in winter. Fragrant white flowers are produced in late summer. Height 10 m (33 ft).

***Tropaeolum majus* Gleam Hybrids** (nasturtium) Trailing annuals with mid green leaves and semi-double orange, yellow and red flowers in summer and autumn. Height 45 cm (18 in).

***Ulex europaeus* 'Flore Pleno'** (gorse, whin, furze) Evergreen shrub with spine-tipped shoots and dark green leaves. The bright yellow double flowers are coconut scented and are in flower for most of the year. This variety doesn't set seed so, unlike the common gorse, it won't spread far and wide. Height 2 m (6 ft 6 in).

Umbellularia californica (headache tree) Evergreen tree with aromatic mid green leaves and pale yellow flowers in winter and spring. The crushed leaves can sometimes cause nausea and headaches. Height 15 m (50 ft).

***Verbascum chaixii* 'Album'** (nettle-leaved mullein) Semi-evergreen perennial with mid green basal leaves and tall spikes of white flowers with mauve centres in late summer. Height 90 cm (36 in.)

Viburnum Easy-to-grow shrubs with white flowers. ***V. carlcephalum*** is deciduous with dark green leaves turning red in the autumn and

fragrant flowers opening from pink buds in late spring. Height 3 m (10 ft). ***V. tinus*** (laurustinus) is evergreen, with dark green leaves. It flowers in late winter and spring, followed by blue-black fruit. Height 3 m (10 ft).

Vinca (periwinkle) Trailing plants for ground cover. These two species are evergreen and are great in dry shade under trees. *V. major* **'Variegata'** has mid green leaves edged with creamy white. Deep blue flowers appear from late spring until autumn. Height 45 cm (18 in). ***V. minor* 'Azurea Flore Pleno'** (lesser periwinkle) has dark green leaves and double, sky blue flowers in spring, summer and autumn. Height 10 cm (4 in).

Viola Large genus of small flowering plants that includes a number of species of perennial violets. ***V. cornuta*** (horned violet) is evergreen with pale green leaves and fragrant violet blue and white flowers during spring and summer. Height 15 cm (6 in). ***V. labradorica*** (Labrador violet) is semi-evergreen. Its dark green leaves are bronze when young and it has pale purple flowers in spring and summer. Height 8 cm (3 in).

Weigela Deciduous shrubs in a range of cultivars with green, bronze or variegated foliage and summer flowers in yellow, pink, cerise, red and purple. Height 1.5–3 m (6–10 ft).

Yucca gloriosa (Spanish dagger) Evergreen shrub with stiff, pointed, blue-green leaves and panicles of bell-shaped creamy white flowers in late summer and autumn. The leaves of *Y. g.* **'Variegata'** have yellow margins and its flowers, which appear in autumn, are sometimes purple tinged. Height 2 m (6 ft 6 in).

Zantedeschia aethiopica (arum lily) Perennial with bright green leaves. Its flowers are large white spathes with creamy yellow spadices, produced in late spring and early summer. Height 90 cm (36 in).

Tamarix ramosissima

Tolmiea menziesii

Viburnum carlcephalum

Vinca major 'Variegata'

Zantedeschia aethiopica

index

Acknowledgements

The publishers would like to thank Charlie Ryrie for her contribution to the text and Steve Wooster for his glorious photography. Thanks also to Garden Picture Library, Unit 12, 35 Parkgate Road, London SW11 4NP, tel +44 (20) 7228 4332, fax +44 (20) 7924 3267 for their assistance, and to Chris Ellis of the Forest Lodge Garden Centre, Holt Pound, Surrey, for allowing us to take photographs there.

SW: Steven Wooster; GPL: Garden Picture Library; HA: Heather Angel; Holt: Holt Studios International Ltd

Page 1 GPL/Juliette Wade; 2/3 SW; 4 SW (Woodstock Garden, NZ); 5 SW (Bellevue Gardens, NZ, designed by Vivien Papich); 7 SW (Ian Fryer's garden, Christchurch, New Zealand); 8 GPL/John Glover; 9 SW (Forest Lodge); 10 Holt/Alan & Linda Detrick; 15 GPL/Michael Howes; 16 SW (design by Ton Ter Linden); 19 S & O Mathews; 20 GPL/Howard Rice; 23 SW (Old Vicarage, Norfolk); 27 Holt/Alan & Linda Detrick; 29 SW (Butterfly Conservation, Chelsea Flower Show 1998); 30 GPL/Jacqui Hurst; 34 Holt/Primrose Peacock; 38 SW (Saddlecombe); 39 GPL/Jerry Pavia; 41 SW (Bourton House Garden); 42/43 Heather Angel (Fisons Roof Top Garden, Chelsea Flower Show 1992, designed by Gillian Temple Associates); 44 SW; 47 SW (Bellevue Gardens, NZ, designed by Vivien Papich); 50 GPL/Clive Nichols; 51 GPL/Lamontagne; 52 GPL/Howard Rice; 53 David Beeson; 54 David Beeson (Longmead House); 55 GPL/Bob Challinor; 56 GPL/Neil Holmes; 59 GPL/Howard Rice; 60 GPL/Howard Rice; 62 top Holt/Nigel Cattlin; 62 bottom GPL/J S Sira; 63 top HA; 63 centre Holt/Len McLeod; 63 right HA; 63 bottom GPL/Christopher Fairweather; 64 left GPL/Sunniva Harte; 64 centre Holt/Nigel Cattlin; 64 right SW; 65 left HA; 65 centre GPL/Lamontagne; 65 right GPL/Vaughan Fleming; 66 top left GPL/Michael Howes; 66 bottom left GPL/Howard Rice; 66 centre GPL/Neil Holmes; 66 right GPL/Michael Howes; 67 left GPL/Michael Howes; 67 centre HA; 67 right Holt/Nigel Cattlin; 68 left Holt/Nigel Cattlin; 68 centre GPL/Mel Watson; 68 right GPL/Lamontagne; 69 SW (Groombridge Place); 71 GPL/J S Sira; 73 GPL/Brigitte Thomas; 74 GPL/Andrea Jones; 75 SW (The Old Vicarage, Norfolk); 76 SW (Mount Usher); 77 SW (Garrets garden, New Zealand); 78 SW (Turn End); 80 SW; 83 top Gill McAndrew; 83 bottom SW; 84 SW (Boardman garden); 86 SW (the garden of Camilla Ross, London); 87 GPL/John Glover; 89 SW (design: Piet Oudolf); 90 Marianne Majerus; 91 SW (Yazdi garden, Holland, designed by Piet Oudolf); 93 GPL/Howard Rice; 94 GPL/Howard Rice; 96/97 SW (Ian Fryer's garden, Christchurch, New Zealand); 98 GPL/Alec Scaresbrook; 99 GPL/Alec Scaresbrook; 100 SW (Pauline Thompson's garden); 102 SW (Kilmokea, Co Wexford, Ireland); 103 SW; 104 top GPL/Lynne Brotchie; 104 bottom GPL/J S Sira; 105 SW (Hyde/Bennett garden); 107 SW (Himeji Japanese garden, Adelaide, Australia); 108 GPL/Neil Holmes; 110 SW (Glenbervie); 112/113 SW; 115 SW (design: Rod Barnett); 116 SW (Little Court, Crawley, Hants); 117 GPL/Didier Willery; 118 GPL/Juliette Wade; 119 GPL/John Glover; 120 Holt/Primrose Peacock; 121 SW (Japanese garden in Auckland, NZ, designed by Ted Smyth); 122 GPL/J S Sira; 123 GPL/Brigitte Thomas; 124 GPL/John Glover; 125 SW (Thijssehof); 127 Marianne Majerus; 128 SW; 129 GPL/Neil Holmes; 130 GPL/Brian Carter; 131 GPL/Michael Howes; 132 GPL/Georgia Glynn-Smith; 133 GPL/J S Sira; 135 SW (designed by Antony Paul); 137 GPL/Steven Wooster; 138 SW (Old Vicarage, Norfolk); 139 SW (Congham Hall); 141 SW (Chelsea Flower Show, design by Rupert Golby); 142 GPL/Zara McCalmont; 143 SW (the garden of Ross and Paula Greenville, Mt Manganui, NZ); 144 SW (Diana Firth's garden, NZ); 145 SW (Knockcree, Co. Dublin); 146 HA; 147 SW (Saling Hall); 148 SW (Old Vicarage, Norfolk); 150 SW (Old Rectory, Sudborough); 151 SW (Steven Wooster's garden) 152 GPL/Christi Carter; 155 SW (Ballymaloe); 156 GPL/Ron Sutherland; 159 HA; 160 top GPL/John Glover; 160 centre GPL/Linda Burgess; 160 bottom GPL/Howard Rice; 162 GPL/J S Sira; 163 GPL/Ron Evans; 164 left GPL/Roger Hyam; 164 right GPL/Mayer/Le Scanff; 165 left GPL/Marie O'Hara; 165 right GPL/Eric Crichton; 167 HA; 168 GPL/Mark Bolton; 169 GPL/John Glover; 170 GPL/J S Sira; 171 GPL/Howard Rice; 172 GPL/Brian Carter; 173 Holt/Nigel Cattlin; 174 GPL/Sunniva Harte; 175 Holt/Gordon Roberts; 177 SW (Ten ter Linden); 178 top to bottom: GPL/Gary Rogers, GPL/Howard Rice, GPL/Erika Craddock, Nicola Stocken Tomkins, GPL/Densey Clyne; 179 top to bottom: GPL/Brian Carter, GPL/Jacqui Hurst, David Beeson, David Beeson, GPL/Steven Wooster; 180 top to bottom: GPL/John Glover, GPL/John Glover, GPL/Marijke Heuff, GPL/John Glover, GPL/J S Sira; 181 top to bottom: GPL/Neil Holmes, GPL/Neil Holmes, GPL/John Glover, GPL/John Glover, GPL/J S Sira; 182 top to bottom: GPL/Neil Holmes, GPL/Howard Rice, Nicola Stocken Tomkins, GPL/Brian Carter, GPL/Brian Carter; 183 top to bottom: GPL/Neil Holmes, GPL/Howard Rice, GPL/Howard Rice, GPL/John Glover, GPL/Geoff Dann; 184 top to bottom: GPL/Clive Nichols. GPL/John Glover, GPL/Mark Bolton, GPL/Howard Rice, GPL/Eric Crichton; 185 top to bottom: GPL/John Glover, GPL/Howard Rice, GPL/John Glover, GPL/J S Sira, GPL/Mark Bolton; 186 top to bottom: GPL/Lamontagne, GPL/Brian Carter, GPL/Christopher Fairweather, GPL/Rex Butcher, GPL/Christopher Fairweather; 187 top to bottom: GPL/Neil Holmes, GPL/John Glover, GPL/Lamontagne, GPL/J S Sira, GPL/Neil Holmes 188 top to bottom: GPL/Brian Carter, GPL/Philippe Bonduel, GPL/John Glover, GPL/J S Sira, GPL/John Glover; 189 top to bottom: GPL/Neil Holmes, GPL/John Glover, GPL/Neil Holmes, GPL/Mayer/Le Scanff, GPL/Neil Holmes